THE
ORGANIZATION OF
GOVERNMENTS
A COMPARATIVE ANALYSIS
OF GOVERNMENTAL
STRUCTURES

JEAN BLONDEL
Professor of Government, University of Essex

Political Executives in Comparative Perspective:
A Cross-National Empirical Study Volume 2

(S)*SAGE Publications* ● *London* ● *Beverly Hills* ● *New Delhi*

For information address:

SAGE Publications Ltd 28 Banner Street London EC1Y 8QE

SAGE Publications Inc 275 South Beverly Drive Beverly Hills
California 90212

SAGE Publications India C-236 Defence Colony.
New Delhi 110 24 India

British Library Cataloguing in Publication Data

Blondel, Jean
   The organization of governments. — (Political
executives in comparative perspective; 2)
   1. Political science
   I. Title   II. Series
   320   JA66

Library of Congress Catalog Card Number 82-80523

ISBN 0-8039-9776-0
ISBN 0-8039-9777-9 Pbk.

pv
12-20-83

CONTENTS

PREFACE

This is the second in the series of volumes devoted to national political executives across the world. The first volume, *World Leaders*, was concerned with a general mapping of the characteristics of national leadership as well as with the backgrounds and careers of leaders. Originally, I had thought that this second volume would achieve for governments and ministers what the first volume had done for leaders. I found gradually, however, that the problems raised by governmental structures were both so numerous and so intriguing that it became necessary to devote an entire volume to those structures alone; the study of backgrounds and careers of ministers will therefore be considered in a further work.

The fact that a separate volume is needed to cover — or should one say to begin to explore — the problems and characteristics of governmental structures is a further indication of the pressing need for a concerted action among political scientists in the field. For the subject of governmental structures is not merely intellectually intriguing; it is also scarcely covered in the literature, except — and indeed even then only partially — on the basis of individual country studies. Problems of cabinet governments are analysed, for instance, from the specific point of view of the specialists of these countries; they are not related to the problems of other types of governmental structures, except in so far as rather simplified comparisons are made between the American and British governments; the lessons which might be drawn from other types of governmental arrangements, including Communist governmental arrangements, are purely and simply ignored. One can therefore only reiterate the point made in the Preface to *World Leaders*, namely that despite their importance, studies devoted to national political executives are still extremely rare. One of the objects of this work is therefore to stimulate studies and to provoke discussions about the current structure of executives and about reforms which might be put forward.

This is fortunately beginning to happen: scholars are becoming increasingly aware that a problem exists; conferences and workshops are being set up to examine it. It was, for instance, particularly rewarding to discuss some of the points which are made in this volume at a Workshop of the European Consortium for Political Research which took place in Lancaster in the Spring of 1981. I wish to thank here all the participants at that Workshop for the help which they gave me, directly and indirectly, and especially Professor G.D. Paige, of the University of Hawaii, for his encouragement and his comments. I also wish to thank Dr T. Dunmore, of the Department of Government of the University of Essex, for his remarks and suggestions, in particular with respect to Communist and Third World governmental arrangements. I also wish to record my thanks to Mrs Desne Harrington for her care in typing the manuscript despite its many corrections. But, above all, I wish to address my greatest thanks to Tess Martineau who in the course of many months has had to bear the brunt of unsolicited remarks and reflections about structures of governments and yet has given me unceasing encouragement.

October 1981   Witham, Essex

INTRODUCTION

This study is an exploration into the main characteristics of government in the contemporary world. It aims to examine the forms that governments take in countries as diverse as the United States and the Soviet Union, Britain and Zaire, Switzerland and Libya. The simplest and most straightforward justification for such an enterprise is that we should be curious about the way men are governed; indeed, perhaps political scientists can rightly be criticized for being insufficiently curious about the world around them — the whole world, not merely the countries of the West in which most political scientists practice their discipline. This justification has indeed become more pressing since, after a short period during which governmental structures were coming to resemble each other, in the early part of this century, they have once more taken increasingly different forms; as the twentieth century draws to a close, the variety is perhaps greater than at any time in the past.

But there is a deeper justification for a world-wide study of executives. Studies of governments have so far been concerned mainly with Western countries; indeed, most studies refer to one or two Western countries only. When they go a little further, they tend to be in the form of compendia, valuable and informative to be sure, but almost always unable to draw more than the most obvious comparisons.[1] As these studies refer only to a limited number of countries in one part of the world, the problems which executives face and the solutions which can be given to these problems are not fully perceived, let alone tackled, in their generality. As a result of our 'parochial' concern with our own patch, we have not elaborated a general theory of executives — rather what has emerged has been a piecemeal and almost anecdotal study of the behaviour of a few governments.

The usual case for country studies is that much needs to be known about every nation and that the socio-political characteristics of each nation have an immense bearing on the nature of the executive. And the usual critique against world-wide studies of almost any political structure, including executives, is the corresponding point that we know very little about most countries and that the problems are posed so differently, in Communist countries, or in the Third World, from the way they are posed in the West, that it is a vain endeavour to try and bring the whole subject under one rubric. There is, of course, some truth in these assertions, and the need for general studies of executives is not a substitute for the need for single-country studies or for two-country comparisons. But the fundamental error of the approach is that it prevents political scientists from even perceiving that governments may be organized differently elsewhere, and consequently from beginning to ask themselves what is the nature of government and what is the range of feasible responses to the problems which governments pose.

Yet this is a time when, in the West, many doubts are being expressed about the structure of governments. All of us have complained occasionally about the exaggerated influence of prime ministers or presidents, and have pointed out the dangers which governments face if they are reshuffled too often or are staffed with men whose technical competence for the subject of their ministerial department is too limited. There has been less widespread concern about the size of cabinets, or about the extent to which decisions are taken collectively or not; but, among specialists as well as among close observers of the political scene, this concern has often been expressed. Yet few solutions have been offered, and those that have been suggested have either been totally ignored or rejected as impractical. For a very long time now — over a third of a century — it has been stated that governments should be based on a 'pyramidal' structure, with a small number of 'superministers' only;[2] as a matter of fact, the size of governments has continued to grow, and the idea of superministers has not been pursued with much energy. Thus the 'overload' of governments is on the verge of being no more than a topic of conversation among the *cognoscenti*, a ground for complaint rather than the starting point of an alternative approach to governmental structure.

What is, of course, generally missing in the field of executives is a long-standing concern for what these governments should be: the neglect is more apparent than in almost any other aspect of political life. Past theorists have never really devoted their attention to the way in which governments should be composed. Classical political theory may not have sufficiently defined leadership or may not have precisely determined the powers of leaders,[3] but at least there has been interest in the way chief executives should be chosen and in the relationship they should have, for instance, with the legislature. In the case of governments, there has been no reflection at all. It is as if it was assumed that the problem of who should be minister and for how long, or in what way ministers should relate to chief executives simply did not exist. Perhaps classical political theorists should not be blamed too strongly since governments were small and informal in the seventeenth, eighteenth and nineteenth centuries; yet, as we shall see, types of governmental structures were different in the past, from the Roman Republic to the absolute monarchies of the post-Renaissance period. But, whatever the rights and wrongs of the neglect in which governments were left, the result is that there has been almost no tradition of studying executives, legalistically or sociologically, institutionally or behaviourally, and that the post-1945 generation of political scientists had therefore almost no guidance and has consequently never been attuned to the need to study governments in a general manner.

Given the difficulties which governments and cabinets currently face, the need to develop such a general theory of governmental structure and behaviour seems both obvious and pressing. It is the contention of this work that the simplest and most natural way to proceed in order to come gradually to a theory of government is to draw, so to speak, a broad map of the contours of governments across the world. No amount of study, however detailed and painstaking, of the British and American governments alone can provide a substitute for a general work. It is true that a comparative study of British and American governments already does provide a source of important reflections of major differences in the structure of executives.[4] But, interestingly enough, because the American and British governments tend to be studied by single-country specialists who occasionally make an excursion into the

other man's patch, the full richness of the comparison, even between the two countries, has so far almost entirely escaped the
observer. Students of British government are mesmerized by the
visibility and prestige of the American president and they consequently concentrate on the question of whether or not British
prime ministers are becoming presidential; there has been much less
recognition of the gradual break-up of the United States government or of the truly structural difference between the virtual
autonomy of United States cabinet secretaries and the great
compactness of the British government. And the fundamental
reason why the point has not been recognized is that neither the
American nor the British government is typically studied in the context or against the background of governments elsewhere. When it
is perceived, on the contrary, that the United States governmental
structure bears many similarities with the Soviet governmental
structure, because, like the latter, it is divided into segments, while
most 'cabinet-type' systems on the British model partake to a different model based on a strong party system, in which parties
dominated by tightly-knit oligarchies come to rotate in office in an
almost perennial manner, the nature of the comparison between the
American and British governments takes on an altogether different
and much richer dimension. Only at this point does the study of
government begin to lead to the truly important questions that need
to be raised about the way in which governments should be constituted while also providing clues to the parameters of the political
and social constraints under which governments operate.

To state that governments must be studied generally is not to
claim that such a study can be conducted easily and that the point
made earlier about the difficulty of cross-national analyses is a
matter to be taken lightly. There are indeed many serious problems
in the comparative study of government — as there are problems in
the comparative study of any aspects of political life. There is, of
course, a common and well-known universal basis for the study of
executives. Every country has a government and the composition of
this government is published in documents which can readily be
obtained.[5] One can also, over the years, easily build a data bank of
ministers and consequently find out without much effort how often
these ministers change; one can further discover, by taking a little
more trouble, the origins of ministers and how far governments
constitute a unified social and political group. But there are many
other, perhaps more important points which are less easy to

monitor. The power relationships between the various ministers constitute one point which is obviously most elusive: tomes have been written about the nature of the British cabinet; major controversies have raged about the relative importance of the prime minister and cabinet ministers in Britain. If it is so difficult to know how far the British prime minister is superior to his or her colleagues, it is clearly very difficult indeed to attempt to compare, on a world-wide basis, the relative power of leaders and members of the executive. As a matter of fact, the problem here is not mainly one of data-gathering: it is essentially the result of our inability — endemic in political science — to have any but the crudest means of measuring political power. For what makes us unable to state whether British prime ministers are a little, much, or strikingly more powerful than their colleagues is not the lack of information about what prime ministers and ministers respectively do, but the lack of analytical tools to locate, ascribe or otherwise measure ratings of strength and weakness within the British cabinet.

Of course, our knowledge is often so small with respect to the governments of countries other than Britain, the United States and a number of European states that we are seriously hampered in our endeavour to trace generally the strength of leaders vis-à-vis those who are sometimes rather generously called their 'colleagues'. But we are also hampered in our attempts at general surveys by our gross inability, so far, even to try and give a definition of what a government is. The matter seems so simple, so straightforward, that the neglect is almost total. We just talk of the government, sometimes of the cabinet, as if these expressions were interchangeable and, above all, self-evident. We do not ask ourselves how far we include advisers of presidents or prime ministers, 'eminences grises', party secretaries, straightforward confidants within the nomenclature. Such is the simplemindedness of these analyses that it is almost impossible — indeed, truly impossible — to find a definition of what government is, not just on a cross-country basis, but even on the basis of individual countries. Indeed, the government which is the most studied, in the country which is the most studied and which has by far the largest number of political scientists, that of the United States, is perhaps the most difficult of all to circumscribe. Studies of the presidency or of individual presidents are, of course, extremely numerous; studies of the president's entourage and cabinet are more rare, although there has been a healthy growth of these works, especially since the

1970s.[6] But these studies never ask themselves what constitutes the American government. Perhaps it is because the question is viewed as obvious; perhaps it is because the matter is deemed uninteresting; perhaps it is because it is felt to be unanswerable. Whatever the reason may be, the question should not be left in such obscurity. If the concept of government is not one to which a definition can be given, let the point be made openly; if there are too many subtle and almost indistinguishable steps between the top — say a president — and the bottom — say very junior ministers, assistants, aides, envoys, special councillors — for political scientists to provide a realistic description of the contours of governments, the matter must not be left unstated. We must continue to believe that it is meaningful to speak of the 'government' of a country. But if such vagueness comes from a lack of serious endeavour to provide an operational definition of government, then the effort must be made to do so; and a comparative analysis, by forcing political scientists to come out of this obscurity and to gradually elaborate the various conditions which have to be fulfilled by government members, will markedly help to clear the undergrowth and introduce rigour to the analysis.

This study does not pretend to solve problems of this magnitude: it aims only to explore, both theoretically and empirically, the questions posed by governments and cabinets. The matter of the definition of government is so complex that what can be done here — and this is the object of the coming Chapter — is merely to look at government in the broadest possible way and see what elements have to be taken into account to arrive at a definition of governments. The operationalization remains somewhat elusive, but the direction in which one must go to arrive at this operationalization begins to be clearer. Even less is it possible to come here to an operational determination of power which might be applied to the assessment of the relative position of leaders and other members of national executives. What is attempted is a more limited and preliminary task, which we referred to earlier as a 'mapping' of the contours of the problem: in this the process is similar to that which political scientists, for want of better tools, have used in many aspects of the discipline. A general typology is being constructed, and, within this typology, a number of similarities and differences are observed and noted. What is clear is that the examination of the structure of governments, as it presents itself outwardly when executives are set up or reconstituted, reveals a number of characteristics of governments; these characteristics may not tell with precision who has more power than whom, but they indicate at least the general manner in which power is distributed within the government. Thus, by comparing these structures, one begins to have an idea of the similarities and differences in power distribution in various governments. This is not to suggest that one must limit the observation to manifest structures — whether there is a cabinet, how large is the body of presidential aides, how far the government is divided into separate councils, etc. — but, by a patient examination of the ways in which the various structures of the government appear to operate, one can detect a number of clues which help to identify the bodies which are most important and the ways in which these bodies, and the men who belong to them, relate to each other.

The first part of this book is therefore devoted primarily to an examination of the nature of governments and to their broad structure. The coming Chapter focusses on the definition of government and on the general political and social forces which account for the way in which the concept of government is 'operationalized' in the various countries of the contemporary world. Chapters 2 and 3 look at the structure of government in the past and at present: because there is a widely-held belief that governments are almost synonymous with 'cabinets', and that the distinction between a large government and a much smaller cabinet in Britain is a peculiar British idiosyncrasy, it is worth exploring how the concept of government emerged and developed in the Western world. This exploration is valuable as it shows that there have been many differences in the course of the centuries and that, consequently, the supremacy of the cabinet form was a rather temporary peculiarity of the late nineteenth and early twentieth centuries. Having seen how varied governments were in the past, one can easily see that the governments of today are also varied, indeed perhaps more varied than ever, and not necessarily along the lines which existed in the past before the period of cabinet predominance.

One of the causes of the diversity of governments is the very substantial variation in the political composition of these governments. For the last one hundred years, Western European and American governments have been dominated by single-party administrations or by coalitions: naturally enough, much of the emphasis of governmental studies in the West has been on the analysis of the ways in which parties form the basis of governments and, interestingly though rather 'parochially', on the ways in which parties that do not have a majority in Parliament appear to have to combine with others. But parties have dominated governments in Western countries and Communist states only, while coalitions of parties have, in practice, played an important part in Western countries only. A general analysis of the political basis of government has therefore to inquire into the role of forces other than parties and, increasingly, into the way in which these forces — the military, but also the civil service and indeed traditional groups — ally with parties to form governments which are, in effect, 'coalitions' of a different type, not so much among parties as between parties and other forces in the society. The basic hypothesis — in fact an assumption which has rarely been questioned — was and still is to some extent that traditional forces are slowly being replaced by parties as the main organizations from which ministers are recruited and on which support for the government lies. The experiences of the 1950s, 1960s and 1970s at a minimum raise some doubts about this view of the modern developments of national executives, as we shall see in Chapter 4.

The examination of general structures of government poses further and more detailed questions about the way in which they meet the problems which governments have to face. Specifically, one major question underlies all the experiments currently undertaken, namely how is the apparently ever-widening gap between leader and ministers to be filled at a time when the requirements of decision-making call for greater coordination and indeed concentration of the policy-making process, at a time when the problems of managing individual ministerial departments — education, the social services, industry, agriculture, trade, etc. — are becoming increasingly large? For here lies, at the highest level of generality, the major difficulty which confronts governments: the demands of a smooth policy-making process are antagonistic with the demands for detailed supervision of the implementation of policies. This problem is at the root of the relationship between leaders and ministers: it is not so much that leaders necessarily *want* more power; it is that ministers are no longer in a position to be truly close to the leader *and* to the whole decision-making machine.

On this point, this investigation is a preliminary exploration. Having seen that governments are diverse in structure, we can only at this stage begin to try and see to what extent it seems that these structures respond to the needs of decision-making. Much more will be needed to come to a definite conclusion: the purpose of this book is to ask the question. If governments are genuinely to initiate policy over the whole range of the public sector, what types of administrative arrangements exist and what types of interpersonal relationships seem to be most suitable? Should there be formally recognized intermediate echelons between leaders and ministers, or can the leader take over the powers of overall policy-making? The examination of the responses, across the world, from the 1940s to the 1980s, which is conducted in Chapter 5, begins to give an idea of the magnitude of the difficulty and of the type of answers which can sensibly be provided.

Since the distance between leaders and ministers is due in large part to the apparently inevitable expansion of the scope of the government, it is worth examining with some care the nature and extent of this expansion. The description undertaken in Chapter 6, of the development of departmental ministries across the world, of their rate of growth, and of the types of new ministries, is a supplementary indication of the apparent ease with which governments are able to cope with the problem of the management of the country's affairs. And a further indication of the extent of the burdens which governments have to face and of the problems which they have to solve is provided by the uneven growth in the number of echelons or levels of the ministerial pyramid: whatever happens at the top, some governments have felt obliged to fill in what seems to be a widening gap between the political 'superstructure' and the administrative elephant with a variety of junior ministers and other assistants in positions of advice or responsibility. Here we come to the very uncertain frontier between government and bureaucracy (Chapter 7), a frontier which becomes all the more uncertain as the administrative duties of the government expand and the government is unclear about the model it attempts to follow. For to create ranks of junior ministers in order to help the ministers is also to increase the hierarchical nature of the government, a point which brings us back to the question of the overall structure and which echoes the matter of the gap between leader and ministers.

This book is about governments and cabinets as organizations. It considers the ways in which these bodies are structured and the forces — political, such as parties or the military, or social — which account for the ways in which these structures developed. The examination of the individuals who compose the governments is left for the next volume. It is, of course, difficult in practice to disentangle matters of personality and matters of organization: whether a government is or is not genuinely a 'group' depends on the characteristics of and especially on the interrelationships among the members of this government. But to have discussed ministers alongside governments and cabinets would have made this book about twice as long, and, in reality, it would have been necessary, even in the context of a single book, to distinguish the analysis of ministers from that of governments. It has therefore seemed more sensible to concentrate on governments as structures and to leave for the coming volume considerations relating to ministers, their background, their duration in office, and their fall, and thus to leave for that volume the question of the extent to which it can be said, in the contemporary world, that governments are, in the true sense of the word, 'bodies' or 'groups', or whether they are merely collections of men filling certain positions at a given point in time.

Notes

1. One of the more recent and informative works in this vein is that which was edited by R. Rose and E.N. Suleiman, *Presidents and Prime Ministers* (American Enterprise Institute, 1980). This study covers in succession eight Western European and North American countries.

2. L.S. Amery, *Thoughts on the Constitution*, which first appeared in 1946; it was published again in 1964 (Oxford University Press). See in particular Chapter 3, 'The Machinery of Government', especially at pp. 90 and following.

3. See my *World Leaders* (Sage, 1980), at pp. 10 and following, for a discussion of the definition of political leadership and its problems.

4. R. Neustadt's reflections on the British governmental structure are a case in point: see A. King, ed., *The British Prime Minister* (Macmillan, 1969), pp. 119-47.

5. The composition of governments is published in a number of reference books, normally on a yearly basis. See for instance *The Europa Yearbook — A World Survey*, published by Europa Publications Ltd or the *International Yearbook and Statesman's Who's Who*, published by Kelly's Directories Ltd.

6. See Chapter 5 and the notes to that Chapter for examples of these works.

1. THE NOTION OF GOVERNMENT

The idea of government is one of the most central in our societies. Whether we believe that rulers are good or bad, effective or inept, strong or weak, we believe in their importance. Even those who, in view of their political and social philosophy, might be led to conclude that governments are merely epiphenomena obscuring the clashes between economic forces in effect recognize the role of these governments: they criticize the deeds of those rulers whom they dislike and extol the virtues — even often justify the excesses — of those rulers whom they support. Totalitarianism has reinforced the power of governments, and democratic states have seen the extent of intervention by governments increase.

Yet, these very influential, ever-present governments are also elusive. It is difficult to state with precision who belongs to them, let alone how they are effectively structured. We talk about governments having taken some decisions and pursuing a particular policy, but it is far from clear, in many instances at least, who took the decisions and who favoured the policy line. 'The most curious thing about the British Cabinet', said Bagehot, 'is that so little is known about it'.[1] The point could be made more generally: the most curious thing about governments is that so little is known about them.

In the eyes of most of us, governments are composed of the rather small body of men who, together with the leader, take the major political decisions which confront the nations.[2] A government appears therefore to be both an institution and a collection of decision-makers. But such an impression does not stand up to close examination. If we look at governments around the world, and begin to attempt to circumscribe their characteristics, the conception of a well-defined group has quickly to be abandoned. First, it is not at all clear, for many countries at least, who are the members of the government. Admittedly, there are official documents which list ministers from time to time and which specify the positions that they occupy. The titles differ: there are administrations, cabinets, councils of ministers, as well as, more recently, revolutionary and military councils. But these varied appellations seem to cover a common underlying reality, the group of men and women who are in charge of the different sectors of the public services.

Yet a closer look at the nomenclature and at the arrangements quickly shows that matters, far from being simple, may in fact be almost impossible to describe adequately and grasp analytically. It is not merely that some governments are very much larger than others, with variations from one to ten between Luxembourg and Switzerland, on the one hand, and the Soviet Union, on the other. It is also that the overall arrangements differ widely, so widely that it becomes difficult to determine, in some cases, what body constitutes the government. The case of the British administration is one of the most striking: there is a cabinet of some twenty members, but there are also ministers outside the cabinet who are of cabinet rank; and there are ministers of state, parliamentary secretaries, whips, members of the Queen's Household. Where does the government end? Is the government to be restricted to the cabinet? Or should one also include some or all of those who are mentioned in the official list which includes over a hundred names? Nor is the British case unique: the American government is also difficult to define since members of the cabinet are advised and helped by assistant secretaries who can be regarded as part of the government.

The question of the boundaries of governments leads to another and potentially more serious problem: should governments be viewed as bodies, or organisms? In the American case, it is not only that assistant secretaries of departments are political appointments and may deserve to be considered as parts of the government, although they are subordinated to the secretaries; it is also that there are, outside the cabinet, in the Executive Office of the president, directors of agencies and of bureaus who seem to be for all intents and purposes equal to cabinet secretaries. Difficulties of this type, only more pronounced, arise when considering Communist states and countries of the Third World: in a substantial number of new countries, in the 1960s and 1970s, leaders have been surrounded by military or revolutionary councils as well as by councils of ministers: which of these bodies should be deemed to be the government or should all these bodies be considered to form the government together? And one could argue with much justification that a similar state of affairs prevails in Communist states where the Politburo of the Communist Party, although not officially the government, manifestly takes many important decisions and deserves to be placed perhaps above, and certainly not below, the council of ministers.

The determination of which bodies constitute the government is therefore at times, indeed often, not simple. It is apparent, in the contemporary world at least, that there is no universally received view about whom a government is supposed to include and how it is supposed to be organized. Every substantive definition has, not just exceptions, but large numbers of exceptions. Governments may be large or small; they may be composed of more than one body; indeed, it is not even clear that they necessarily constitute a 'body'. In a previous volume, we found it almost impossible to define leadership conceptually, and we found it frankly impractical to give an operational definition except by using a positional approach to which some substantive conditions were attached.[3] With governments, the problem seems even more complex: what substantive conditions should be attached to a pure positional definition is far from clear. We defined leaders as heads of governments and heads of state, provided the latter did not exercise purely formal functions: in the case of the vast list of the British governments, the point is not that anyone holds a purely formal position, but that some of the positions seem to be rather 'lowly'; but we do not know where to draw the line. Conversely, we added to formal leaders those holders of positions which manifestly were of crucial importance, such as Communist Party secretaries in Communist states. It would seem rather arbitrary to add similarly to the 'official' government all those advisers, assistants, or directors on the grounds that they 'seem' to hold power, often behind the scenes, at times quite overtly; yet it also seems unrealistic to exclude them altogether.

The Analysis of Government

In view of these manifest difficulties encountered in defining
governments with precision, it is surprising that the political science
literature should not provide help and guidance. Yet the study of
government has so far been undertaken generally. The literature on
executives is vast, but it addresses itself in the main to the description of the characteristics of power within individual governments:
there are numerous studies of the American presidency or of the
British cabinet; there are also many works on other Western
cabinets, as well as on Communist executives and on some Third
World governments.[4] But these country-based analyses tend to be
primarily historical and almost anecdotal in character: there is considerable emphasis on the legal framework and on the extent to
which the practice differs from the formal arrangements. More
recently, some of the analyses have been sociological and
psychological and the backgrounds and the attitudes of ministers
have begun to be examined.[5] But the nature, boundaries, and even
characteristics of the government are not fully assessed: as the work
is not comparative, the more fundamental questions do not need to
be asked. The executive is studied as it exists and its idiosyncrasies
are taken for granted.

Two general questions have been raised, admittedly, and appear
repeatedly in the literature. The first is that of the 'hierarchical' or
'egalitarian' structure of the government. The point was examined
in earlier decades in a normative context and viewed as a consequence of the constitutional distinctions between presidential and
parliamentary systems. Gradually, however, it became fashionable
to stress the fact that the reality did not conform to the legal
distinction: the view that the British prime minister was becoming
as powerful as the American president with respect to members of
the government was strongly put forward, especially by R.H.S.
Crossman in his Preface to a new edition of Bagehot's *English
Constitution*.[6] The controversy which followed led to a recognition
that the British cabinet was still, in many ways, a collective body.[7]
But even this matter has been discussed primarily in terms of Britain alone. Whether governments *are* collective or not, in a variety
of countries, has scarcely been examined; how coalitions, for
instance, affect the effective structure of governments remains
grossly understudied. Thus a potentially general issue is still examined almost exclusively in the context of one country.

Nor has the other problem which has exercised political scientists been examined in a general context either. From the 1930s, students of public administration in Britain have been concerned with the effectiveness of the cabinet as an organ of coordination.[8] The Lloyd George war cabinet was found to be effective; Churchill's war cabinet followed the same model and had similar results. It seemed, on the other hand, that the multiplication of cabinet committees in peacetime situations led to a loss of time, to uneasy compromises and to a lack of real coordination. The idea of appointing 'superministers' was put forward: a number of experiments followed, some of which were successful, in the fields of defence, economics, and more recently in the social services. But, while the same questions arose in countries other than Britain, the matter was not discussed in a comparative framework.[9]

The Problems Posed by Government

Yet even if these matters had been studied generally, they would not have exhausted the problems which the notion of government poses. For, beyond the question of whether or not a government is collective, or whether or not it has 'superministers', a number of more fundamental questions need to be resolved which strike at the root of the concept of government itself. The first of these questions is perhaps the simplest: it relates to what might be called the 'vertical' depth of government. We encountered this problem earlier when we described the uncertainty relating to the size of the British government. The British government is composed of a number of levels: the first of these is made up of the cabinet, to which should perhaps be added at least the ministers of cabinet rank. These are the men and women who are the apex of the hierarchy of public decision-making; in many countries, for instance in most of continental Europe, the government is officially composed of men and women of this rank only. But the British government also includes a second level (ministers of state) and a third level (parliamentary secretaries). These help the ministers, often by concentrating on one section of a department only; they are hierarchically subordinated to the ministers and, theoretically at least, it is always the minister who takes the formal decision. Clearly, in countries where ministers do not have subordinates of this kind within the government, help and advice does still come from some men and women: it may be that ministers have a personal staff; it may be that civil servants provide the advice. Thus the substantive function is fulfilled, but it is fulfilled by men who are not officially recognized as belonging to the government.

The fact that there is some ambiguity here does not mean that there is not also, so to speak, some 'certainty'. What is certain or unproblematic is the fact that governments are concerned to an important extent with the running of various sectors of public administration. The leader needs some help with respect to finance, defence, international relations, and the like; in recent years the number of sectors of administration that is being covered has increased as states have everywhere, though to a varying degree, interfered more and more in the economic and social life of nations. But this development has only made it more difficult to answer the general question of the point in the hierarchy where the line has to be drawn between what is the government and who does not belong to it. For if one way of solving the problems of the increased burden falling on government departments consists in splitting what was previously one department into two or more units each of which is headed by a minister, it becomes apparent that the size and composition of a government largely depends on accidental decision. Consequently, 'second level' ministers may be viewed as merely formally distinct from full ministers. Customs and different practices decide, here, that the government will include only the 'top layer' of the decision-makers, while, in another country, the government might include men and women who are officially subordinated to one of the ministers. So far, there has not been a clear answer on this point, although there have been a variety of theoretical justifications of different arrangements. The British practice is among the most 'pyramidal', although, on paper at least, some other experiments echo aspects of the British arrangement.

The second area of ambiguity relates to the 'horizontal' extension of the government and in particular to the extent to which the personal staff of the leader belongs to the government or not. This horizontal extension leads to a degree of diffuseness of the government whose sides and edges become blurred. In the United States at least, many of the 'president's men' outside the cabinet have to be treated as belonging to the government. Indeed, formal changes occur from time to time as a result of which a position becomes part of the cabinet or is excluded from the cabinet to become part of the Executive Office and, especially, of the White House Office.[10] This may be because a position is viewed as being more or less significant, but it is often also because of differing views held by presidents or their advisers about the best way of organizing the government. Formal variations in nomenclature are therefore not the most important criteria to adopt when one attempts to describe the boundaries of the government, in the United States or elsewhere; it seems on the contrary highly realistic to include in the government those who are close advisers whatever their precise position and whatever the way in which they relate to the rest of the government.

For, while the present structure of the United States government makes the role of advisers more obvious, the idea of the 'eminence grise' is one which has had considerable importance in the history of governments. Kings and presidents have often appointed advisers, sometimes in secret, to handle delicate questions which they felt unwilling to unload on the official government. It seems somewhat incongruous to exclude such men from the government merely because they do not happen to be listed under the relevant rubric. The appointment of special assistants, envoys, or counsellors is clearly a sign that there is often a desire to extend the government, and to create parallel lines of communication, even when — and perhaps especially when — the leader is fully in control.

The third difficulty which the nature of government raises goes even deeper and strikes at the root of the idea of government as a body. We noted earlier that a number of Third World countries had a revolutionary or military council distinct from the council of ministers; Politburos of Communist parties in Communist states are similarly distinct from the 'administrative' councils of ministers. The division contrasts sharply with the arrangements which prevail in Western European states where, on the contrary, the councils of ministers are fully in charge of affairs.

The idea that there are two (or perhaps more) governments in some countries challenges the commonly-held view that 'the' government is at the top of the pyramid of the state and forms a compact organization. But this is a view which has come to be accepted without clear theoretical grounding or systematic empirical evidence. This conception was not universally held in the past.[11] The fact that there are two or more governments in the Communist states or in a number of Third World countries may not therefore constitute as much of an exception, or a novelty, as might perhaps seem at first sight. And it is questionable as to whether current trends in the American government are not a more extreme move in the same direction. For what is characteristic of modern American government is not merely that the Executive Office has grown to such proportions that it constitutes a second or parallel government but that also, at the same time, the solidity of the organization of the 'regular' government is also in question. It seems that the government of the United States has come to be a diffuse concept, made up of 'strangers'[12] rather than forming in a real sense a united body. This development seems to correspond to the view which has become fashionable in French journalistic and even academic circles according to which one should refer, not to a 'government' but to *le pouvoir*, an amorphous concept which covers those who rule the country but does not bother to consider specifically whether these men and women belong jointly to an 'organization'.

Meanwhile — and this is the fourth ambiguity — it is not clear whether it is permissible, in many situations, to refer to a 'government' in the sense of a body having a clearly defined beginning and end. In Communist states, ministers and leaders tend to be replaced successively, not simultaneously; indeed, even when there is a very substantial 'reshuffle', it normally takes place over a period of some days or weeks, as if the appearance of continuity had to be preserved. A similar practice can be found in many Third World states, except when a military coup or other revolutionary take-over leads to the desire, on the contrary, to break with the past. Indeed, in Western Europe as well, the Swiss practice is one of considerable continuity, although (or because) the chairmanship of the Federal Council rotates every year.

Thus, while every country is governed, not every country has *a* government that can be distinguished from other governments which preceded it. The concept of government is therefore truly ambiguous on this point; not only are governments more or less 'collective' at a given moment, but the concept of government may refer either to a clearly definable body of individuals or merely to the collection of office-holders who happen to be running affairs at a given point in time. From this it follows that a number of questions which agitate political scientists (and others) have absolutely no meaning in some countries while they are important in others, the question of the stability of governments being a prime example. While it is possible to discuss everywhere the question of the stability of *ministers as individuals*, it is possible to discuss the stability of governments only where cabinets or administrations have a beginning and an end. For large numbers of countries, typically outside the West, this matter has simply no meaning.

The uncertainties relating to the notion of government are thus considerable: the boundaries of government are unclear; it is not even always the case that governments are sufficiently coherent internally to deserve being given a collective label. The idea of government is more an abstract concept than a universal reality. What therefore needs to be done is to try and circumscribe more precisely the types of governmental arrangements that can be found in response to the problems which governments face. We start from the notion that there is, at the top, a little group: as the group expands, it can extend downwards as well as sideways; there can be ministers of equal rank or there can be a pyramid with different levels. As this development occurs, the leader may be in danger of losing control: there is therefore occasionally a move to expand the personal staff of the leader and thus to create an internal government alongside the regular cabinet, with the side effect, however, that the regular cabinet may become even more distant from the leader and even less united as a result. But there are other developments. 'Second' governments may be composed, not of the most loyal servants of the leader, but of important politicians whom the leader must involve in decision-making whether he is, or is not, close to them. And even more complex arrangements may emerge. There are thus cohesive governments and loosely structured administrations; there are single governments whose members play a multiplicity of parts and more complex organizations where the roles are more differentiated. The notion of the government as an all-purpose cabinet, so commonly accepted intuitively, is only one formula, even if this formula is widely adopted. Why are there these differences?

The Variety of Governmental Arrangements and their Raison d'Etre

The variety of governmental arrangements is such that it would be absurd to believe that one single set of explanations could account for the differences. Indeed, at least four factors play a part, although the precise extent of their influence cannot be adequately measured. The first factor is the most obvious and the least controversial: it relates to the effect on the government of the expansion of the public sector and of the activities of the state in general. This expansion has affected the government, and is directly responsible for the increase in the number of ministerial posts everywhere. This increase has in turn led to problems of organization: a government of twenty departmental ministers cannot be run in the same way as a government of four or five. Yet, while this increase has rendered more obvious and more acute a number of problems of governmental structure, it did not create these problems for they were already present. It simply made it more difficult to stick to arrangements which so far had uneasily contained administrative tensions and political contradictions. The expansion of modern government is not the original cause of the problems faced by governments; it is at most a catalyst which increased the consciousness of problems which were already present.

A second explanation for the variety of answers to the structure of governments is ideological. To an extent at least, governments are structured in the way they are because politicians and indeed political theorists have wanted them to be organized in that manner. The most obvious way in which ideology made an impact has been the extent to which governments should be collective and egalitarian rather than hierarchical or pyramidal. For some, in particular in Western Europe, the idea of an egalitarian government is a logical consequence of the process of democratization. Hierarchical government smacks of the tyranny of kings; collective government seems on the contrary to fit with the idea of parliamentary responsibility and accountability to the people.

Thus many governments have formally been structured in a collective manner but, as we noted, the facts of political power and of administrative decision-making have made collective government appear rather impractical, if not indeed simply impossible to achieve. Hierarchical or pyramidal government seemed to reemerge even in countries in which liberal democratic traditions were well entrenched and where collective responsibility was one of the tenets of the constitution. Thus, without dismissing altogether the role of the ideology of collective decision-making in the fabric of modern government, one has to recognize that the influence of the idea is, or has become, relatively small. Indeed, the maintenance of the reality of collective government may in fact be due more often to the reality of political forces than to a prevailing ideology.

For political arrangements — the configuration of political

forces — are probably a more important factor in the structure of governments than ideology, as is the existence of a number of different tasks which governments have to perform. By and large, governments seem to be organized differently, essentially because they are confronted with activities which have to be undertaken and have a variety of political resources to achieve these tasks. These are the two main factors accounting for the differences in the structures of modern governments.

The Tasks of Governments

What are the tasks, activities, or functions of governments? The word 'function' is used here with some hesitation as it has such a history of controversy in political and social science that it would at first seem wiser to try and avoid it. But it does seem possible to define a government without referring (openly or not) to its functions as soon as we recognize that a purely formal definition (based on published lists) is insufficient; we need therefore to explore what the activities, operations or 'functions' of governments are. But, before doing so, we need to see whether the use of 'functions' in the definition will automatically lead to controversies and to a subjective assessment.

This seems avoidable, by virtue of a fundamental difference between governments and other political and social institutions. Functionalism arouses controversies not because institutions do not have effects or lead to activities, but because these effects and activities are so numerous that we are confronted with what seems to be an infinity of functions. Basically, social institutions, and even political institutions, do not exist or do not exist only 'in order' to achieve a particular goal or set of goals. A tribe exists: it encompasses a multitude of relationships and it is only in part concerned with making decisions. It is certainly the case that it has the effect, among other things, of creating certain patterns of representation, or of elite recruitment, or of implementation, but it does not exist *to* do these things. While political institutions have often been created at a given point in time in 'order to' achieve a set of purposes (e.g. a legislature is set up to elaborate and pass legislation), they are also social groupings which have activities well beyond the legislative purpose. Thus the problem with functionalism is not so much that structures do not exercise activities or fulfil functions,

but that they fulfil such a multiplicity of functions to such a varying
extent that it seems impossible to describe them at all accurately; if
one does so, one becomes unable to distinguish one institution
from another as every institution appears to fulfil every function.
Functionalism therefore seems to lead to undue abstraction and to
oversimplification.

These objections do not apply to the analysis of governments,
because governments are the apex, the kernel of the political
machine and therefore do exist in order to take public decisions
relating to the nation, albeit with or under pressure from other
bodies. Government is directed towards an aim, however general is
the aim of governing: this gives a global unity of purpose to the
idea of government. The purpose of the government is thus embedded in the very existence of the government. But there is more:
because the government is at the apex of the political machine, it is,
so to speak, concerned with the major problem which the political
machine has to solve, namely the 'conversion', to use Almond's
terminology, of ideas, suggestions, values (internally produced or
externally suggested, but, in this latter case, after having been inter-
nalized) into specific programmes, decisions, rules, arrangements
(these, too, having to be discussed with or forced upon others).[13]
Governments can therefore be correctly described as being concerned with — as having the function of being concerned with —
the conversion of 'inputs' into 'outputs'.

Moreover, if this operation of conversion of inputs is examined
closely, one can further observe that it consists of three distinct
sub-'functions' or sub-'operations' which have to be taken into
account in governmental activities. The first consists in monitoring.
listening to, but also rejecting a number of policy proposals; this
activity has primarily a political character in that it consists in
weighing the intrinsic and tactical importance of a number of suggestions, and being ready to accept or to refuse them.

The second operation consists in elaborating and developing
practical policies for the nation and seeing that these policies are
consistent with each other, or at least not antagonistic to each
other. This will mean exercising 'coordination' and 'arbitration'
between claims coming from different sections of the community
and establishing priorities. This activity, too, is primarily political:
an element which has to be taken into account is that of the consequences of following one line of action rather than another, in
particular for the popularity of the government. To this extent, this

stage of activity bears some similarity with the previous stage, but it differs from it by the fact that considerable weight has to be given to the implications of one policy on another.

The third operation of governments is very different in character from the other two: it consists in overseeing the administration in its role of implementation of policies as well as in its role of manager of the public services. An element of this activity is political — for instance, judgements must be passed on the chances of implementing more or less speedily decisions which have been taken as well as deciding on complaints which may be made about the way in which the administration is managing the country. But, in the main, the activity of members of governments as supervisors of departments is of a managerial and administrative kind. It is concerned with the best means of implementing policies already agreed to, rather than with the strategy to be followed. It is also essentially a detailed and specialized activity, which implies knowledge on the part of government ministers of the activities of administrators and technicians in their department. While supervision can be undertaken by amateurs, it benefits from being undertaken by specialists.

Three Types of Skills

This outline of the activities of governments begins to give some clues as to what 'running the affairs of the nation' might entail. In particular we discover that members of the government, taken together, have to display various skills of a very different character; this therefore helps to answer questions about the ways in which governments 'should best be run', for instance in terms of efficiency. If we consider the three stages of activities which have been described, the skills which are required to undertake these activities successfully fall into three types (although each skill does not necessarily relate to one of the stages of activity). To begin with the most obvious skill, members of governments must have some expertise of an *administrative and managerial* character. How much they need to have is open to question and might indeed vary from situation to situation: more administrative and technical know-how will be required if the public sector is very large and centralization very high. But, in all countries, members of the government must be able to supervise some services. Otherwise others will do it — and the effectiveness of the government will be very limited. Hence the frequent tendency in the contemporary world to appoint specialists in the government itself.

Yet the appointment of specialists in the government raises serious questions in relation to the other two types of skills which members of governments must possess. One of these is the ability to *coordinate policy*. Governments have to establish priorities between demands over the whole spectrum of public activities: they cannot merely let demands be turned into policies. This is a very different type of skill from that which is required of a good administrator. The ability to coordinate depends on an understanding of the feasibility of various policies. It entails weighing the strength of various demands; it involves balancing the short-term against the long-term. Specialists are most unlikely to perform these tasks adequately; they are likely on the contrary to press for policies in their area, as, if they are good specialists, they are convinced of the almost indefinite usefulness of the development of the sector of policy-making with which they are concerned. At the lowest level, policy coordination within the governmental machine requires an understanding of the need for bargains and trade-offs; at the highest level it entails an ability to see the development of the state in an organic manner. It entails the capacity to unfold a programme for the nation in which the various arguments form part of a coherent whole.

But governments have also to be endowed with *policy-making* capability. In sifting, indeed, in eliciting inputs as well as in ensuring that outputs are implemented at a certain rate and in a certain manner, governments have to be able to induce populations to accept policies which they may be reluctant to follow. The establishment of priorities at the policy-making level entails that sufficient attention be devoted to the ultimate capability of the government to see that policies are carried out. While policy coordination relates to the internal mechanisms of decision-making among government members and their immediate entourage, the need for policy-making skills stems from the fact that governments have to be 'credible' vis-à-vis the population as a whole and the various actors in the political system. While leaders in particular have to be endowed with these skills, it is unthinkable that the government could be entirely shielded by the leader or be unwilling to trespass into the policy-making field.

The complexity of the functions of governments and the variety of skills required of ministers provide ample justifications for the differences in structure that governments display. The emphasis may be on the policy-making functions: if so, the government is likely to be structured, composed and indeed conceived of in a manner which will give priority to the elaboration of policies. The emphasis may be placed on the need for coordination or on the need for efficient management: the result will be a different view of what the government is for and a different set of mechanisms in the decision-making process. But, whatever the model adopted and the principles which politicians attempt to implement, the tensions arising from the different tasks that governments have to fulfil will often tend to surface: the reality will therefore be different from the formal structure. There is no way of avoiding the multiplicity of the tasks, and there is therefore no way of avoiding uncertainties and ambiguities in the structure of governments.

The Notion of Government and
the Structure of Political Authority

The nature and characteristics of governments also differ because of the nature of the political authority of the government and of the equation of political forces supporting the government. For the way in which these forces are distributed has a direct effect on the distribution of power among those who compose the government, and in particular on the relative strength of the leader and of the other members. In a situation in which a leader is the main beneficiary of popular authority in the nation, this leader is at liberty to organize his government as he chooses. He can appoint whom he wishes and structure the members with respect to each other in the way he wants: members of the government know that they depend on the leader while the leader does not depend on them. In a situation where, on the contrary, no one leader has a majority of popular support, and ministers depend for their authority on the strength of each of them with respect to a variety of different groups, the freedom of each of these politicians is narrowly circumscribed. The leader will not be in a position to organize the government in the way he wishes, and individual ministers will have to consult regularly with others.

Thus, the more political power is concentrated on one man, the more the government is likely to be organized by and under this man, in a manner which is likely to be hierarchical; the more political power is distributed among a variety of groups, the more the government is likely to be 'collective', or, at the limit, 'diffuse' in that no-one will really have the authority to control the activities of others and governmental policy-making will develop on a trade-off basis. This means that, in principle at least, in a traditional monarchical system in which the link between people and government takes the form of a broad acceptance of the principle of 'divine right of kings', the monarch is very likely to be able to organize the government in the way he pleases and at the limit to reduce the members of the government to being a number of subordinates, although, as we shall see in the next Chapter, the 'absolute' monarchies often had (and the current monarchies also have) to deal with very strong bureaucracies which were not, and are not, easily circumvented. Similarly, and again in principle, in a presidential system in which a direct popular election gives the leader, for a time at least, an 'anointment' which other politicians cannot challenge, this leader may be able to organize and direct the government in the way he wishes.

On the other hand, where the beneficiary of popular authority is a group, and specifically a political party, and indeed, even more when popular allegiance is divided among a number of political parties, the structure of the government is not likely to be as strongly hierarchical. Admittedly, if a single party commands a majority in the country (de facto or by way of election), and if that party is united strongly around its leader, indeed if the leader has set up the party and helped it develop, the government may be organized and directed by the leader. But if the majority party is not united, or if there is no majority party, power has to be shared among a number of politicians and the role of the leader is much less decisive. There are thus two well-differentiated types of extreme models of government, with an infinite number of intermediate positions, which correspond directly to the relative positions of personal leaders and groups in the political system.

But the government can also be affected by the configuration of political forces in another way. There may be no popular leader; parties may be weak or banned: the political system as a whole may enjoy very little legitimacy. The problem for the leader and his government is therefore to establish their credibility in the nation, for this very endeavour will have an effect on the structure of the government and even on the notion of what the government is. Leaders may for instance feel obliged to enlist the support of some groups in order to reduce opposition and thwart attempts at their physical overthrow. They may therefore feel obliged to accommodate within the government some of the 'representatives' of these groups in a military or revolutionary council. But leaders and ministers will also realize that one of the prerequisites for their success is the continuous support of the civil service whose knowledge is essential for the elaboration of policies and their subsequent implementation: consequently, they may feel obliged to enlist their collaboration by giving them a share in the government and adapting that government's structure accordingly.

The need to achieve support in the nation may therefore lead to the incorporation in 'the' government of individuals who 'represent' in their various ways a number of forces in the nation which cannot be antagonized if the government is to be successful. This may well lead to sets of arrangements which will make the government very diffuse and its real composition very unclear. These arrangements underline the many ways in which parties, the bureaucracy, the military, as well as occasionally trade-union and business groups, overtly or covertly, by design or by accident, participate in governments in the contemporary world. Sometimes it is the leader who, unsure of his own power, finds that it is wise for him to associate with the ruling group prominent 'representatives' of various power hierarchies; sometimes the group configuration is so complex that no-one is in a position to construct a government without taking into account some of the many groups which figure prominently in the national power structure.

In such situations, the notion of government becomes truly obscure. It is a government whose structure and boundaries are fluid and in which decisions are taken as much on the basis of negotiations as in the form of either 'hierarchical' or 'collective' action. But this form of government is in fact very common, and the complexity of modern administration suggests that the fluidity will increase in the future and the structure will be more, rather than less, clear-cut. The government is the most central of institutions: its central position, as well as the multiplicity of its tasks, makes it liable to depend closely and directly on the nature of patterns of legitimacy which prevail in the nation. A realistic description of governments has to take into account these patterns and these tasks in analysing the ways in which the problems faced by governments are met and at least temporarily solved in concrete national situations.

Notes

1. W. Bagehot, *The English Constitution* (Watts, 1964), p. 68.

2. The *Oxford English Dictionary,* for instance, gives as the seventh of its eight definitions: 'The governing power in a State; the body of persons charged with the duty of governing'. This is not a very illuminating definition. The first meaning of 'to govern' is given as 'to rule with authority...; to direct and control the actions and affairs of (a people, etc.), whether despotically or constitutionally'.

3. See my *World Leaders*, pp. 20-3.

4. See the bibliography for a selection of works on specific executives.

5. The most systematic study of the psychological attitudes of ministers is that of B. Heady, *British Cabinet Ministers* (Allen and Unwin, 1974). It is a unique work which needs to be repeated systematically across large numbers of countries. There have been studies of the social backgrounds of ministers, but even these are patchy: much more can be found on the backgrounds of parliamentarians or even of civil servants: see M. Dogan, *The Mandarins of Western Europe* (Wiley, 1975). On United States secretaries and their subordinates, see D.T. Stanley, D.E. Mann and J.W. Doig, *Men Who Govern* (Brookings Institution, 1967).

6. R.H.S. Crossman, Preface to Bagehot's *English Constitution* (Watts, 1964), especially at pp. 51-7.

7. See for instance A.H. King, ed., *The British Prime Minister* (Macmillan, 1969), pp. 168-210.

8. For a survey of the problems as they were viewed both before and after the Second World War, see W.J.M. Mackenzie and J.W. Grove, *Central Administration in Britain* (Longmans, 1957), pp. 336-68 and D.N. Chester and F.M.G. Willson, *The Organisation of British Central Government, 1914-64* (Allen and Unwin, 1968), passim.

9. See Chapter 5 for a discussion of the development of 'superministers'.

10. This happened for instance to the position of postmaster general, which ceased to be part of the United States cabinet in 1970 as a result of the reorganization of the postal services administration.

11. See next Chapter on the evolution of government.

12. From the title of a work by H. Heclo, *A Government of Strangers* (Brookings Institution, 1977).

13. See G.A. Almond and G.B. Powell, *Comparative Politics* (Little, Brown, 1966), pp. 11-12.

2. THE DEVELOPMENT OF MODERN GOVERNMENT

It is sometimes suggested in the rather limited literature on the history of the institution of government that cabinets headed by and advising a chief executive have been the normal pattern of policy-making and administration. R. Fenno, for instance, says, 'Cabinet is modern terminology for an ancient institution. A "cabinet" originates in the universal need on the part of any single chief executive to consult with others and draw upon the advice of others in exercising his political power'.[1] And he continues: 'Scattered anthropological findings suggest that there is an element of universality in the advisory function which the Cabinet performs and in the existence of the Chief Executive-Cabinet relationship'.[2] He quotes E. Adamson Hoebel: 'The one universal instrument of government is the Council. No tribe or nation does without it. No man can govern alone, nor is he permitted to. Monarchy, if taken literally, is a misnomer. Every King or Chief Executive within the network of his advisers and cronies'.[3]

These views exaggerate the extent to which councils and cabinets played a part in the history of governments. While it is true that no man governs alone, it has not been true in the past, nor is it true at present, that all governments are based on a chief executive relying on a cabinet. The notion of council which Hoebel describes has a rather special character. It may have been inherited from widespread feudal traditions, but it has not extended universally. Over the centuries it did lead to the notion of the modern cabinet in Britain and in some other countries. Later, under British influence, which was crucial in this respect, the cabinet system of government extended both to parts of the Continent and to large segments of the Third World. For a while, at the end of the nineteenth century, it indeed seemed to be about to prevail everywhere. This is perhaps why this form of government has been regarded as the 'norm', in both senses of the word — a common practice and an ideal — in the contemporary world. But there have been other traditions which have been at least as important.

Perhaps the simplest way of approaching the complex history of the development of government is to view the model which Hoebel and Fenno describe as occupying a middle position between two arrangements. The king or chief executive-and-council model is based on an equilibrium between men each of whom has authority, but not overwhelming authority. They all need each other, rely on each other and generally respect each other. Such an equilibrium has not always existed in the past, nor does it always exist at present. On the one hand, one extreme alternative position is occupied by the absolutist ruler, who chooses his subordinates in the way he wishes and individually. This model implies that the ruler is politically very strong and therefore does not depend on the support of ministers. As a matter of fact, the pure absolutist model is rarely applied: it can be found more frequently in a somewhat 'impure' form, in part because rulers often need to rely on the advice and strength of one or a few men, and in part even more because these rulers create or inherit a large bureaucracy, which in turn limits their freedom of decision. Thus, absolutist governments often turn out to be bureaucratic governments, with civil servants establishing practices and arrangements against which rulers have to defend themselves.

The other extreme governmental model is that of the old 'republican' arrangement whereby most of the policy-making power, at least, is in the hands of a council, but not of a council in the cabinet sense: this council is a body of independent men, often with a power base of their own and constituting an 'aristocracy' debating the affairs of the state, while functions of 'management' are divided among office-holders rotating rapidly. This model was modified and gradually abandoned in its pure form, as it was seemingly impractical for large polities. The changes have gradually brought the arrangements nearer to the chief executive-and-council system which Fenno has described, thus perhaps accounting in part for the fact that, even where it exists, the 'cabinet' system is far from being uniform.

1. The 'Republican' Tradition: From Senatorial to Presidential Government

At the start of his analysis of the evolution of Roman politics from the end of the Republic to the principate of Augustus, R. Syme describes in these terms the structure of government in the early and classical periods of the Republic:

> When the patricians expelled the Kings from Rome, they were careful to retain the kingly power, vested in a pair of annual magistrates... The Senate again, being a permanent body, arrogated to itself powers, and after conceding sovereignty of the assembly of the People was able to frustrate its exercise. The two consuls remained at the head of the government, but policy was largely directed by ex-consuls. These men ruled, as did the Senate, not in virtue of written law, but through *auctoritas*.[4]

Much later in the work, before analysing the changes in government and 'cabinet' structure brought about by Augustus, Syme states: 'In a sense, the consulars of the Republic might be designated as the government, "auctores publici consilii"',[5] but he adds immediately: 'But that government has seldom been able to present a united front in a political emergency'.[6] Syme does not examine precisely what is meant by 'government': he tends almost to equate government with 'ruling class' or at any rate ruling families. The question of coordination between the various activities of government is not raised. What is noted is that it was not possible for Augustus to manipulate the Senate, or, in Syme's words, for Augustus 'to retain the semblance of constitutional liberty with free elections and free debate in the Senate' ...without 'expert preparation and firm control behind the scenes of all public transactions'.[7] And Syme concludes: 'The era of Cabinet government had set in'.[8] One could put it differently: the Senate had ceased to be a 'council of government' and become an assembly.

The distinction made by Syme between the government of republican Rome and the government of Augustus provides the basis of the sharp contrast which has existed between what may be described as the traditional 'republican' approach to government and the 'monarchical' or 'imperial' form which Fenno presents as universal. This 'republican' form, which was adopted in city states in Italy and elsewhere from the Renaissance, was not based on the idea of a chief executive sharing, because he needed advice, some of the policy-making and much of the coordination and management tasks with a number of advisers, but on the division of specialized areas of government among a number of office-holders, while the power to decide on policy was in the hands of a deliberative body, usually composed of ex-office-holders, of which the Roman Senate of the classical period was the outstanding example.

Such an arrangement makes it possible to claim either that there was no government, and certainly no cabinet, in the strict sense of the word, in the traditional republican arrangement, or that the government was widely spread among the members of the ruling oligarchy. Office-holders had considerable power in their own field, but they did not share in overall policy-making. Rapid rotation was indeed the means of ensuring that office-holders did not overstep their function; the hierarchy of offices (the Roman *cursus honorum*) also ensured that a person holding a minor position was naturally anxious to go up the ladder and therefore willingly abandon the office which he had held with the result that there was rarely collusion between the various office-holders and therefore no informal or embryonic 'cabinet'.

This model of government became impractical towards the end of the Roman Republic when the *imperium* extended over a vast area and when financial and other problems became extremely serious. But while the model was abandoned by Augustus, it was revived, but also modified during the Renaissance, in many of the free cities, in particular in Italy. To take but two examples: Florence and Venice had a modified 'senatorial' government of this kind, the modifications going in the direction of giving powers to an 'inner council', more closely resembling a 'cabinet', as well as some influence to a chief executive. In Florence, the 'traditional form of government' was based on 'the Councils of the People and Commune. . .fully in charge of legislation and financial policy', with 'the Signoria appointed by lot'.[9] The Signoria had powers to initiate Bills, but 'rapid rotation of office was a fundamental feature of Florentine government administration. The length of appointments ranged from two months to one year, office-holders being normally allowed to be reappointed only after intervals of up to three years'.[10] The constant changes and the many 'extraordinary' arrangements which took place in Florence in the fifteenth century make it difficult to describe any form of government there as being truly 'normal', but there was never a model based on a chief executive surrounded by a council. The influence of the Medici was indirect as much as direct; it occurred through the 'packing' of various bodies by their supporters.

Venice went a little further away from the 'true' republican model, but it did not adopt a chief executive-and-council model either. Indeed, the stability of the Venetian political tradition was ascribed to the fact that the Republic had adopted a 'mixed' system which combined, in the Aristotelian manner, elements of democracy, aristocracy and monarchy. In the Venetian arrangement, the Senate — which constituted the 'oligarchical' or 'aristocratic' element — was the central governmental body.

> The Senators, known collectively as the 'Pregati' (literally, those 'summoned') exercised a general supervisory authority over all agencies of the State. They administered foreign policy, waged war and concluded peace, appointed military commanders and ambassadors. . . ., they dealt with taxation and other problems of internal policy; and they chose, as a kind of executive committee, various categories of *savi* or counsellors, who, with the heads of the criminal judiciary and with the Doge and his counsellors, composed the full College of the Senate.[11]

Alongside the Senate, the Council of Ten, created early in the fourteenth century, was assigned certain tasks and did increase its powers, but it did not substitute itself for the Senate, any more than the Doge, whose position was 'essentially honorary'[12] as he symbolized the 'immortality of the Commonwealth'.[13]

Thus, neither Florence nor Venice, nor for that matter most republics of that time and of subsequent centuries were governed on a model based on a chief executive advised by a council. The original idea of a deliberative council, of an oligarchical character, which delegated the management, but only the management, of the government to individuals or to little groups, usually rotating frequently, was maintained, although it became slowly distorted. But it was thought that it had been distorted by the very oligarchical character of the basis of the government and by the ambitions of some individuals and some families, as Rousseau was to state;[14] this 'republican' model, far from being thought impractical, was often considered to be 'ideal'.

Perhaps it should have been clear from the start that the republican system was, indeed, unworkable without major distortions: it might have been recognized that the ability of the Roman

Senate to rule at all depended on the existence of a small number of
leading families. Perhaps it should have been seen not only that a
large empire such as that of Rome in the first century BC, but that
almost any state beyond a tiny size required continuity of action
and coordination of government and that, in their very corrupt and
oligarchical manner, the Roman families, and later the leading
families in Florence or elsewhere, provided continuity and even,
after a manner, coordination. Perhaps, if this had been the case, a
modified version of the old republican model would have been
preserved. As it turned out, while the new French Republic of 1792
quickly collapsed in a vain attempt to organize government on a
'Roman' basis in the midst of a European conflict and of civil war,
the new American Republic moved one step further than Venice
had done in the direction of establishing a chief executive and of
combining the 'monarchical' element (in part imitated from Bri-
tian) with the 'aristocratic' and 'democratic' elements.

The American constitution of 1787 is a turning point in the
history of republican government. From then on, 'republicanism'
became associated with 'presidentialism'; in the early decades of
the nineteenth century, a number of presidential republics were
established in Central and South America; these were to be organized on the basis of structures more resembling absolutist regimes
than chief executive-and-council arrangements, let alone the old
republican model. In 1848, when France became republican again,
a 'presidential' model was viewed as the only possible arrangement
— although it was to fail after after a few years. Thus, the tables
seemed to be turned: absolutism, or at any rate strong executive
leadership, seemed inextricably associated with the idea of a
republic, in complete contrast with the situation prior to the eighteenth century.

Yet, in the late eighteenth century, and to a large extent to this
day, the American constitution and the American practice kept
alive a number of features of 'traditional' republicanism, because
they were based on a compromise which may be viewed as one of
the reasons for the felicitous development of the American Commonwealth, as an earlier compromise has been viewed as the reason
for the felicitous development of the Venetian Republic. For the
part played by the United States Senate, both in the constitution
and in practice, is clearly reminiscent of the role of the Roman
Senate. In essence, American government is based, as Aristotle
deemed necessary, on a *mélange* of democratic, aristocratic and

monarchical government, but a new *mélange* with features and a type of interaction which proved well-adapted to the problems of modern government.

First, the democratic element was 'improved' in that the representative character of the House of Representatives provided the continuity which the people's assemblies did not have in Rome or Florence. The senators themselves, even though they came to be elected directly by the people only in the twentieth century, did not view themselves as belonging to a purely 'aristocratic' element: they collaborated with the House on matters of legislation; they were part of the Congress of the Nation, dependent on the representative principle, and not exercising power in their own right. Second, the presidency had enough strength and continuity to enable its holders to organize government on their own and in particular to appoint personal advisers and a cabinet. These are not primarily, let alone exclusively, dependent on the Senate, although the Senate ratifies most appointments and takes the job seriously, and indeed insists in putting its *auctoritas* in the balance. But there is enough distance between executive appointments and the Senate to make the link between these appointments and the Senate relatively tenuous.

American government is thus not of the 'old republican' kind; yet it still has features of the old model — and this can be viewed in the light of the fact that the Senate is still a half-way house between a 'chamber' and a deliberative council, a state of affairs which has not prevailed in most other 'presidential' republics where, on the whole, the Congress is merely a 'Congress' (and often, but not always, has limited powers). In the United States, the partially 'Roman' character of the Senate remains. This accounts for the fact, which we mentioned in the previous Chapter, that the United States government is, to some extent, a government of 'strangers', that is to say, that the 'managers' are not so much linked to each other as anxious to establish direct communication, individually, with the Congress. While preventing American government from being overly 'bureaucratic' in the continental European sense, the strength and *auctoritas* of the Senate make it almost axiomatic that members of the various agencies will be tempted to lobby senators (and representatives by osmosis) in order to obtain the appropriations which they want, and that the president and his immediate advisers are impotent to stop this move towards 'segmented' government. Thus, to take Syme's expression, the United States government is 'merely an administration, not an organ of authority'. The president of the United States is in a position not unlike that of Augustus at the beginning of his reign, as if the early Augustan system had remained in permanent equilibrium instead of moving towards a bureaucratic structure. There is a 'tendency' to build a cabinet, to unite the various positions, but there is at the same time a contrary 'tendency' for the government to remain divided and to have separate lines of communication with the 'aristocratic council', the Senate. So far, the equilibrium has been maintained: we shall examine in the coming Chapters the extent to which it might currently be upset.

2. The Chief Executive-and-Cabinet System of United Government: British and Swedish Experience

While the republican tradition was maintained in Renaissance Italy, the monarchical form of government which was to lead to the cabinet system began to emerge in Northern Europe and especially in Britain and Sweden. Monarchical cabinet government has a double origin, patrimonial and feudal: surprisingly, perhaps, at first sight, this double origin was to give cabinet government its unity. For, while the desire of the king to rule the country as he ruled his estates led to the central position of the king as chief executive (or in the name of the king to the central position of the chief minister), the existence of a feudal bond with the nobles obliged the monarch at least to take account of the views of some of the members of the aristocracy. Cabinet government resulted from the very tension between the two forces, a tension which was never solved, as it was to be in absolutist government, to the benefit of the king. Where the power of the aristocracy was never fully broken, the transition from feudal government to a modern government, was, paradoxically enough, relatively smooth and a united cabinet form of government emerged without major hurdles. Difficulties were to arise much later, in the twentieth century.

The origins of this chief executive-and-council form of government in Britain appreciably precede the development of the cabinet under Charles II, although the Restoration period is often said to have been the start of modern British government. The basis for the arrangements were in fact established after the Wars of the Roses when the Tudor kings set up a government composed of an 'outer' circle and an 'inner' circle, noblemen often constituting the outer circle while middle class protégés of the king (Wolsey and later Thomas Cromwell, for instance) were the kernel of the inner circle. The English king did not eliminate the nobles from the government.

It is commonly asserted that Henry VII innovated when he surrounded himself with a council of men from the 'middle class'. As a matter of fact, Henry's Council included noblemen — Lancastrians...and reformed Yorkists...Such a Council was typical of nothing new, but of the older, pre Lancastrian Councils...When Henry VII chose advisers from non-magnate ranks, he was following not only Yorkist examples but the general practice which was only abandoned when the Crown lost control of the government.[15]

And Elton continues: 'The Tudors were not against aristocracy as such; they were against obstreperous men, whether noble, or gentle, or common'.[16]

What was therefore characteristic of Tudor government, and, as Elton says, of previous governments in England, was that there was a blending of noble and middle class, of aristocracy and 'people', of men who had standing in their own right and of 'king's men', the important point being that they were all part of one body, the council of the king. This council is therefore very different from the Senate of Rome or indeed of the United States: it is the council of the king; it advises the king; it centres around the king. The king determines its activities and indeed its organization, although he bows to the need to include in it men from outside his immediate circle. Feudalism and the general role of the aristocracy had seen to it that, even under the Tudors, English kings could not simply get rid of these 'outsiders'; but the strength of the king was such that he could bring the aristocracy in combination with his own men, exclude some of the nobles and make the others feel that they should work with him.

This situation was scarcely altered by men as powerful as Wolsey and Thomas Cromwell, although they did attempt to diminish the power of the aristocracy in order to rule more personally, albeit in the name of the king. As Elton says of the Elizabethan privy council:

The councillors were not equal because they included great men as well as lesser, and because the leaders of faction naturally loomed larger than the followers. More important for good government was that they did not all attend with equal zeal. The ordinary work was in fact done by a smaller group of executive ministers.[17]

From the point of view of the relative power of the monarch and chief minister, it is interesting to note the differences between Henry VIII and Elizabeth. Elton points out that Elizabeth was keen to keep factions within the council in order not to have to rely too much on one man. But from the point of view of the organization of government and of the cabinet, the difference was not very important, any more than it is important from the point of view of the existence and role of the cabinet to note that a modern British prime minister organizes a balanced composition of the representatives of the various factions in his party or tries on the contrary to have a united cabinet. What is essential is that the Tudor council, composed as it was of active ministers and less active 'hangers on', provided what had become the traditional blend of aristocrats and new men, laymen and specialists which paradoxically gave British government its overall unity and its effectiveness.

This tradition is the crucial element which accounts for the fact that the sixteenth century council became the seventeenth and eighteenth century cabinet. The functions of the council were naturally passed on to the cabinet because, by then, it had become normal (it was regarded as ideal) that the body surrounding the king (acting under his initiative or, as in the eighteenth century, on his behalf), should deal with policy-making, but also comprise men especially engaged in managing the affairs of the state. What Elton says about the Elizabethan council of the late sixteenth century applies to the modern cabinet: 'The Privy Council concerned itself quite simply with everything that went on in England, and it often dealt with these matters directly, though at other times it delegated them to a particular minister (in the main the principal secretary), a lesser official, or a different court'.[18] Charles II or William were not to innovate in this respect: they simply transferred to the cabinet the powers which the council could no longer exercise because it was too large.

The unity of the government in Britain was therefore achieved because the privy council, first, and, though to a lesser extent, the cabinet later, was composed of men belonging to three groups whom the king felt obliged or convenient to bring together. First there were the 'representatives', that is to say in earlier times the feudal lords and later those who had a standing in the country and in Parliament. These were the men who, if they had been excluded, might have either led a warring faction in Parliament or a rebellion in the country or who might have indeed attempted to give to

Parliament, and in particular to the House of Lords, a function of council analogous to the function of the Roman Senate. Of course, the privy council and even more the cabinet included only a small proportion of these men, but the proportion was large enough to avoid the formation of an alternative source of power elsewhere. Those who felt strong enough to lead a faction and were not included simply became leaders of the opposition and, occasionally, entered the government. However, probably because these aristocratic members of the privy council had other interests, they often constituted the 'outer circle' of the council. But this was their doing in so far as, if they wished to, they could achieve greater influence, and some of the aristocrats did, from time to time, emerge as real leaders. But most of them seemed, in most cases, satisfied with their representative and somewhat decorative function. Their role was therefore to legitimize, and occasionally to veto, decisions felt to be controversial.

The second group on the council was composed of the executive ministers whom the king chose at will and to whom he from time to time gave particular responsibilities because he wanted to work with and through them. They were the 'full-time directors', so to speak, of the governmental structure. They were thus managers of specific aspects of government, occasionally coordinators of policy, either as individuals or collectively; they were also the main elements in the policy-making process, although the members of the 'outer ring' of the council could also occasionally play a part. The situation was always fluid, in that the king could rely more on one minister than on another, or on a group of ministers than on others, but it was fluid within the framework of the privy council and later of the cabinet. The advantage which this flexibility gave the king, and which, later, the prime minister was to inherit, was compensated by the fact that the king never completely abandoned the idea of a council, that is to say that he never completely eliminated the 'outer ring' of the representatives from some participation in affairs.

Between the 'representatives' and the 'executive ministers' was a third group of members of the council and cabinet: these were the men in various 'sinecures' who played a crucial part by being available for any special missions which the king might wish to see them undertake; prime ministers of modern British government were also to use them in this way. They were also entrusted occasionally with tasks of coordination or acted as arbitrators if some of their colleagues were engaged in factionalism. And they constituted a link between the outer ring and the executive ministers; indeed, kings and prime ministers were to gradually place 'representatives' whom they wanted to include in the government in some of these sinecures. As the 'outer ring' as such slowly disappeared, the holders of sinecures were often to fulfil the same role. Thus, the unity of the government as a whole was maintained through the realization that it could be achieved only if diversity of origin and skills was kept in the council and, later, in the cabinet.

The development of governmental arrangements in Sweden occurred along parallel lines, although the distinction between representatives of the nobles and king's men was never as clear cut as in Britain and although, as a result, the king of Sweden did not have to bring the two groups together in the same rather contrived manner as in Britain. Modern Swedish government was organized by Gustavus Adolfus and his chief minister Oxiensterna by the charter of 1611. 'The Charter embodies both the old ideas and new but definitely redirected the constitutional structure.... It provided explicitly for the power of the nobility. ...Aristocratic monopoly of high office was fixed for a long time to come'.[19] And F.D. Scott continues, 'The King accepted the conciliar machinery and then used his own dynamic personality to guide the machine set up to control him'.[20] Five offices were incorporated within the council, but one of the offices, the chancery, 'touched almost every aspect of government, including commerce, education, hospitals, and, of course, all foreign affairs'.[21]

What had been achieved was a fusion of the nobility and the bureaucracy under the leadership of the king. For what was to be peculiar to Sweden for the coming decades and even centuries was that the nobles were also providing the administrative and technical personnel which the country needed. The system was based at the same time on a parliamentary principle, a democratic principle, a bureaucratic principle and a corporative principle.[22] Thus when, in 1809, the new constitution was adopted, the government, or Council of State, continued in the same tradition and, indeed, throughout the nineteenth century, Swedish government succeeded in being a body combining a considerable amount of 'representation' (first from nobles, and later from other classes) with a high degree of administrative and managerial skills. Perhaps this blending was possible because of the relatively small size of the population, but perhaps it was also due to the fact that, very early on, a substantial part of management was severed from the government and given to administrative boards whose origin stemmed from the eighteenth century.[23] These boards were set up in order to avoid tyranny and it was specified, in 1720, that members of the government could not be members of the boards.[24]

No equivalent distinction between ministers and members of administrative boards was instituted in Britain, or in the other European or Commonwealth countries which introduced a cabinet system in the nineteenth century. On the contrary, the British cabinet was viewed as the effective centre of political power as well as of administrative decision-making. This was Bagehot's view in the middle of the century, and it was also recognized by the politicians, as an episode reported by J.P. Mackintosh aptly indicates:

> Ministers assembled to consider all the principal questions before the government and the decision was final. When Kimberley decided to refuse the post of Viceroy of India in 1872, he reflected that 'the office of Cabinet minister is really higher. It sounds grandly to be Viceroy over 180 millions of men, but it is in truth a much greater thing to be a member of the governing committee of the whole Empire, India included'.[25]

Thus, the British cabinet was both the equivalent of the Roman Senate of the Republic, in that it effectively took the major policy decisions, and the equivalent of the Roman office-holders, as ministers decided on administration and were markedly involved in the management of affairs.

This concentration of all important matters on cabinet members was to lead gradually to difficulties, at the very moment when the cabinet form of government was being imitated in parts of Europe and throughout the Commonwealth. Indeed, difficulties might have arisen before the twentieth century had not two developments reduced to some extent the pressure on the cabinet. First, the British government was increased in size and came to include non-cabinet ministers as well as undersecretaries; these were politicians of either House who hoped to move eventually to cabinet level and meanwhile were willing to carry out loyally on behalf of the cabinet some of the managerial tasks which had to be undertaken. Second, the introduction of civil service reforms patterned on the model of the Indian civil service helped to establish a philosophy of ministerial control, as a result of which civil servants remained somewhat nervous of taking major decisions: the fact that the top civil servants were 'amateurs' rather than technicians reinforced this caution.

But world wars were to show, in Britain as in other cabinet systems, that the combination of policy-making, coordination and management within the cabinet was becoming inefficient and, indeed, unrealistic. Various suggestions were made and various experiments attempted to meet the problem, but no truly acceptable solution was found. Meanwhile, some of the reality of power began to escape the cabinet: aspects of policy-making and coordination were increasingly dealt with in bodies smaller than the whole cabinet; management, on the other hand, was increasingly undertaken by administrators or even technicians. Thus, the experiment of a united 'chief executive-and-council' government appeared, in the post-1945 world, no longer to be the ideal compromise by which the various aspects of governmental activity were reconciled and blended, but to lead to difficulties and to the realization that formal authority no longer corresponded to the reality of decision-making. Hence, perhaps, the resurgence of the third form of governmental structure which had been in existence since the Renaissance, but had suffered a decline in the late nineteenth century, the model of the authoritarian, bureaucratic and rather divided government.

3. Absolutist and Bureaucratic Governments

Both what we have called the 'republican' system and the 'chief executive-and-council' arrangement were primarily political ways of organizing government in the face of contending groups which needed to be placated: 'republicans' believed that decisions should be taken within a relatively large oligarchical body; supporters of the 'cabinet' system found the 'chief executive-and-council' method particularly valuable in striking a compromise between the needs of 'leadership' and the imperative of 'consultation'. Where, however, as a result of the victory of monarchs over the aristocracy, there was no need to placate outside groups by including them in the government, an 'absolutist' model began to prevail which was theoretically devoted to the principle of governing things rather than men, that is to say, that the purpose of government was to establish a number of services and run these as effectively as possible. Thus, enlightened despotism, as it emerged in the second half of the eighteenth century, was a direct and logical consequence of the growth of absolutism of the French seventeenth century variety. Needless to say, it seemed that such a government should be composed and based entirely on the loyalty of civil servants. Absolutist government seemed to be the triumph of administration over politics.

It may therefore seem surprising to discover that the governments of the absolute monarchs and of the 'enlightened despots' who succeeded them were far from being simple hierarchical structures with straightforward lines of command. Admittedly, the various monarchical governments which were built on this model included a number of ministers or secretaries, often drawn from families with a civil service tradition and whose function was to carry out the broad policies of the head of state with respect to various aspects of administration. But there were also other bodies alongside the ministers. In France, for instance, there were no less than four councils which could be said to share in the business of government (although one of them had a partly judicial function). In Prussia, after the disappearance of the Council of Nobles, the administration was run by as many as nineteen departments: this structure was so unwieldy that it was replaced in 1728 by a *Kabinetsministerium* to which, however, a number of councils were attached.[26] In Russia, the Council of the Boyars was replaced by Peter the Great in 1711 by a Senate, together with, a few years later, eleven 'colleges', each of which was composed of a number of civil servants.[27]

There were two main reasons why these complicated arrangements were set up in absolute monarchies. First, even strong monarchs were not always able to abolish the older councils without replacing them by an ostensibly similar consultative mechanism. Absolutist leaders had at the time, as many authoritarian rulers have at present, to establish their power gradually: even if they had wanted to, even if they had perceived (which was not always the case) that a simpler and more streamlined hierarchical structure would serve their purposes better, they simply politically could not do so. Monarchs had to some extent to keep the pretence of 'consultation'; even a 'charismatic' usurper such as Napoleon felt it necessary to build a variety of councils within his governmental structure. Thus, councils played a 'symbolic' political part — and the government was not fully 'administrative'.

But the political role of the administration was even greater as

the 'civil service class' came to acquire increasing influence and to
be viewed as the only basis for a 'traditional' administration. A
government based on a number of councils was thus felt to be a
good government: in Central and Eastern Europe, the councils of
the absolute monarchies were therefore replicas of the
administrative boards which were set up in Sweden in the eighteenth century. But, while in Sweden the Council of State provided
the political leadership, the secretaries and ministries of absolute
monarchies had a less clear position. They were the agents of the
monarch, but, being drawn from the same groups as the members
of the councils, they were more often in the position of buffers than
in that of real decision-makers.

Thus, although absolute monarchs were deemed to be all-
powerful (and in the Russian case were claimed to be autocrats) the
structure of government was not based on a clear and hierarchical
line of command. The practice more resembled a confederacy of
semi-autonomous agencies, each of which produced semi-
representative mechanisms from within. For the councils were in
effect corporate bodies of the civil service. The fact that the problems faced by absolute monarchs came from within the
'implementing machine' did not make these less serious, especially
since these rulers claimed that they were attempting — and indeed
often were genuinely attempting — to transform and modernize the
economies of their countries. Their *dirigisme* implied a technically
competent and efficient civil service; in practice their efforts were
often thwarted by the bureaucratic machine.

Some of these difficulties were alleviated as, from the early part
of the nineteenth century, governments were reorganized: councils
saw their role decreased; arrangements resembling the British
cabinet system were introduced. This was particularly true in post-
revolutionary France which adopted a constitution patterned on
that of Britain; Central European states also adopted at least the
trimmings of a cabinet structure, although the cabinet was rarely
responsible to Parliament. It seemed that, as time passed, most
European states would simply move gradually to an 'executive-and-
council' system of government.

Yet, even in France, let alone in Prussia, Austria, or Russia,
many characteristics of the absolutist and bureaucratic governmental structure remained: specifically, ministerial councils remained staffed with civil servants and the idea of collective government spread only very slowly. In reality, only in the 1870s did the

French government finally become composed of politicians; between Napoleon I in 1800 and the end of the Second Empire in 1870, civil servants played a very large part in France, sometimes in association with politicians, but often on their own. There was interpenetration between business, public service and politicians, and, except for relatively short periods, there was no collective responsibility of the government. Indeed, the power of civil servants has remained very close to the surface ever since, even during the Third and Fourth Republics: thus, not too surprisingly, in the first two decades of the Fifth Republic the government displayed characteristics more akin to the 'absolutist' period of the kings and of the Empire than to those of a 'cabinet' arrangement.

In Prussia, and later in Imperial Germany, as well as in Austria and Russia, there was not even the pretence of a 'political' cabinet before 1914. Governments were first and foremost of a bureaucratic kind: emperors, often helped (and occasionally overshadowed) by a chancellor or prime minister, were the major political elements in the governmental machine. Governments did not constitute 'councils' in the real sense; nor did they even advise emperors or chancellors in the strict sense of the word. The purpose of the government was, as in the eighteenth century, to see that the services were run efficiently on behalf of and for the emperor. Only in Hungary did the cabinet system gradually prevail — possibly because the Austro-Hungarian emperor remained, primarily, an Austrian emperor. But in the new states which were gradually established out of the slow disintegration of the Turkish Empire, the prevailing 'absolutist' model of a bureaucratic government also became the norm.

While their ministers remained confined within their own sphere and often did not pretend to be more than administrators, Central European monarchs relied heavily on advice from outside the government: even the chancellor or prime minister was not necessarily the man to whom the king or emperor listened for advice. This state of affairs contributed to the maintenance of a tradition of dualism throughout the nineteenth century in Central and Eastern Europe, although the reasons were different from those which had originally led to 'dualism'. In the early absolutist period, monarchs relied on ministers and secretaries to counterbalance the power of the aristocracy. As the whole structure of government tilted towards the bureaucracy, and, indeed, as the bureaucracy appeared to acquire an overwhelming role in the implementation of decisions, monarchs seemed to wish to disentangle themselves from the exclusive advice of public servants, while avoiding dependence, as far as possible, on the representatives of new, more 'democratic' political forces. The result was an increasing reliance on a small number of personal friends and advisers, often very unrepresentative, which probably contributed to the increased divorce between the rulers of these regimes and the new groups in society.

This distinction between political advice given by some courtiers and administrative management provided by the government did not have time to take a fully settled shape in Central Europe, as the three empires collapsed in the aftermath of the First World War. But a similar structure was maintained in some of the Balkan states in the interwar period and in a number of Middle Eastern countries after 1945, including a few monarchies which have remained in existence up to the 1980s. In Weimar Germany and in post-1918 Austria, as well as even more so in Czechoslovakia, a cabinet system of government was ostensibly introduced, although it was more akin to the French than to the British form in that loose coalitions of politicians were superimposed on a civil service structure which controlled the mechanisms of implementation. Thus, German and Austrian cabinets in the 1920s were never truly in charge of policy-making, coordination and the supervision of management.

Meanwhile, the most important developments in the organization of government were occurring in the Soviet Union. By accident more than by design, the Soviet practice came to build on and expand the dualist structure which had mostly characterized Russian government since Peter the Great. Soviet leaders inherited an almost unbroken tradition of purely administrative government, the only period during which a political government, loosely resembling the British cabinet, had been in existence in Russia having been that of the Provisional Government of 1917-18. Thus, Russian and Soviet ministers, and the Council of Ministers as a whole, were the direct heirs of the ministers who, from the early eighteenth century, had been drawn from the civil service class, had moved gradually up the ladder of their departments and had usually found themselves at the top after a long career in that department. Whether or not this model was felt to be the best possible, it was obviously the only one which had operated the heavy and complex bureaucratic machine of the tsars. The natural sequence was therefore not so much to change the characteristics of the government as such, especially as the Soviet government was engaged in a massive expansion of the public sector, but to let the Council of Ministers perform the task which it had always performed, ever since Peter the Great had created the colleges of administration, while entrusting the Politburo of the Communist Party with the functions of policy-making and coordination, which Peter the Great's Senate had fulfilled and to which a few close advisers of the tsars had been entrusted up to 1917.

Dualism in the Soviet structure of government is thus only in part an invention of the twentieth century and of Communist rulers; rather it is an adaptation from the authoritarian tradition which, because it became naturally bureaucratic, had to contend with the problems of coping with the very bureaucracy which it had created. Here lies the reason why this dual model has spread widely in the post-1945 world. The cabinet form of government based on the single, all-purpose council was set up, or developed naturally, in order to cope with a primarily political situation, the situation resulting from the conflict between the king and his subjects (nobles in the first instance, 'Third Estate' later). This form of government proved increasingly inadequate, in the twentieth century, as managerial problems increased: Sweden may have, better than Britain, been able to maintain the cabinet system without major problems, but this has been because the system of boards, in itself already more akin to a 'bureaucratic' structure of government, prevented ministers from being involved very deeply in matters of administration. The dual government model developed naturally from the bureaucratic structure because, once the monarchs were able to control the nobles through the bureaucracy, the need to control the bureaucracy in turn began to arise. Not surprisingly, new states which have given major emphasis to economic development have had to rely on the bureaucracy to implement these aims, and, in these states, the bureaucracy is usually one of the very few forces which emphasize the need for national unity and for modernization. But the problem of controlling the bureaucracy inevitably arose and this in turn led naturally, in many cases at least, to a dual or divided structure of government.

Modern government has thus three main origins. The 'republican' oligarchical form, one of the most ancient, also proved to be the least able to survive; it seemed primarily adapted to small city-states, as Rousseau noted, but it also provided the basis for one very important element in presidential government, in the United States at least, by stressing the need for 'councils' of a deliberative, rather than purely executive character. There is indeed a broader legacy: it is the legacy of the 'unbureaucratic', 'participationist' government, which may not 'work' efficiently in the context of a massive state, but which is perhaps for this reason preferable if consensus is to be achieved and regimentation avoided. The influence of these ideas can be found in certain forms at least of 'cabinet' government, those where the chief executive is less able to dominate the rest of the government. This cabinet form of government, which emerged as a compromise between the desires of monarchs to rule and the wishes of subjects to be represented, indeed seemed for a period to constitute an ideal way of combining the new democratic ideas of participation and the more traditional aims of leadership; but it has in turn proved increasingly ineffective in the face of the development of bureaucracy which has multiplied problems of management and exercised considerable pressure on the time of cabinet members. Thus, the form of governmental structure which Europe inherited from absolute monarchs and which was the first to give much power to the bureaucracy while reserving the policy-making functions to small, often informal, and usually secret groups, has increasingly appeared able to meet some of the requirements of the contemporary world. The fall of empires which followed the 1914 war did not lead to the victory of the cabinet system of government over the bureaucratic system: on the contrary, new bureaucratic forms of government emerged, while the cabinet system had to increasingly adapt to circumstances with the result that not merely collective government, but indeed united government seems, at least on the surface, to be increasingly challenged by a divided form of hierarchical and bureaucratic government.

Notes

1. R. Fenno, *The President's Cabinet* (Harvard University Press, 1959), Vintage Edition, p. 9.

2. Ibid., p. 10.

3. E. Adamson Hoebel, *Man in the Primitive World* (McGraw Hill, 1949), p. 387.

4. R. Syme, *The Roman Revolution* (Oxford University Press, 1st ed., 1939, paper ed., 1960), p. 10.

5. Ibid., p. 387.

6. Eod. loc.

7. Ibid., p. 407.

8. Eod. loc.

9. N. Rubenstein, *The Government of Florence under the Medici (1434-94)* (Oxford University Press, 1966), p. 88.

10. Ibid., p. 30.

11. W.J. Bouwsma, *Venice and the Defence of Republican Liberty* (University of California Press, 1968), p. 61.

12. Ibid., p. 62.

13. Ibid., p. 63.

14. Rousseau, *Social Contract*, Book 3, Chapter X, footnote 1.

15. G.R. Elton, *England under the Tudors* (Methuen, 1955; 1974 ed.), pp. 44-5.

16. Eod. loc.

17. Ibid., p. 407.

18. Ibid., p. 406.

19. F.D. Scott, *Sweden: The Nation's History* (University of Minnesota Press, 1977), p. 183.

20. Ibid., p. 184.

21. Eod. loc.

22. Ibid., pp. 240-2.

23. Ibid., p. 184.

24. B. Chapman, *The Profession of Government* (Allen and Unwin, 1959), p. 18.

25. J.P. Mackintosh, *The British Cabinet* (Stevens, 1st ed., 1962), p. 246.

26. L. Dupriez, *Les ministres dans les principaux pays d'Europe et d'Amérique* (Rothschild, 2 vols, 1892 and 1893), Vol. I, p. 352.

27. M.S. Anderson, *Peter the Great* (Thames and Hudson, 1978), pp. 128 and 132-3.

3. THE STRUCTURE OF MODERN GOVERNMENT

Although many nineteenth century national executives were controlled by monarchs and staffed with civil servants, most observers probably felt at the beginning of the twentieth century that governments were moving towards a collective cabinet system. By and large, governments were then viewed as belonging to one or the other of two types, hierarchical and centred around one leader, or collective and based on a cabinet of near-equals. And the evolution of governments in Central Europe indeed seemed to suggest a gradual and almost inevitable ascendancy of the cabinet form. The American system remained very different, admittedly, but it was exceptional; it was unique among Western countries, as if there was a fundamental contradiction between democratic government and a hierarchical executive in which a president could appoint his subordinates at will. With that one, admittedly major, exception, cabinet governments of a collective character seemed to prevail all over the 'modern' world.

Less than a century later, the picture has changed dramatically. Cabinet government has survived, admittedly, but it no longer exerts the attraction which it once did. In the Third World, only a small majority of new countries are ruled by a collective or even near-collective government. Furthermore, the cabinet system itself is under attack: some claim that it is an inefficient system, wholly unsuited to the complexities of modern government, while others remark that it is gradually disappearing where it previously prevailed; it is suggested that cabinet governments are moving in a hierarchical direction and specifically that prime ministers are becoming 'presidential' and are taking over powers hitherto shared among the whole cabinet.[1]

This view is controversial and it is, so far, exaggerated. But other forms of government have been as successful as the cabinet system in many parts of the world and especially in new countries. In much of the Third World, hierarchical or strongly-led governments have been set up, either from independence or after only a few years of apparently relatively ineffective collective government. Traditional monarchs, charismatic presidents, and military leaders have set up executives in the same way as the eighteenth century enlightened despots once did, in which the civil service plays a large part alongside parties and other groups.

But other recent developments have perhaps been even more remarkable, not least because they have raised major doubts about the wisdom of dividing all governments into hierarchical and collective only. First, at the very moment when questions were being asked about the feasibility of a collective structure of government in Western Europe, the hierarchical model which United States governments had previously embodied was being transformed. While British governments were described as 'prime ministerial' or near-presidential in many quarters, the American government was ceasing to be presidential in the strict sense of the word: it seemed on the contrary increasingly characterized by the presence of a number of semi-independent units which the president had difficulty in coordinating, let alone in leading. Observers noticed that the United States president's role was more to induce and influence than to direct. From this realization began to emerge the view of an American government composed of a number of independent chiefdoms and no longer forming an integrated whole in which the lines of decision-making all led to the president. Thus, even if it was the case that the British and other European governments were inexorably moving towards a hierarchical model (a point which remains quite controversial), the United States government was moving away from this model, not towards a collective formula, but towards a new set of arrangements in some ways reminiscent of the origins of republican government, when, as we saw, the various sectors were administered by independently appointed 'ministers'. While the full implications of this new development have still not been assessed (in part because of the traditional lack of broad comparative interest in governmental structure), it seems at least necessary to conclude that developments in the United States suggest that a different model of government is slowly emerging.

The complexity of the administrative machine was the main root of the changes occurring in governmental structures in the United States. Meanwhile, an even more complex set of governmental arrangements has been adopted in Communist states. Although these arrangements are not usually observed systematically in the West (in part because of the difficulty of discovering the reality behind the facade), there is no doubt that the government structures in the Soviet Union and other Communist systems cannot easily, if at all, be accounted for by the distinction between cabinets and hierarchical or bureaucratic governments. Admittedly, for a long time, and especially for as long as Stalin ruled the Soviet Union, governmental structures in Communist states could be described as resulting from an endeavour to impose a strong, indeed ruthless, form of political control on a public service which in turn was in control of the society. Indeed, the Soviet government, and other Communist governments in its wake, seemed to attempt an impossible task: they had to maximize the influence of the bureaucracy by eliminating or drastically restricting the scope of private initiative in the economic and social spheres. This meant a vast expansion of administrative services and, consequently, a dramatic multiplication of the problems raised by administrative management and coordination, let alone overall policy-making. Yet Communist leaders wanted at the same time to ensure that the political controllers remained on top; theirs was the opposite approach to that of American government, in which the various agencies which were also less overwhelmingly powerful than their Soviet counterparts were basically left relatively free to bargain with each other and to come to compromises by way of trade-offs. The Soviet leaders wished to impose a line and see to it that the line was implemented throughout the many agencies of the bureaucracy: this led to the setting up of complex governments in which state bodies were constituted alongside and under party organizations.

The political conditions under which these developments occurred were such that it was difficult to know for at least a decade after the Second World War whether these arrangements were more than a massive cover-up for a ruthless autocracy. Communist governments had special problems of policy-making, coordination and administrative management arising from the endeavours of Communist states to control and direct, in a detailed manner, most aspects of society; but Communist governments also seemed organized primarily in a totalitarian, or at best very authoritarian manner. The model seemed to be neither collective nor even hierarchical: it had elements of both, the ostensible collective elements being a modernized facade for a wholly personalized system, not merely in the Soviet Union under Stalin, but in East European and North Asian states as well. It seemed unnecessary to lay much emphasis on the formal structures, and especially on the formal state structures. Power appeared to be concentrated in the Politburo, if not on the first secretary alone.

The same kind of attitude prevailed in relation to experiments taking place in the Third World, especially in parts of Africa and the Middle East from the 1960s. At first, the newly independent countries had usually adopted a Western model, formally at least; this of course had been the case for over a century in Latin America, where almost all the states set up governments on the United States presidential pattern, often in a somewhat caricatural manner. The result was that any differences which occurred there usually seemed to be the consequences of the basically unstable, indeed, unruly character of these polities; it seemed unnecessary to examine Latin American governments to see whether they had brought about an alternative model. Similarly, the newly independent states of the post-1945 period did not appear to warrant a reassessment of existing models: any variations were almost automatically ascribed to the fact that underlying patterns of legitimacy were low and problems posed by the setting up of an efficient administration particularly acute, especially since these countries often had development goals that required sophisticated bureaucratic structures and the presence of men in government endowed with high managerial skills and benefiting from large political resources.

Indeed, for a period, the first generation leaders of new Third World countries, often possessing 'charismatic' popularity, introduced collective or in most cases hierarchical arrangements based on a presidential system. But from the late 1960s, some changes began to occur: second generation leaders, especially those coming to power through a military coup, experimented with more complex structures of government. Because they lacked personal support, they needed to rely on their military colleagues; but they also needed the support of the bureaucracy to achieve development goals or even simply to 'clean up the mess' which they claimed to have inherited; and, in some cases, they also wanted to give a socialist, or Marxist, ideological base to their regime. They thus began to adopt governmental arrangements resembling those of Communist countries. Revolutionary or military councils were set up alongside regular administrative governments.

Two Dimensions of Governmental Arrangements

The second half of the twentieth century has been characterized, not merely by the return to a hierarchical form of government in many countries, but by the institutionalization of complex Communist governments, by the emergence of executives organized on a similar basis in the Third World and by the evolution of the American government towards a looser but also more divided structure. These changes suggest that forms of government are becoming more varied in the contemporary world. Governments are not merely hierarchical or collective, they can also be 'united' or based on two or more bodies. As multi-level governments are becoming more numerous, we are witnessing the gradual development of a second dimension along which structures of government need to be analysed.

This is not an entirely new development, but it has acquired more importance than in the past, almost certainly as a result of the expansion of governmental activities and of the consequential difficulties which governments based on traditional arrangements are experiencing in coping with them. For, while the existence of a particular set of governmental arrangements depends on many factors, among which tradition, political ideology and the socio-economic structure of society obviously play a part, three specifically institutional characteristics have an essential and direct role — the personal strength of the leader, the weight and character of the main political groups, and the role and importance of the bureaucracy; and the last two, and perhaps the bureaucracy in particular, have been instrumental in leading to divided governments in the contemporary world.

Personal leadership is obviously the element which has traditionally pulled government in a centralized and hierarchical direction. If leaders are strong, they can decide, not just on the composition of the government, but on the extent of influence which they

wish to exercise. But, in the contemporary world, leaders are rarely
very strong: as we saw in the previous volume, the only situations
from which long-duration leaders still emerge are traditional
monarchies, of which there are very few, the early post-independence period, which is a once-and-for-all occurrence, and Communist arrangements. But we also noted that the duration of Communist leadership was probably due, more than in part, to the dual
character of this leadership. Other long-duration leaders are the
product of circumstance, and these circumstances are relatively
rare.[2] And, while long-duration leadership cannot be equated entirely with strong leadership, there is a manifest relationship between the two characteristics. Moreover, as many leaders come to
power as a result of military coups, they have to engage in difficult
operations designed to build their political and administrative
strength. This suggests that most leaders have, for one reason or
another, to depend on a number of groups to exercise their influence; they may temporarily have great power, but they cannot long
resist the erosion of this power under the pressure of groups, the
complexity of problems which they face or simple sheer ill-luck.

The power of leaders thus depends on the configuration of the
forces which led them to power. Traditional elites, the army, a
political party, will determine the parameters of the influence of
leaders and set the conditions under which they will be able to
govern. As most leaders realize that they need the support of these
groups to remain 'credible', they also have to accept the consequences for the composition and structure of the governments
which they form.

Leaders also depend on bureaucracies; these may enhance their
strength — their role may be better assured against parties, the
military, or other politically important groups — but, while leaders
are helped in this way, they also become the prisoners of the
bureaucracies. Large numbers of states view socio-economic
development as the means of diminishing their dependence on
traditional elites and their representatives, but this means that they
have to rely more heavily on the technical know-how of the civil
servants. Thus, the bureaucracy has acquired almost universal
influence, although its strength has been particularly noticeable in
Communist countries and in Third World states adopting a
populist or programme ideology.

Leaders who are not naturally strong have to include at least
some of the representatives of these groups in the governmental

decision-making process. They may include them all in a united governmental council, and they may let the members of this council exercise much influence: this is indeed what happened with collective cabinets. But this is becoming more difficult as a result of the combined power of the political groups — elites, military, party — and of the bureaucracy; this is also clearly at the expense of the power of the leader himself. It is difficult to accommodate the bureaucracy in a single government based on a collective model: the normal consequence is for the bureaucracy to be subordinated to the political leaders, and this may be detrimental to both public sector efficiency and to organizational morale.

Thus contemporary governments come to be divided if the weight of the bureaucracy is such that it is in equilibrium with the political groups in the society, or they may be divided if the leaders attempt to strengthen their hold by keeping the political groups, party or military, on the one hand, and the bureaucracy on the other, in two separate spheres. Governments may be divided as a result of a natural evolution simply because, as in the United States, the administrative and political machine has become so complex that efforts at coordination are in many ways thwarted by the sheer impossibility of keeping effective control over bodies which find it useful to relate to many important spheres outside the government, such as Congress, or interest groups. But, the division of the government may be formal as well as informal, where, as in the Soviet Union and several Third World states, a sharp distinction is drawn between 'administration' and 'policy-making'. From a tightly knit nucleus to a 'government of strangers', the structure of modern government comprises almost all possible types of arrangements along the two dimensions of unity *v.* division and hierarchical *v.* collective decision-making.

1. Hierarchical Governments

A government may be said to be united when decisions emerge from one centre, be it composed of one man, a few men, or a whole group. If the centre of this nervous system is composed of one man, or, at most, of two or three, and if the rest of the government depends for its guidance on the initiatives or 'impulsion' from this centre, the government may be said to be both united and hierarchical. Obviously, even in a hierarchical structure, the ministers will be expected to take many important decisions, but, if these decisions are derivative from the decisions taken by the centre, the government may still be said to be hierarchical. In practice, a distinction will tend to be drawn between broad policy-making and coordination which will remain primarily in the hands of the leader and his immediate entourage, and managerial activities which will, perforce, be undertaken mainly by the ministers; but, even there, in a truly hierarchical government, the continuous guidance and influence of the leader will be felt.

One of the ways in which leaders are able to make their influence felt on the whole government is through the power to appoint and dismiss ministers. Obviously, if a leader can appoint whom he wishes to the government and dispose of anyone with whom he is not satisfied, he will be able to ensure that his views are taken into account and his suggestions carried out. But such a power of leaders over members of the government is less common than might outwardly seem to be the case. While many leaders may be legally entitled to select and dismiss ministers at will, there are often constraints to the full exercise of this power. This is true in parliamentary systems, where leaders have, in practice, to choose their colleagues from among members of their party in Parliament, at least in most cases. They also often find it embarrassing to dismiss many of them, as they may fear the consequences of such an action for their own prestige and popularity; many ministers thus become indispensable and, for all intents and purposes, unremovable. But, even in governments in which the leader is very strong, there are limitations on the leader's effective power to appoint and dismiss his colleagues: politically and administratively, some of these may, also, be indispensable. Thus, there are also clear limits to the hierarchical structure of the government as a result of the de facto constraints exercised on the leader with respect to the composition of the government.[3]

In practice, therefore, hierarchical and collective governments are two extreme poles in a continuous dimension. There are very few, if any, 'true' collective governments. There are perhaps more hierarchical governments, although, in the past and perhaps even more at present, general societal conditions, as well as internal relationships within governments, contribute to reducing the number of those which are fully hierarchical, for a number of characteristics have to be present for full 'hierarchical' goverment to occur. One of these is that the bureaucracy should be relatively small; this means that economic and social 'interventionism' has to be relatively low; hierarchical government is difficult in a 'welfare state' context. Another characteristic relates to the position of leaders: leaders must be able to wield very strong influence, and ultimately be independent of the authority of those whom they appoint to government; this means in particular that leaders must not be obliged to rely on strong party structures existing independently from their own influence. Clearly, neither condition applies in Western Europe, nor do they obtain in Communist states, or indeed in a substantial number of Third World states. Hierarchical government prevails where, as a result of a variety of circumstances, a leader has emerged and dominates the political scene in a framework of relatively low governmental action. These conditions tend to be met in four types of situations, those of traditional monarchies, of charismatic presidencies, of some constitutional presidencies and of some, rather traditional, military regimes.

Traditional Monarchical Governments

The first, and by now the least common, of these situations is that of traditional monarchies. These are located in the Arabian peninsula and in the Himalayas. They are based on the very strong leadership of the monarch who can realistically claim to have a right to rule as a result of traditions and customs: the leadership aspect of governmental activity is thus fully in his hands. Coordinating functions are also in the hands of the monarch, largely because these countries are small and often primitive or because the wealth (in oil-producing countries) is concentrated in the hands of an (often extended) ruling family. In some cases, a prime minister is in charge of coordination; when the post does not exist, some coordination and some general policy-making is probably also conducted by advisers (in a few cases foreign advisers) of the monarch.

As a result, the official governments of these countries have almost exclusively managerial and administrative functions. Indeed, because of the nature of these countries, the emphasis is not on technical specialization, but on administration in the broader sense, although technical positions have increased in number, in particular in oil-rich countries. But, because of the social structure of these countries, the government is still composed primarily of ruling families rather than of civil servants: the modernization of these countries will lead to an increase in the influence of civil servants, as can already be seen in states where the monarch places heavy emphasis on technical change. In Iran under the Shah, in Jordan, in Morocco in the periods during which the king exercised personal rule, the government was largely composed of members of the administrative groups. This means a gradual reduction in the truly hierarchical character of the government.

Charismatic Presidencies

The second group of countries in which the hierarchical model prevails are the presidential systems at or very soon after independence in Third World states, and especially African states. The arrangement can be found both among countries which used to be under French rule such as Ivory Coast under Houphouet Boigny and, for a period at least, Senegal under Senghor, as well as among countries which used to be under British rule, such as Kenya under Kenyatta, Tanzania under Nyerere or Zambia under Kaunda. These countries sometimes acquired independence under a parliamentary system, but the leader soon introduced a presidential system which made him independent of Parliament; and while he appointed his ministers from among members of a single (or at least dominant) party, this party has been so much under the control of the head of state that it rarely constituted a constraint on the powers of selection and dismissal which the president could exercise. These governments are truly hierarchical with most of the powers of policy-making and coordination retained by the president and a very small entourage.

Yet, as time passes, the situation tends to alter somewhat in these countries (independently of the fact that military coups have led to a new form of governmental structure in some countries). Problems of internal coordination of governmental activities, and even problems of policy-making are among the main reasons which induce a number of these charismatic, 'historic' leaders to appoint a prime minister.[4] Systems of dual leadership are gradually becoming more numerous, and, as this happens, the power of the president to concentrate policy-making and coordination on himself diminishes. However, by the early 1980s, the hierarchical system had none the less broadly been maintained in the majority of countries which were still ruled by their founders: the bulk of the government remains concerned with administrative matters only;

the appointment and dismissal of ministers remains in the hands of the president (with perhaps some advice from the prime minister where there is one); and matters of policy-making and coordination are still dealt with, to a very large extent, by the president himself.

But the situation remains in a state of flux and, in some cases already, the position of the charismatic leader has been undermined while the role of the government has increased. There is little doubt that the increasingly technical character of many development matters enhances the power of at least some of the ministers, who do not merely occupy a managerial position, but who come to play a broader part. Yet the main reason for the decline in the hierarchical structure comes from the gradual undermining of the position of the president: his position as an unquestioned ruler becomes less secure; his attention to detail diminishes. He may become so involved with foreign affairs that problems of policy-making with respect to the internal life of the country are left to the prime minister and other ministers. The government ceases to be a hierarchy in the strong sense of the word and develops an embryonic collective element.

By and large, 'second generation' leaders of a civilian type do not succeed in providing the same kind of leadership as original leaders, and their government is consequently usually less hierarchical. There are exceptions, admittedly, such as that of President Stevens in Sierra Leone, who came to power after an experiment with 'collective' rather than hierarchical government; President Bongo of Gabon also succeeded in creating around himself an aura of prestige which placed him in a position very superior to his (extremely large and complex) government. But the modes of transmission of power in single-party systems of the African model (admittedly so far relatively untried) lead to a reduction in the strength of the leader. If hierarchical government is to remain in operation, the power of the leader has to come from another source, mainly military and, occasionally, through electoral support.

Limited Presidencies

Electoral victory explains why, in some cases, heads of state of constitutional presidential systems can succeed in acquiring sufficient strength to exercise alone, or almost alone, policy-making and coordination powers. The extent to which a regularly elected president may be able to exercise leadership wholly or almost wholly on his own depends on the way in which the political forces which contribute to his election are organized. Constitutionally, the president is elected directly (in law or in practice) by the people: thus he does not depend formally on a regularly elected body, such as a Parliament, for his leadership; the fact that such a president is elected for a fixed term also contributes to enhancing his authority. However, in practice, presidential candidates are nominated through, and by, political parties; these parties are more or less dominated by these candidates. We just considered the case of parties strongly dominated by leaders when we examined the case of founders of states; in the normal way, regularly elected presidents in pluralistic systems do not dominate their parties to the same extent, but there are cases when they do, for instance when they are populist leaders who built their power in one area and gradually extended their influence across the country, usually by means of a party which they created. This happened in several instances in Latin America, as with Vargas, Quadros and even to some extent Goulart in Brazil, with Peron in Argentina, with Velasco in Ecuador.

Thus, the more a president dominates the party which helped him to come to power, the more he can exercise independent leadership. But the ability of a president to exercise leadership on his own also depends on the extent to which the channel through which he was elected remains distinct from other channels of power. In effect, the more the party system is centralized and the power hierarchy outside the presidential network is identical to the power hierarchy which contributed to his election, the less the president can exercise full and independent leadership. An extreme case is Colombia, where the party system is strong and well-established, both in Congress and in the country, and where the selection of presidential candidates, from both parties in succession, results from arrangements over which these presidential candidates have little or no control. As a result, not merely administration and policy coordination, but policy-making is exercised in Colombia through a party network and through 'representatives' of the parties in the government. Other Latin American presidential systems are more hierarchical, but, in a general manner, the more the leader emerges at the polls as a result of his personal pull, the more he is likely to be able to organize his cabinet in the way he wishes. On the other hand, presidents who are selected by a party, as in Mexico or, especially since the mid-1960s, in Venezuela, have to rely more heavily on prominent leaders of the party or parties involved in the selection process: the government is as a result more collective than hierarchical.

The United States governmental structure was traditionally rather hierarchical: indeed, in the nineteenth and early part of the twentieth century, a distinction was occasionally made between the more hierarchical American cabinets and the more collective Latin American cabinets.[5] The character of the United States party system has always been such that presidential nominees have been able to be largely independent from the party 'bosses' in the selection of their ministerial colleagues. Moreover, the primary system further reinforces (and probably helps to maintain to this day) the decentralized character of the party system, as it enables presidential candidates to build up a faction of their own which they control. American presidents had therefore in some ways a position similar to that of leaders who created a party which they subsequently dominated. The fragmentation of the power situation in the United States meant that the external limits of presidential power were always very clear: presidents had difficulty in having their own way vis-à-vis Congress, let alone vis-à-vis states and municipal governments. But, within the area of power of the executive, American presidents always exercised considerable influence: they were true policy-makers and coordinated the policies between the departments. Traditionally, the cabinet was confined to the function of administration and management, and the president always chose its members precisely in order to achieve managerial results, even if posts were also given to reward those who had helped him politically.

The situation has become different, however, since as a result of the growth of the American government from F.D. Roosevelt, the system began to develop horizontally to such an extent that the control which the president and his immediate aides could exercise over the various departments became rather limited. Thus, although the formal structure remains hierarchical, it is unrealistic to describe the American model as being any longer based on a set of lines of command emanating from the president; it is becoming closer, as we shall shortly see, to one in which a series of autonomous agencies act independently.

Thus, presidential systems in which the president is elected in a competitive manner do occasionally give rise to hierarchical government, but three conditions have to be met. First, the electoral process must be sufficiently competitive to enable the president to acquire authority as a result, and therefore to enable him to choose ministers who will feel effectively dependent on him; second, the presidential candidates, rather than the parties, must be an essential element; and third, the administrative and decision-making structure must not be so complex as to make it impossible for the president to exercise full control.

Governments of 'Usurpers'

Governments can be hierarchical in strong authoritarian regimes resulting from a coup, and especially a military coup, but this is not always the case. Such leaders probably want in the main to establish a hierarchical government, if only because, among military leaders, the idea of applying the 'efficient' military hierarchy to civilian government more than occasionally prevails. It is sometimes assumed that the smooth running of society as a whole must be on hierarchical lines, a conception which the Nazi and fascist dictators of the interwar period thought essential to put into practice. Some postwar dictators have adopted a similar model for reasons not altogether dissimilar from those of the fascist experiments.

As a matter of fact, however, the ability of dictators to implement a hierarchical mode has come increasingly into question: they have sometimes displayed this ability when, relatively quickly, they have also been able to acquire a personal following and therefore been able to eliminate potential or actual opponents. But this is far from always being the case, and it seems that 'usurpers' are less able to do so, since the 1970s, than they were in the past. As a result, experiments based more or less genuinely on some form of collective government are increasingly common; and, in particular, the leader has to contend with a group of 'advisers' ranging from a small number to a body having almost the dimensions of a council.

Thus, while hierarchical government still exists in a substantial number of states in the 1980s, the model seems to encounter difficulties and to be highly dependent on special circumstances. The difficulties are political and administrative. By and large, the administrative problems result from the near impossibility of a single leader keeping full control of the government as the administrative complexity of public decision-making increases; while the hierarchical structure has the apparent merit of simplicity and, on the surface, of clear devolution of responsibility, it is also too rudimentary to allow for the effective running of a modern bureaucratic state. Moreover, such an administrative arrangement does depend on the political position of the leader. This is why fully hierarchical positions are relatively rare; this is also why the hierarchical character of the government often does not survive the founder of the state; and this is also why, ultimately, the emergence and maintenance of a hierarchical structure is often largely dependent on the accident of strong leadership.

Indeed, the political and administrative aspects of the problem become intertwined as the government experiences loss of efficiency if the managers are not associated to some extent with policy-making and coordination. Modern organizational theory stresses the need for group action by opposition to hierarchical fiat. Morale will be higher among the managers if these participate to some extent in the general running of the organization to which they belong and the same idea surely applies to governments as well. It seems, therefore, wise from the point of view of the smooth running of affairs to associate all members of the government with policy-making and coordination activities.

Moreover, some spread of decision-making is also required if responsibility is to be spread. In a pure hierarchical model where members of the government merely carry out orders, full responsibility rests with the leader alone. This means that the system will be maintained only as long as the leader alone has enough authority to carry the political consequences of governmental decisions. This situation may obtain in relatively traditional societies where the leader is, in the terminology we used in the previous volume, 'anointed';[6] in most contemporary societies, both developed and developing, this is not the case. Where leaders are 'appointed', a hierarchical structure will simply use the capital of credibility of the leader too quickly.

2. Collective and Semi-Collective Governments

Since a hierarchical structure is both administratively and politically relatively rare and rather accidental, governmental arrangements tend in practice to be based either on a 'modified' hierarchical model or, indeed, on an entirely different premise. At the opposite extreme of the hierarchical structure is the wholly 'collective' arrangement, on which some governments are based in principle — in part to avoid the difficulties of a hierarchical structure, in part because a cooperative framework seems altogether more justifiable among 'colleagues' in a government. But a collective structure in turn raises difficulties, when the arrangement is fully collective or even when members of the government are not fully equal. To begin with, some degree of specialization must take place, at least as far as management is concerned: this was indeed the main value of a hierarchical structure. Although such a structure is ruled out on other grounds, the 'collective' character of the government cannot be extended to the managerial area: thus a collective system can be collective only with respect to coordination and policy-making, and not with respect to all aspects of governmental activity.

But such a division, which corresponds roughly, at least in principle, to the kind of structure which exists in many cabinet governments on the Western European model, has a number of drawbacks, while it does admittedly obviate some of the problems raised by hierarchical structures. A collective system involves members of the government, more or less fully, in the general affairs of the state; consequently, responsibility becomes shared and, if the leader does not possess considerable authority, he can be buttressed by the authority of other ministers. The solitary position of the 'hierarchical' leader is avoided. But this is at the cost of placing ministers in a somewhat ambiguous position: they have to be both generalists and specialists — and this may lead to tensions. Moreover, the collective character of decision-making will mechanically lead to a loss of efficiency, as the numbers of persons involved inevitably entail a multiplication of committees and an increase in the activities designed to achieve better 'communication'.

In practice, this means that collective governments have to be small: a large cabinet will not have the time to spend on more than a small number of decisions; moreover, calls on the time of ministers are made by their other roles. It follows that a fully collective arrangement can be expected to be viable only when problems are limited, for instance, because state intervention is small: the expansion of state activities in the course of the last decade means that the probability that fully collective government will be effective, or indeed be maintained at all, has sharply declined. In the contemporary world, only Switzerland can be said to be a truly collective government on a permanent basis: it is a small, highly decentralized country, where state intervention has traditionally been limited. Elsewhere, not surprisingly, efforts are made periodically to reduce the size of governments; not surprisingly, too, these efforts have had only limited success: the activities of governments tended to expand over the same period.

Moreover, true collective government implies that members be 'equal' in most respects, and especially with respect to their power base and to their attitude to collective decision-making. In practice, neither occurs frequently, and the larger the government, the less either of these characteristics will obtain. Politicians have to have a power base, in their constituency, in their party, in a group — tribal, ethnic, religious, occupational; naturally, this power base varies from one man to another, and it is very improbable that the power base of one man will be as strong as that of another. Nor is the desire to participate in decision-making equally spread among government members: relatively little exploration has been conducted up to now among ministers about their approach to decision-making, but what has been done clearly shows that not all wish to participate equally, as we shall examine later in greater detail.[7] As a result, collective decision-making may often occur simply because some members of the government prefer to remain spectators rather than full actors.

But, perhaps, the main problem posed by collective arrangements stems from the fact that ministers cannot normally be expected to show qualities in the policy-making, coordinating, and management fields to the same degree. An emphasis on the technical expertise of members of the government is somewhat inconsistent with the ability to coordinate or become involved in broad policy decisions. As a result, a differentiation tends to occur between types of ministers; as a result, too, the problem of the control of subordinates becomes acute in those departments whose ministers are primarily policy-makers. The supervision of administrators is often weak and, the more the government is collective, the more the 'technocrats' are likely to be influential; they may even at the limit evolve specialized policies of their own.

Because of these difficulties, governments which are formally collective have become in practice somewhat more hierarchical in the sense that all members of the government are not equal. Much of the controversy which arose about the position of the prime minister in Britain is thus only one sign of a much broader problem that affects in various ways all or nearly all governments which are formally collective as well as those governments which, like some of the constitutional presidencies which we mentioned earlier, are hierarchical in name but somewhat collective in practice, such as the Venezuelan, Colombian or Mexican presidential governments. But, in the same way as, for hierarchical governments, the nature of the party system leads to variations in the character of the presidential government, the nature of the party system leads to variations in the extent to which a government of a 'parliamentary' kind is in fact collective.

Thus, the first and most crucial element which will drive a particular governmental structure towards the 'collective' or the 'hierarchical' pole is the party system. To the extent that the leader needs the continuing political support of his colleagues in order to be able to run the affairs of the state, the government will be, in some important regard at least, relatively collective. This is true of some presidential arrangements, as we saw; this is even more true of 'prime ministerial' arrangements, as prime ministers can normally be described as being 'appointed' rather than 'anointed': they owe this 'appointment' to colleagues in the party who will be rewarded by becoming members of the government.

This means that, in general, governments in parliamentary and cabinet systems are usually endowed with at least part of the policy-making functions as well as with the functions of coordination and administrative management. Members of the government are, in the main, politicians with a power base; the reasons why they are in the government are related, at least in part, to this power base. It follows that prime ministers not only cannot be said to be wholly free to appoint or dismiss them, but they cannot exercise their leadership over the country without taking into account the possible reactions of members of the government. They see their role as that of men who belong to a team, which may be somewhat hierarchically structured, but which is none the less a team.

The reason why the power of prime ministers has often been presented as strong is because the reality of the leadership of the prime minister does contrast with the theory of 'pure' collective government, and it is clear that, as we saw, true or full collective government is rare or even impossible to achieve. But parliamentary or cabinet governments are not hierarchical either; nor are a number of limited presidential systems. In fact, the arrangements which exist in those countries in which the government remains united and is not hierarchical fall within three broad groups, with Switzerland being unique in having a governmental pattern of behaviour truly very close to the full collective model. The three types are: the 'leader-based' government, the 'team' government and the 'consociational' government.

(a) Leader-Based Governments

Leader-based governments are those in which the authority of the leader is substantially greater than that of other government members. They occur because the leader has a position of strength within the nation which does not depend on other members of the government. These leaders may be presidents, who owe their authority to a line of authority which by-passes the government and the assembly, or prime ministers who benefit from an authority of their own, acquired as a result of their past actions: they have a 'charismatic' authority which transcends the power of their colleagues. This authority may have been acquired because they founded the state or reconstructed it: Nehru or Adenauer had such a position. Both used parties which already existed, but expanded them and gave them a truly dominant position; their colleagues were dependent on these leaders. A somewhat diluted form of the same type of authority is exercised by leaders who benefit from the aura of a major success which the population attributed to them alone. Churchill had such a position during the Second World War; other examples are, or were, those of Mrs Gandhi in India, Manley in Jamaica, Trudeau in Canada, Burnham in Guyana, even Macmillan in Britain. All of these leaders had, at least for a time, a seemingly unassailable position, which enabled them to play a major part in policy-making and coordination.

In a 'leader-based' arrangement, members of the government have only limited influence over policy-making; the coordination of policies is also often carried out by the leader. Yet, an element of collective decision-making remains: the leader has at least to discuss matters in the cabinet, even if the outcome is a foregone conclusion. In parliamentary systems in particular, but also in party-based presidential systems such as those of Venezuela or Costa Rica, the leader has to defend his policies in the assembly, directly or through members of the government, and this contributes to reducing the distance between the leader and his colleagues. Leaders are not usually in a position to create an effective coordinating machinery which is directly at their disposal and which is distinct from the government. Every president or prime minister has his personal staff, to be sure, and it has been noticed that some leaders have been able to expand this staff appreciably. But this does not amount to a truly unofficial coordinating government, at least for very long, probably because the system is so structured that coordinators have to be politicians of some stature, capable of appearing in front of Parliament and of speaking on behalf of the government. Finally, unless the authority of the leader is exceptional, as in the case of the founder of a state, this authority is rapidly reduced: the examples of Macmillan, Trudeau and Churchill suggest that presidents or prime ministers dependent on parties cannot easily escape the erosion of their strength. Indeed, this erosion was noticeable even in the case of Adenauer and Nehru, although age and consequential declining strength may also have contributed to the loss of authority. Leader-based governments are leader-based only as long as the population recognizes the superiority of the leader, and the structure of the system gives other members of the government an area of action from which they can expect gradually to reduce the influence of the leader. These members, too, become entrenched in the positions which they hold; they, too, increase or acquire power bases which are often strong enough to prevent the leader from dislodging them. If he did, moreover, he would do so at the risk of showing that he does not fully control his government; he would thus indicate some weakness — and ultimately undermine his own base.

This is why leader-based governments result in somewhat unstable types of governmental structures: these are potentially collective and only temporarily hierarchical. This is also why, in order to establish their position more firmly, many strong leaders have tried to move in a more hierarchical direction: prime ministers have sometimes felt that a presidential system would increase their power. And, when the leader was endowed with the prestige of having founded the state, he has been able to achieve a more hierarchical structure. This has happened in a number of African countries, both English- and French-speaking. By formally demoting the government and by establishing their sole right over policy-making and over the coordination of policy, these leaders have underlined their special position and reduced that of their colleagues.

In some cases, systems of dual leadership have constituted an alternative way of reducing the role of the government, as they have enabled both the president to be above the rest of the government and the prime minister to rely on the authority of the head of state to prevent members of the government from being markedly involved in policy-making and coordination. This has notably been the case in France in the Fifth Republic: there, as in Adenauer's Germany, the leader has been sufficiently above the rest of the politicians to impose his policy line. A dual leadership system is thus a half-way house. It constitutes a means by which a strong president attempts to draw the structure of government in a hierarchical direction, but it can also be a point in a movement in the opposite direction where presidents have abandoned, or are prepared to abandon, part of their coordinating role to the prime minister and, through him, to the government. Systems of dual leadership may be viewed as transitional or not, as we argued in the previous volume:[8] they are at any rate mostly hierarchical or intermediate: they do not have characteristics of near-collective governments, except when, as in Finland or Lebanon, they are associated with a consociational system which, left on its own, would be dangerous in view of its extreme 'collective' characteristics. A compensatory 'unifying' strength must be provided by the leader.

(b) Team Governments

When the leader is less exalted and is dependent on his colleagues in a real, as well as in a formal manner, parliamentary or cabinet government can be described as 'team' government. This situation characterizes a number of Western democracies, mainly parliamentary, but also a few Latin American presidential systems, for instance Venezuela, especially where the government is wholly, or almost wholly composed of one party (though some single-party governments, as we shall see, do not belong to this type). Team governments can be found in particular in Britain, in the old Commonwealth, in several Scandinavian countries, and occasionally in some continental countries, as in Austria since 1966.

For a team government to exist, two broad and somewhat contradictory tendencies have to be in equilibrium. There has to be loyalty to the leader on the part of members of the government — he must not be threatened with rebellions and he must have an

expectation that the broad line of his action will be acceptable —
but there must also be respect on the part of the leader for the views
and initiatives of the members of the government. These conditions
can be fulfilled only if the government is composed of one party (or
is overwhelmingly composed of one party), and indeed of a party
which has been in existence for a substantial period, as, in such a
case, patterns of relationship between members of the party are
well-established and predictable. The process by which one reaches
the leadership, and in the first instance the government, must be
well-known and not subject to the whims of individuals or to
'palace revolutions' or conspiracies which might undermine the
relative positions of leaders and their colleagues; there must be a
belief that a well-organized party with well-known structures is a
source of strength and a boost at elections.

In particular, there should not be organized factions: these tend
to undermine the 'team spirit' and force leaders to appoint men and
women who exercise influence by virtue of being representatives of
these factions, not because they belong to the government. In its
'ideal-type', a team government is one whose members relate to
each other because of past actions. Influence depends partly on
seniority, and partly on the ability shown earlier to deal with problems. The role of the leader also depends on his own experience
and personal prestige acquired in this instrumental manner, rather
than on his charisma among the population. Thus, in one sense, the
government is collective — management, coordination and policy-
making are collectively undertaken — but, as there is a hierarchy of
talent, seniority, and recognized experience in the government, the
collective appearance does cover an oligarchical structure where the
man at the top plays a determining part.

This ideal-type presentation is, of course, only approximated in
practice. Few parties avoid factions altogether; loyalty to leaders is
often the result of negative attitudes, such as fear of alternative
leaders or, on the contrary, the absence of strong alternatives. But
a number of single-party governments in Northern Europe and in
Commonwealth countries come fairly close to this model. Some of
these governments are clearly oligarchical in character, not merely
informally but formally, particularly British governments, where
the cabinet forms only a small part of the government (twenty
members out of one hundred or more). The collective character of
team government is clearly limited in law or in practice, but the
oligarchical role of some members and generally the team character

of the relationship do appreciably reduce the position of the leader.

(c) Consociational Governments

Governments which are nearest to the collective pole of the continuum and in which individual members are at their strongest can be labelled 'consociational'. These governments are characterized by the presence of well-established groups which agree to work together on the basis of compromises. The government as a body therefore plays a very large part in policy-making and co-ordination.

The groups which form the elements of the government can be of three types. They can be factions of one party which are so strong that they have each to be represented in the government. Some single-party governments are of this type — indeed, perhaps the majority. In many countries, socialist or social-democratic governments have to include representatives of broad ideological groups (a left and a centre) as well as some occupational groups, trade unions in particular: the British Labour Party is factionalized in this manner. But some right-wing or centre parties also have factions which are well-established, such as trade unions and middle-class groups in several Christian parties, language or ethnic groups in other parties (in Belgium or Canada). And in a few countries, factions are built around leaders or 'chieftains', each of whom has an established following, perhaps of a geographical kind. The Japanese Liberal Democrats and the Italian Christian Democrats are particularly riddled with factions, and in these two cases, governments have to include representatives of most, if not all factions. The role of the prime minister in appointing his cabinet and in steering its policy-making process is consequently limited.

A second type of consociational government is the coalition government. The existence of a coalition implies that there is agreement between parties, which are represented in the government after difficult bargains involving a number of leaders. The result is sometimes a compromise programme which is adopted for a substantial period (occasionally, as in West Germany after 1969, for a whole legislature) and sometimes more temporary arrangements which are almost continuously in question. Even where there is a dominant partner, as in West Germany after 1969 and where, also as in West Germany or in the Netherlands, the agreement has a long-term character, negotiations have to take place and the cabinet has to be involved to a considerable extent in policy-making to avoid break-ups of the coalition. In effect, governments are then composed of a number of 'pillars' which have all to remain solid if the coalition is to be maintained. Yet, coalition governments form the majority of governments in continental Europe and some countries are ruled permanently by coalitions. With variations, these countries all experience permanently consociational forms of government.

Finally, groups other than parties may be part of the government and thus contribute to a form of consociationalism. This case is much less common; it is in fact very rare in Western Europe, where parliamentary government is almost exclusively based on parties. But, occasionally directly and more frequently indirectly through the parties, some groups are represented in the government, for instance business groups, trade unions, ethnic minorities. Governments in 'plural' societies have occasionally had this character, with Lebanese, Malaysian, indeed Indian and Sri Lankan governments being markedly of this type. The government which is the closest to a pure collective model, the Swiss government, owes its collective character to the fact that, not merely parties, but language and religious groups are represented regularly on the basis of a customary arrangement. Overall, these governments can be said to have many of the characteristics of pure corporatism; at the limit — and Switzerland comes very close to that limit — all groups of significance are permanently represented in the government which develops national policy on the basis of a continuous series of bargains.

But, with the exception of Switzerland, these governments are not fully collective as they are oligarchical rather than truly egalitarian. They do not represent all the groups in the society, or even all the important ones: as we saw, parties tend to be the only groups which are represented. Moreover, the government is usually composed of a number of blocks, each of which includes members of the same party who tend each to follow their own leader. Here again, the Swiss government is exceptional because it is the only one in which each of the members of the executive does have a 'constituency' and where, as a result, with some variations admittedly, all members are truly equal. In other consociational governments, members are not equal and the arrangement is therefore oligarchical.

But the elements of such an oligarchy are stronger than in team governments because of the relative absence of an overall loyalty to the government. The prime minister is in a weak position as he can only appeal to a spirit of compromise among members. Occasionally, admittedly, he carries considerable weight; his political strength may indeed be buttressed by that of a president in the few dual leadership systems which are of this type (Lebanon, Finland); in some consociational governments, the prime minister may have been instrumental in winning an election for the coalition or he may have national or international prestige (Tindemans in Belgium for a period, for instance). In the large majority of cases, however, consociational government corresponds to a situation in which power is diffused among the parties and where, as a result, the leader's strength depends more on the art of manipulation than on personal power.

Consequently, in consociational governments, there are serious difficulties arising from the potentially very wide involvement of ministers in all aspects of policy-making, coordination, and management. These are the governments which are most threatened with 'overload', and whose members are most likely to be 'politically', rather than 'administratively' inclined. This is perhaps why this form of government is mostly found in the smaller, traditionally stable democracies of Western Europe, in which there is (normally) a basic consensus and problems are technically less complex, while the civil service has a long tradition of competence. But there are exceptions, which arise from what appears to be the inability of the political system to move from 'consociational' to 'team' government, despite the seriousness of the problem. Italy is an example, and the linguistic difficulties experienced in Belgium since the 1960s have clearly brought the consociational system there close to breaking point. Elsewhere, the consociational system might purely and simply give way, as it did in France in 1958.

There are palliatives, however, which enable consociational systems to avoid having to choose between very serious policy-making problems and the abandonment of the consociational system. In France, before 1958, many of the managerial tasks — and indeed some policy-making tasks as well — were purely and simply abandoned by the government to the civil service. The situation in Japan is, in practice, rather similar. The role of the government appears to be one of providing legitimacy to the political system as a whole, but not to 'take decisions' in the strongest sense of the word: the rapid turnover of ministers has the (perhaps not altogether unintended) result of ensuring that these ministers are simply unable to control their departments. British governments have solved the problem by sharply distinguishing cabinet from non-cabinet members, a distinction which is rarely as marked elsewhere (Australia being the other clear example), but this is in the context of a team government. The British government can perhaps be based officially on several levels because it is not consociational; the more consociational the government, the more its members wish to be equal and the less a formal or even informal distinction among members of the government becomes practically enforceable.

Consociational government is often regarded as relatively clumsy and perhaps ineffective. On the whole, the larger European countries have moved away from such an arrangement. But the tradition and the need for coalitions between equal partners or with parties which have a pivotal role, as in Italy, Belgium, the Netherlands, Finland, will probably maintain consociational forms of executives in many Western European democracies in the coming decades.

3. Divided Governments

The structure of government is usually discussed in terms of the extent to which ministers participate in overall decision-making; it is rarely described as being based on a number of groups kept together more or less tenuously. Yet, many governments are sharply divided. This was true in the past to some extent, as we saw: both the republican tradition and the authoritarian bureaucratic arrangements led to divided governments. But divisions have become sharper and perhaps also more common among the governments of the contemporary world.

The four factors which we mentioned in Chapter 1 all contribute to the division of governments, although the normative-ideological element has usually played only a limited part: governments are not kept divided because it is felt that, as a result, the structure of the decision-making process at the top will conform better to the broader philosophy of government prevailing in the state. While governments are kept hierarchical or made collective in part because leaders wish thereby to stress the authoritarian or more liberal nature of the polity, divisions in the government are not viewed as consequential upon an overall normative political blueprint. By and large, the division of governments into two or more semi-autonomous units is more the product of necessity or, if consciously desired, motivated by instrumental rather than ideological considerations.

Yet, certain of the overt considerations — or rationalizations — leading to the division of governments into several units sometimes come close to a normative justification. In the Soviet Union and other Communist states, for instance, as well as to a lesser extent in some recently-created military regimes, the distinction between a revolutionary, military, or party 'council' and an 'administrative' government is often presented as being a means of ensuring greater political control over the machinery of government. The parallel development of party and state institutions in Communist countries arises from the ostensible fear that the bureaucracy might not naturally be willing to implement the decisions of the party: the distinction between a party government and an administrative government corresponds logically, at the top of the political structure, to the duplication of institutions further down the hierarchy.

The division of governments into two or more units is more commonly the result of pressures stemming from the increased complexity of administration, however, and especially from the rapid increase in state bureaucracies in many Third World countries, as well as from the problems arising from the limited political legitimacy of leaders and ruling elites. Indeed, ideological considerations have usually tended to operate in the opposite direction and succeeded in maintaining unity or at least reducing the pull towards a division. Thus, the ideology of collective government which prevails in many Atlantic countries and elsewhere tends to keep the bureaucracy more united, even though the supervision exercised by the ministers over their respective departments is relatively tenuous. Thus, paradoxically at first sight, it is in the United States, where the structure is nominally hierarchical, that the trend towards divided government has been most marked. This is due both to the fact that the American federal government is particularly large and to the fact that formal hierarchical norms scarcely correspond to the prevailing American ideology of bargaining and trade-offs, these in turn being reinforced by the elements of 'republicanism' which continue to give to the Senate (and to the House) a significant say in matters of governmental decision-making. Thus, among Atlantic states, the one example of divided government is that of the United States.

Elsewhere, both in the Communist states and in the Third World, the division of government has occurred less spontaneously than in the United States. It has usually taken the form of a more rigid distinction between two or more segments of the government, often in order to stress the division between political and administrative functions. In practice, however, the distinction is not always as clear-cut, in part because of an overlap of membership between the bodies; nor is the scope of activities of these bodies always as precise as the original division suggests or aims at fostering.

The Gradual 'Atomization' of the American Government

Ostensibly at least, the American government is hierarchical: the president appoints the members of his cabinet at will, not just in theory but in practice as well, although the Senate can, and occasionally does, exercise a veto. The initiative to appoint and the power to dismiss is fully in the hands of the president; the range of groups from which the president chooses the members of the government is also much wider than in other Western democracies, wider even than in most countries of the world, including most presidential systems which, as in Latin America, are modelled on the American government. The American president is free from the behavioural constraints which other heads of government have — he does not need to rely on party influentials, or on groups of civil servants. And experience has shown that American presidents make extensive use of the opportunity to select the various secretaries from all walks of life.

Yet, while American presidents are free to compose their government at will, it does not follow that the government which is thus created is — or is any longer — hierarchical. Quite the contrary: what has happened is a transformation by which the president can scarcely be said to be in command of the overall structure. A more realistic way of describing American governmental arrangements is to view them as 'pluralistic' or perhaps as 'atomized'. As R. Fenno pointed out in the late 1950s: 'The general conclusion which emerges most clearly from this study [is] *the relative difficulty of promoting unity in the face of the basic pluralism of the American political system*'.[9] The rather early publication of this work (1959) perhaps accounts for the fact that a generation later the comment seems almost like an understatement. Writing in the 1970s, H. Heclo referred, not to pluralism, but to a 'Government of Strangers' (1977).[10] It might indeed be said that the members of the United States cabinet are the poor relations of the American executive. In another work, Heclo begins his analysis of the 'executive establishment' by stating: 'The connection between politics and administration arouses remarkably little interest in the United States, the Presidency is considered more glamorous, Congress more intriguing, elections more exciting, and interest groups more troublesome...'.[11] And he adds, with perhaps not quite as much justification, 'This lack of interest in political administration is rarely found in other democratic countries, and it has not always prevailed in the United States'.[12]

This situation of relative neglect of the American cabinet and of the link between politics and administration is indeed not strictly speaking confined to the United States: it echoes the relatively low level of interest shown in the Council of Ministers and the state administration in the Soviet Union and other Communist countries,[13] and it stems basically from the fact that, by and large, it seems 'intuitively' true that members of the United States cabinet are, ultimately, administrators, or managers, and not 'real' policymakers. That is to say that the American government is viewed as fundamentally divided into two segments and that the second layer is perhaps viewed increasingly as atomized.

The relatively low position of the members of the United States cabinet has, as Heclo rightly points out, tended to be more pronounced in recent years, but the seeds of such a state of affairs were sown in the past, although a number of factors have combined to increase the trend. Four elements can be identified as being of particular importance in this context. The first is the absence of a 'team spirit' among the members of the cabinet, this in turn being the result of the way in which they are appointed. Members of the United States cabinet may enjoy good relations with the president, but they do not normally relate to each other. Appointments tend to be made for one or more of three reasons: there are men who have helped the president to be elected and are in a sense rewarded for past services; there are men who are known to be good administrators and who are selected because they are assumed to be efficient (these are the 'technicians', such as Macnamara, whose previous contact with politics may have been very limited); and there are those who are drawn because they will cover, or almost 'represent' a particular group or section of the community (workers, farmers, blacks, women, etc.). A cabinet is therefore based on a careful 'balance' between a variety of quite distinct considerations.[14]

The result is that the cabinet cannot constitute a team in the strict sense of the word because the men and women who belong to it come from a wide variety of backgrounds and have never been together in any organization or group prior to becoming members of the cabinet. In this respect, the composition of the United States government differs from that of almost every other government in the world, parliamentary, but also Communist or Third World: elsewhere, government members are parliamentarians, or civil servants, or members of a 'social elite' (in a traditional monarchy for instance). In the United States, the hand-picked character of the members of the cabinet and the individual nature of the choice mean that the potential for genuine interaction among cabinet secretaries will be small and will tend to result from the necessities of the job and not from pre-established friendship or even acquaintance.

This state of affairs alone would not lead to a 'break-up' or 'atomization' of the cabinet were it not for three other factors which push the various secretaries to 'retreat' into their departments and to view these as fortresses which they must lead, but also defend. The growth of the bureaucracy is a first element. In countries where 'collective' governments exist it has had the effect of creating tensions between the demands made by policy-making and coordination and the demands made by management. But, while in collective and semi-collective governments, the result is a 'tight-rope' performance which often results in management not being given the attention it deserves, the effect in the United States has been to push members of the cabinet and their immediate subordinates into their departmental 'ghetto'. And, since one important consideration in the selection of cabinet members is acceptability to a constituency while another is technical expertise, it is not surprising that, faced with a huge and complex bureaucracy in their own departments, cabinet secretaries should feel that their task as department heads is sufficiently vast to warrant their almost undivided attention. Were they not to devote their minds to their departments, these would simply not be run at all.

This tendency is reinforced by the role of Congress which, as is well-known, is strikingly more influential than other legislatures in terms of scrutiny and even control of administration. As congressional committees have a manifest say on appropriations and even on departmental policy, it is incumbent on departmental heads to ensure that the projects of the department have as safe a passage as possible through these committees. Cabinet ministers are therefore more than inclined to play an 'individualistic' game as far as their relations with Congress are concerned: the president might help occasionally, but the president is not all-powerful, to say the least, and the president is unlikely to be very happy with a cabinet secretary who continuously asks for his help; other cabinet secretaries are competitors for the favour of Congress. Thus, each secretary is on his own, whatever ideological gloss may be put on the situation of the 'administration' as a whole: the structure of political power imposes on cabinet ministers an individualistic and sectional mode of behaviour.

Finally, and perhaps most important of all, the growth of the Executive Office of the president has contributed markedly to the 'rejection' of cabinet members into their departmental positions. Admittedly, the Executive Office has developed since F.D. Roosevelt to help the president in a number of ways, not the least of which was the hope that it would counteract the trend towards the atomization of the cabinet and government. As Wildavsky says: 'After all, if the President were able to be sure that Cabinet members would follow and enforce his preference, he would not need the large Executive Office he has now'[15] (and the office has grown larger since). However, the mushrooming of the Executive Office has not had the desired effect of bringing the cabinet and the departments more closely under the control of the president: the effect has been to create a second (or first) government which forms a screen between president and cabinet. A large number of men and women in the office duplicate the activities of cabinet secretaries and their subordinates, ostensibly to supervise, control or coordinate these activities, but in practice the result is that the president is more distant from the departments and their heads. These are consequently forced to take even more of a departmental position; they are also forced to rely even more on their special access to Congress to obtain the advantages which they wish to have or their subordinates feel they must have. Thus, the comparison which we have already drawn between Ancient Rome at the time of Augustus and modern American government is quite apposite: on the one

hand, there are a number of departments headed by men who com-
municate mostly with the Senate (and House) and do so on an individual basis; on the other, there is a presidential 'government' in
which the Executive Office makes constant, but Sisyphus-like efforts to control the rest of the administration but does not succeed
in having a firm grip on the management of the affairs of the
Republic.

Divided Governments in Communist States

Although the effective structure of the governments in Communist
states is better known than in the past, much remains obscure about
the way in which power is distributed among the various bodies
which compose these governments. Two things are certain,
however. One is that, almost from the start, and more markedly
since the Khruschev era, the governmental structure has been formally divided, not merely between a party 'half' and a state 'half',
but into a number of organizations whose membership overlaps to
some extent. And the other characteristic is that there is a significant degree of collective decision-making within these organizations, despite the predominance of the party leader and, to a lesser
extent, of the government chairman. Moreover, it also appears to
be the case that the division among the various bodies which constitute the government corresponds to the different tasks which the
executive has to fulfil. Communist governments constitute
interesting experiments in modern political and administrative
decision-making.

The Communist system is based, first and foremost, on the
parallel and long-standing existence of two hierarchies, the party
hierarchy and the state hierarchy, the party hierarchy being the
prevailing one. In the last years of his life, Stalin was at the top of
both hierarchies and neither the party nor the state organiztion probably had a significant part to play at the time. With the loosening
of the autocracy, however, both hierarchies were led in a more collective manner and the various top bodies within each hierachy
acquired correspondingly more influence. A similar development
occurred in most Communist states, at least in Eastern Europe,
though not necessarily at the same rate, or indeed regularly. By the
1970s, however, it became realistic to view the governments of
Communist countries as being composed of five different bodies,

each of which had a somewhat different role ascribed to it. First, the party 'half' of the government is composed of two somewhat interlocking bodies, the Politburo and the Secretariat. Many secretaries, and especially the first secretary, belong to the Politburo, which unquestionably takes, under the leadership of the first secretary, the most important policy decisions. To an extent, the relationship between Politburo and Secretariat resembles the relationship between president and Executive Office in the United States, but the Politburo is a collective organ, whose members are appointed as a result of the long-standing part they have played in the party, while the Secretariat is headed by a number of very influential members of the party oligarchy.

Second, the state 'half' of the government is composed of a hierarchy of three bodies. First, there is a collective presidency, sometimes called Presidium (of the Supreme Soviet of the Soviet Union, for instance) and sometimes called 'State Council' (as in East Germany). The Council of Ministers also has a collective chairmanship, normally known as the Presidium of the Council of Ministers. And, lastly, the Council of Ministers itself includes all the departmental ministers. Even if one or more of these last three bodies plays only a symbolic role, their existence is an indication of an approach to the structure of government which is at considerable variance from the deliberately united structure which parliamentary governments have traditionally followed and indeed fostered; and this model is particularly interesting since it has now begun to spread outside the Communist world.

To the extent that Communist governments are divided into a party 'half' and a state 'half', there is a clear resemblance with the American government; but the way both 'halves' of the government are organized in Communist states suggests considerable differences from America. Indeed, it is not an exaggeration to view the Communist systems, in the 1970s at least, as based on 'collective' arrangements: leaders are not, vis-à-vis the rest of the members of government, in the exalted position which presidents enjoy. This is because leaders are ultimately appointed by, or at least proceed from the bodies which they lead; there is a 'team' relationship which resembles that which we described for prime ministerial systems of this type. It is true that leaders have, for a variety of reasons, a superior position to that of their colleagues. In the most extreme cases, their status is truly above that of everyone else in the government: the founders of Communist states in

Albania, Yugoslavia, North Korea, Vietnam, had impregnable positions; nationalistic fervour also occasionally gave to some leaders a dominating status, as in Romania to Ceaucescu and in Poland, for a while at least, to Gomulka; and the sheer length of tenure of many leaders (Kadar, Zhivkov) also places them in a strong position.

But the other members of the 'team' also have considerable influence in part because they, too, remain in office for long periods. By and large, the second generation leaders have to be content with a position of relative influence which places them comparatively close to many of their colleagues. Authority has to be shared, even though the closed character of the system means that the broader base on which the various members might rely cannot be appealed to directly, as is the case in Western European team or consociational governments. But, channels of communication do exist between the top and the bottom of the party structure: members of politburos and of councils of ministers 'represent' different segments of either party or state. The Communist leaders of the 1970s have, to some extent at least, to take these different segments into account.

The semi-collective character of the decision-making process in Communist states is maintained and indeed strengthened by the division of the government into at least two elements. By and large, members of the Politburo and members of the Council of Ministers come to office through different channels; their constituency is different. Their interests are also different: members of the Council of Ministers, who come to office after long periods in the civil service, often in the same department, tend to have 'managerial' rather than 'policy-making' aims, but the converse is true of members of the Politburo. This leads to an accepted division of functions which reduces the urge for overall involvement and overall supervision characterizing many ministers in parliamentary systems. Members of Communist councils of ministers have a narrower conception of their job; they behave more as ministers in a presidential government than as ministers in a prime ministerial system, while members of politburos are more similar to the members of a 'collective' White House office than to ordinary ministers of a 'team' or consociational government. The accepted character of the division of functions probably makes for greater efficiency or, at any rate, for less inefficiency than would otherwise obtain in a system where much of the economy is centrally controlled. It also makes

for the emergence of a relative equilibrium between the contradictory demands of 'collective' decision-making and of relative
specialization. Communist leader-government relationships are
often, and probably increasingly, of a 'semi-collective' type, but
the collective framework is bounded by the accepted institutional
limits arising from the existence of other bodies in which decisions
are also taken in a semi-collective manner.

The special character of the government in Communist states
stems in part, but only in part, from the dual character of the
leadership. It is not dual leadership per se which is at the root of the
governmental division: the American government is divided, but it
is not based on dual leadership; conversely, many dual leadership
systems exist in the context of a hierarchical or even collective
governmental structure (Finland). But in divided executives, such
as those of Communist states, where the managerial half of the
government is very complex, the dual leadership structure probably
prevents the administration from being atomized. The chairman of
the Council of Ministers exercises some coordinating functions,
and, in so doing, he has the effect of keeping the ministers together
and providing a focus and a link (and he is helped, in this respect,
by the vice-chairman of the council).

Communist governments have a multi-level, semi-collective
structure. The extent to which the structure is collective varies over
time and space, but the extent to which the structure is collective
also varies in parliamentary and other non-Communist systems. It
is, therefore, not surprising that there should also be variations
among Communist systems. Taken together, the semi-collective,
multi-level arrangements which have characterized Communist
systems have enabled these systems to endure, to do so in a gradually less authoritarian manner, despite the complex, indeed heavy,
bureaucratic structures which the nature of Communist government has so far appeared to entail.

Emerging Dual Governments in the Third World

Dual government emerged gradually in the United States as a result
of the natural development of organizations; a mixture of ideology
and bureaucratic pressure led to the division of governments in
Communist countries. In the Third World, another and more
directly political aim led to a similar trend in a number of countries

in the 1960s and 1970s, namely, the need to strengthen, and sometimes almost to create, the legitimacy of the ruler. For dual government emerged in the Third World in conjunction with the coming of 'second generation' leaders, often drawn from the military, in a context in which the credibility of the previous regime had diminished, while no clear alternative had manifest roots in the population.

New military rulers are often confronted with a number of requirements which are difficult to fulfil in the context of a united government. First, because they have to achieve change in the social and economic fields, there has to be heavy reliance on technical expertise if new programmes are to be elaborated and implemented: 'technocrats' have therefore to be included in the governmental structure. However, given the suddenness of many military coups, given the small number of persons endowed with managerial skills, leaders have to call for the help of men, often drawn from the civil service, who have typically been employed by the previous regime (although they may have been frustrated in their efforts in the past). Meanwhile, they have rapidly to acquire political support: they have to ensure the loyalty of the army, and, through the army, of at least the important sections of the community. They have, therefore, in effect to associate some elements of the army with the government and, indeed, other elements as well, at least as long as they cannot rely on an organization, a party for instance, which could contribute to the maintenance of their authority. It is possible to achieve both military and civil service presence in the government in the context of a united executive. In some cases, for instance in Latin America, the two groups have indeed often been associated. Such a development resembles the type of arrangements characteristic of early European cabinets, especially in England, when the king brought together within his council representatives of the aristocracy and a number of technical advisers. But such a merger implies a fairly high level of legitimacy on the part of the ruler; he must be sufficiently above the rest of the members of the government to be able to resist demands for special representation from members of his peer group. If, on the other hand, the new ruler is selected by colleagues all of whom believe that they have an equal right to become the head of state, the practical solution is to set up a 'junta', or 'presidential council' on the Latin American model, or a military or revolutionary council, on the African or Asian model.

Before the 1960s, these councils had been created only in Latin America and, in all cases, for short periods only. In 1962, a Revolutionary Council was set up in Burma as a result of the coup which overthrew U Nu for the second time and placed General Ne Win in power. This Revolutionary Council was to be different in two ways from the Latin American juntas. First, it was to last: instead of being a temporary arrangement designed to give some credibility to the ruler but which the ruler was quickly to find an impediment to his power, the Burmese Revolutionary Council was, in reality, set up by Ne Win himself and not merely tolerated by him for as long as he was not strong enough to dispense with it. It was viewed by him as a governmental council designed to give legitimacy to his own power by achieving some element of representation. This representative character was further emphasized by the fact that, unlike previous juntas, the Burmese council was a large body: it had seventeen members when it was set up in 1962; in 1973, it was expanded to twenty-eight members while being renamed Council of State. This meant that the council was, in the true sense of the word, a council, composed of various elements from the army and the party which Ne Win had by then organized. Such a council compares fairly closely in size to the American Senate at the time of American Independence (twenty-six members) and to the Swiss Council of States (forty-six members). Thus, the Burmese council stands half-way (as did the American Senate) between a government and a representative assembly and, in the theory of the Burmese arrangement at least, is deemed to achieve both functions.

The Burmese development remained unique for a number of years, but it was then followed by similar developments in other countries. Nigeria was the first to follow by setting up a Supreme Military Council — of four members only — in 1966. In 1967, the Yemen Arab Republic set up a Presidential Council of three members and, in 1968, Iraq and Mali set up respectively a Revolutionary Command Council of seven and a National Liberation Committee of five. In 1969, while the Iraqi Command Council was expanded to fifteen members, a Revolutionary Council of eleven was set up in Libya, a Supreme Revolutionary Council of twenty-five was set up in Somalia, a Revolutionary Command Council of ten was set up in Sudan and a Presidential Council of five was set up in the Popular Republic of South Yemen. Thus, by the end of the 1960s, nine countries, mainly in the Muslim world and especially in the Middle East, had set up a council around the head of state. Four of these councils (those of Nigeria, Mali and the two Yemens) were of the 'junta' type and were small — three to five members — while five of them (those of Burma, Iraq, Libya, Sudan and Somalia) were appreciably larger.

For half a decade, the experiment remained virtually static. The only new development occurred in Ghana with a National Redemption Council set up in 1972 when the military took over for the second time, but, except for the transformation of the Sudanese Command Council into a Presidential Council of four members only, the bodies created in the late 1960s remained in existence, experiencing very little change. Then, from the mid-1970s, revolutionary or military councils were created in a number of other countries, especially in black Africa, although the first council of the second wave was the Portuguese Supreme Revolutionary Council set up in 1974 (it was renamed Council of the Revolution in 1976). By 1978, there were revolutionary or military councils in eleven black African countries: alongside those of Nigeria, Ghana, Mali, Somalia and Sudan, there were those of Burundi, the Congo, Ethiopia, Madagascar, Mauritania and Zaire, while, outside black Africa, revolutionary councils had been set up in Afghanistan and Thailand. Altogether, there were councils around the head of state in eighteen countries. Only two of those which had been set up earlier had been abolished, those of Libya (in 1976), after a gradual depletion of its members from eleven in 1969 to four in 1975, and of the Central African Republic, which lasted only a year, in 1975.

While some of the councils of the first wave of the late 1960s were relatively small and resembled Latin American juntas (two of which were set up in the 1970s and have indeed lasted for a long period — in Chile and Argentina) the councils set up in Africa and Asia from the mid-1970s were relatively large, except in Mauritania where the Military Committee for National Recovery had only six members; elsewhere military or revolutionary councils had between eleven and twenty-five members. Thus, by and large, these councils have a semi-representative and legitimizing character, bearing some relationship with the politburos of Communist parties, on which they are sometimes modelled; indeed, in Zaire, Somalia and Ethiopia the councils have largely become committees of the ruling party.

These councils are given different titles, the two most popular being those of 'revolutionary council' and 'military council'. The difference between the two types is not immediately clear, as some

FIGURE 1
Evolution in the number of military
or revolutionary councils

of the 'revolutionary' councils have been created by military leaders after a coup and are staffed with military men. There may be an ideological difference, although, on the whole, regimes which created 'second governments' of this type have tended to be of the 'Left': only two clearly 'non-left-wing' regimes have had such councils (Ghana and Zaire) while the rest were divided fairly evenly between (ostensibly) left-wing regimes and somewhat more moderate ones. [16]

The future of revolutionary and military councils is still somewhat unclear: while they have multiplied and exist in about a sixth of the countries of the Third World, they depend primarily on the extent to which the new leaders can establish their position. They have clearly helped to give a base to leaders who have come to power by a military coup: indeed, on occasion, as in Nigeria, they have been the instrument through which a leader was deposed and replaced by a new leader, but this has been rare. By and large, the institutionalization of these councils has not taken place to the extent achieved by politburos in Communist states, although the setting up in the late 1970s of revolutionary councils or of party councils instead of military committees may be a step towards better institutionalization. Overall, however, the multiplication of these bodies indicates that they correspond to a need felt by the leaders to share the government with men who, in their eyes and perhaps in those of the population, give a wider political base to the new regimes and thus contribute to their greater stability.

Governments have always been organized on the basis of different conceptions, but differences are becoming more marked in the contemporary world. Far from there being a universal trend towards prime ministerial 'hierarchical' government, current developments suggest that the uneasy equilibrium between hierarchical and collective governments continues to flourish, while the number of divided governments is on the increase. Governments need authority as well as technical competence. Such authority can come from the leader, from his colleagues, from a combination of leader and colleagues or from 'representatives' of broader forces associated with the government; thus, the structure of government reflects in large part the political equilibrium in the country by means of the political origins from which its members are drawn. But technical competence is also a major problem; it creates major tensions because, where the political basis of government is weak, the problem of the reliability of technicians seems almost in-

superable. After examining the political composition of governments in the next Chapter, we shall have to see how the different
structural arrangements which we have described help cope, more
or less satisfactorily, with the different 'functions' or activities of
governments and what changes or amendments have had to be
made to the overall structure for these functions to be fulfilled, or
to be seen to be fulfilled, in the contemporary world.

Notes

1. See Chapter 1 and references in notes 6 and 7.
2. *World Leaders*, pp. 230-56.
3. The limitations on appointment and dismissal of ministers are very often
quoted in the British context. Prime ministers, such as Macmillan, who dismissed
many ministers were subsequently in trouble. But the problem is wider: detailed
studies would almost certainly reveal that few leaders are really free to appoint and
dismiss their ministers, because of constraints from ruling 'families', political parties, the military, geographical origins; and many leaders probably owe their subsequent overthrow to having dismissed ministers without sufficient concern for the
consequences.
4. See *World Leaders*, pp. 63-76.
5. See for instance J.N. Matienzo, *Le gouvernement représentatif fédéral dans
la République argentine* (Hachette, 1912), passim. Already in the mid-nineteenth
century the 'cabinet' was formed on the basis of men 'whose observations must be
accepted and from whom not only the signature but conscious and sincere agreement must be sought for every act of the government' (p. 132). President Urquiza
said to the cabinet — in sharp contrast with American practice — 'You have the
majority and I accept your decision' (p. 133).
6. *World Leaders*, pp. 265-9.
7. See B. Headey, op. cit., especially at Chapter 3, pp. 56-79.
8. *World Leaders*, pp. 67-72.
9. R. Fenno, op. cit., pp. 270-1.
10. H. Heclo, *A Government of Strangers* (Brookings Institution, 1977).
11. H. Heclo, 'Issue Networks and the Executive Establishment', in A.H. King,
ed., *The New American Political System* (American Enterprise Institute, 1978),
p. 87.
12. H. Heclo, eod. loc.
13. The standard text comparing American and Soviet governments, that of Z.
Brzezinski and S.P. Huntington, *Political Power, USA/USSR* (Chatto and Windus,
1964), scarcely discusses the structure of the executive in either country.

14. R. Fenno, op. cit., p. 77. See also D. Truman, 'Presidential Executives or Congressional Executives' in A. Wildavsky, ed., *The Presidency* (Little, Brown, 1969), p. 486.

15. A. Wildavsky, 'Salvation by Staff: Reform of the Presidential Office', in A. Wildavsky, op. cit., p. 698.

16. Of the 'Left' were Afghanistan, Iraq, Congo, Ethiopia, Madagascar. Of the 'more moderate' were Burma, Thailand, Burundi, Mali, Mauritania, Somalia, Portugal (at the time). Of the 'Right' were Ghana and Zaire.

4. THE POLITICAL COMPOSITION OF GOVERNMENTS

Differences in governmental structures may not be apparent unless one looks carefully at the way governments are organized: the existence of marked differences in the political composition of governments, on the other hand, comes as no surprise. The distinction between party government and military government, even the distinction between single-party and coalition government, are among the political divisions which are most commonly perceived by a wide public; it is probably also generally realized that some governments are still run in a traditional or 'pre-modern' manner by kings and other rulers with their courtiers and the rest of their entourage. There is, therefore, little doubt that the political character of the governments of the contemporary world is widely recognized as being divided into a number of sharply distinct types.

Indeed, the differences in the political basis and composition of governments are probably greater in the contemporary world than at any time in the past, largely because of the emergence of party government in its various forms in the course of the nineteenth and twentieth centuries; the variety of governments clearly owes much to the widening role of parties and to the relatively recent spread of new forms of party systems throughout the world. Yet, paradoxically, differences in the political composition of governments owe perhaps even more to the weaknesses of parties and party systems than to their strength. For if parties had truly succeeded in what have often been the claims on their behalf, namely that they are *the*

institutions which are able to control the political system in the contemporary world, the old forms of government would slowly have
been replaced and parties would no longer be challenged by other
bodies in their monopoly over governments. In reality, not only
have a few traditional governments survived, although these were
very few at the end of the 1970s, but, more strikingly, the military
has provided a major challenge to the dominance of parties over
modern political systems and over governments in particular. It is
clearly not the case that the second half of the twentieth century has
seen parties gradually dominating all types of governments: there is
no advance of party government.

Yet the forces which challenge the hold of parties on governments — the military, and to an extent the bureaucracy as well,
normally in combination with the military — have for their part
failed to emerge as a genuinely positive alternative to party government. They exercise substantial control over many governments, but
this control is more the result of a protest against what is regarded
as the failure of party government than a consequence of a marked
appeal. The military appears on the governmental scene as a group
able to stop the excesses of parties, to 'clean up the mess'; it does
not appear as an organization widely recognized as being able to
give governments a true mark of their own. It is because party
government has been weak or even impotent, because the effective
hold of parties on the government, let alone on the country, is often
more nominal than real, that the military seems able to take over
power. Even more strikingly, the process of civilianization which
military governments often undergo constitutes a further proof of
the longer-term inability of military men to maintain themselves
and to be viewed as a genuine alternative to party leaders.

The strengths and weaknesses of parties thus explain in large part
the fact that governments are so obviously diverse in the contemporary world. And these strengths and weaknesses indeed account
for an even greater diversity than is immediately apparent. For not
only are there different forms of party government (single and
coalition being the best known examples); not only is party government often replaced over the years by military rule, although party
government may subsequently return; but military government has
also come to be combined, in a number of ways, with party government, as well as with governments which are organized on a traditional basis. The study of the political composition of governments
thus becomes the study of the variety of ways in which the major

types of governments — party, traditional group, military, as well as the bureaucracy — enter into combination in order to form governments. Some of these constructions have only been in existence recently both since the worldwide spread of the idea (if not always the reality) of party government is a post-1945 phenomenon, and since, consequently, the emergence of the military as an 'anti-party' phenomenon is even more recent. Nevertheless, these combinations gradually fall into patterns which can be described and assessed, at least in terms of their duration and apparent hold on governments. Thus, the contemporary world is one in which governments are formally composed primarily of parties but in which the challenge to parties, principally by the military, takes complex and subtle forms which need to be examined carefully.

1. Party Governments

Let us begin by examining the hold which parties currently have on governments and the form which this hold takes. Ostensibly, and in the most global analysis, this hold is strong, but not overwhelming. Taken together, parties have always, at least formally, controlled about two-thirds of the governments of the world in the post Second World War period: in 1980, among the countries which had had an independent life for at least ten years (one hundred and thirty-seven countries), ninety-three or 68 percent lived under one form or another of party government.

Yet, this hold becomes less impressive when we look at the evolution of party government since 1945 and at its geographical spread. In 1945, among an appreciably smaller number of independent countries, admittedly, the percentage of governments ruled by one or more parties was fractionally higher than it was in 1980: 70 percent against 68 percent (fifty-one countries out of seventy-three). Thus, from the beginning to the end of the period, there was almost no change — just a little drop in party government. But this overall near-stability conceals some substantial movements in the intervening period, and these movements point to fundamental weaknesses in the attractiveness of party government (Figure 2). At first, during the late 1940s and even more during the 1950s, party government spread: by 1959, almost 80 percent of the countries of the world were ruled by a party government. But this was followed

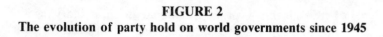

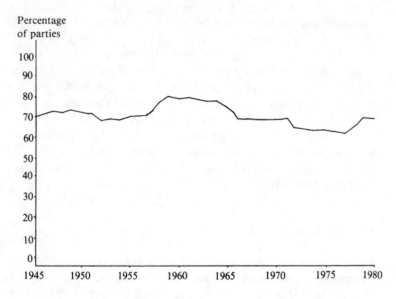

FIGURE 2
The evolution of party hold on world governments since 1945

by a decline from the mid-1960s, at first very sharp, and then more
gradual until only about 60 percent of the governments were ruled
by a party in 1977 — a drop of 20 percent or one-quarter of the
total. Party government spread again fairly rapidly in the late
1970s, to reach 69 percent in 1979, but in 1980 there was a small
decrease — perhaps party government had once more reached a
plateau.

The hold of parties on governments is thus substantial, but not
very impressive, and the interpretation of the evolution in the
1945-80 period for the future of party government is ostensibly not
altogether favourable, on the basis of aggregate figures. Party
government seems vulnerable: perhaps this vulnerability was due,
in the 1960-75 period, to the fact that many new countries were led
to independence by parties which were relatively weakly implanted;
and perhaps, therefore, the upward trend of the late 1970s indicates
that parties are gradually becoming better implanted; but perhaps,
too, these movements are of a cyclical character and parties may
still continue to find it difficult to extend their hold beyond the
levels which they have achieved so far.

TABLE 1
Types of governmental composition
across the world, 1980
(percentages)

	Atlantic Area	Middle East and North Africa	South and South East Asia	Africa South of the Sahara	Latin America
Traditional	—	49	23	7	2
Military (Pure)	1	7	8	15	19
Military (+single-party/mixed)	2	11	3	11	5
Military (dominant but some competition)	—	—	10	—	9
Single-party	6	8	18	41	21
Single-party government in pluralistic systems	46	10	33	19	35
Coalition	45	15	5	7	9
	100	100	100	100	100

TABLE 2
Evolution of types of government hold
(Third World only)
(percentages)

	1945	1950	1955	1965	1975	1980
Traditional	38	30	28	16	13	12
Military (pure)	9	12	16	10	20	11
Military (single-party mixed)	2	4	—	8	14	15
Military (dominant but some competition)	—	—	4	4	5	6
Single-party	16	12	13	27	24	22
Single-party government in pluralistic system	28	34	30	25	18	20
Coalition	7	8	9	10	6	14
	100	100	100	100	100	100

This somewhat pessimistic conclusion is reinforced if one looks, not at the percentage of countries which, each year, live under a party government, but at the number of countries which have consistently been under party rule since 1945 or since their independence. While at least three-fifths and normally over two-thirds of the countries of the world have a party government, and while only ten countries have never been ruled by a government controlled by parties, only sixty-five countries — somewhat under half (48 percent) — have had *uninterrupted* party rule throughout the post-1945 period and this number grows only to seventy (just over half) if one adds those countries which were controlled by parties continuously throughout the 1970s and to eighty (58 percent) if one includes those countries which were ruled by parties during three-quarters of their independent life during the post-1945 period. Whereas nearly all countries have had some period of party rule, those which have been ruled predominantly by parties, especially in the more recent period, are a bare majority and those which have been ruled consistently by parties are a minority. This means that there is a considerable turnover of countries living under party rule: perhaps groups other than parties do not succeed in controlling governments very effectively, but the hold of parties on governments is not very impressive either.

Indeed, the weaknesses of parties are perhaps further stressed by an examination of the geographical spread of countries which have consistently been under party rule. Basically, half of them come from the Atlantic area or the Communist world (thirty-three out of sixty-five countries): all the Communist countries of East Europe and North Asia belong to the group, and only three Atlantic countries (Spain, Portugal and Greece) have not been under continuous party rule since 1945. On the other hand, only one-third of the Third World countries (thirty-two out of 102) have been under continuous party rule since 1945 or independence and under half were predominantly under party rule (three-quarters of the period), although only 10 percent of them were never under party control at all. Differences across the Third World are not very marked geographically, although they do exist: the Middle East and Latin America are the two regions where the percentage of countries with constant party control of the government is lowest (25 percent); in South East Asia and in Africa South of the Sahara, the percentage is higher but it does not reach 40 percent. One major difference relates to countries belonging to the Commonwealth or having previously been British dependencies: over half of them have been under continuous party rule (seventeen out of thirty) while only fifteen countries outside the Commonwealth — barely a quarter of the total — have had continuous party rule, only two of which are in Latin America (10 percent), six in Africa South of the Sahara, three in South East Asia and four in the Middle East and North Africa.[1] The very low percentage of Latin American countries in this category is particularly striking: Mexico and Costa Rica alone have had continuous party rule, but it should be pointed out that a further five Latin American countries had continuous party rule in the 1970s, while another two, under military rule in the second half of the 1970s (Chile and Uruguay), have been dominated by parties in the post-1945 period.

Continuous party control is thus relatively uncommon in Third World countries, especially outside the Commonwealth; on the other hand, the hold of political parties on government is an almost universal characteristic of Communist and Atlantic countries, although the types of party systems are vastly different in the two regions and although the hold of parties on government manifests itself differently. But, while all Communist systems are based on one form of party rule — single-party government —, Atlantic countries have been controlled by two types of party government, those by a single party and those by coalitions (although there are,

TABLE 3
Countries with continuous party rule in government since 1945 or independence
(Third World only)

	Number in group	Single-party always	Single-party govt. in pluralistic system always	Coalition government always	Single-party govt. in pluralistic system or competition	Single party or pluralistic
North East and North Africa	5 / 21	South Yemen / Tunisia		Lebanon / Israel	Cyprus*	
South and South East Asia	7 / 18	Taiwan / Singapore*	India* / Japan / Malaysia*		Sri Lanka*	Philippines
Africa South of the Sahara	14 / 38	Guinea / Ivory Coast / Kenya* / Malawi* / Tanzania*	Botswana* / Gambia* / South Africa		Mauritius*	Cameroon / Gabon / Senegal / Zambia* / Zimbabwe*
Latin America	6 / 24	Mexico	Barbados* / Costa Rica / Guyana* / Jamaica* / Trinidad*			
	32 / 101	10	11	2	3	6

* Denotes Commonwealth countries.

admittedly, a number of 'forced' coalitions in the Communist world). We shall examine these two forms of party government in succession.

(a) Single-Party Governments

Single-party governments — based on a competitive party system — are by far the most common form of government across the world: for 54 percent of the time, the countries of the world have been ruled by a government controlled by, if not necessarily exclusively composed of, representatives of one party. Single-party government is also the only form of government which can be said to have been experienced, during the post-1945 period, by almost all countries: only twenty-one nations have never had any form of single-party government, while 117 (85 percent) have been for shorter or longer periods ruled by one party.

But single-party rule also has its manifest weaknesses: in only forty-five countries did single-party rule prevail continuously and in another seven did it prevail for three-quarters of the years or more. Single-party rule is the most common form of government: it has been 'tasted' nearly everywhere, but it has so far been resilient only in limited parts of the world.

The two main forms of durable single-party government are Communist single-party systems and two-party systems on the British model. The forty-five countries which have been ruled continuously by a single-party government since 1945 or since independence fall into three groups of about equal size: thirteen countries have a strong single-party *system* based on the Communist Party; twelve countries are or have been members of the Commonwealth and have a two-party system or a near two-party system; they also mostly have a single-member, first-past-the-post system (all except Australia, Guyana and Malta); and the twenty other countries (several of which belong to the Commonwealth) have a variety of single, dominant or two-party systems. Thus, strong single-party government appears to be markedly associated with either a Communist system or British political influence.

Communist single-party governments. The fact that Communist single-party governments are strong and, by the late 1970s at least, had successfully resisted any challenge to their overthrow is both well-known and very impressive when it is contrasted with the instability of Eastern European governmental systems before the Second World War and the inability of parties to rule continuously in the Third World. Indeed, the same type of strong control seems to be emerging in those countries which have been taken over by Communist governments from the late 1950s, Cuba, first, Laos, Cambodia and some of the former Portuguese colonies in the second half of the 1970s, though the hold of the Communist Party on the governments of these countries is seemingly less strong and appreciably more vulnerable than in the original thirteen Communist states: coups, civil wars and international conflicts have occurred in Guinea-Bissau, Angola, Laos, Cambodia and Afghanistan. These events make it more difficult to believe that the maintenance of Communist governments is assured in these countries, while, of course, the hold of the Communist Party on several Eastern European governments appears essentially due to the military power of the Soviet Union and only secondarily to the internal ability of Communist governments to exercise full influence.

Indeed, primarily in two Eastern European Communist countries, Poland and East Germany, and to a lesser extent in a third, Czechoslovakia, the government is not strictly speaking run by the Communist Party alone, but by a permanent coalition composed of the Communist Party and other parties, in which the former has, of course, a predominant voice. The presence of other parties in the government is alleged to correspond to the fact that these countries are still in a transitional stage; what it also signifies is that Communism was established with considerable difficulty in these countries: the hegemony of the Communist Party was introduced only after a period of some years during which coalition governments were established, sometimes under Communist leadership, as in Czechoslovakia, but sometimes, as in Hungary, under the leadership of other, appreciably more popular parties. Thus, while the domination of the Communist Party is marked in all thirteen East European and North Asian states, this domination, even in the context of Soviet presence, is restricted in some East European states while it is complete in the Soviet Union, Albania, Yugoslavia and the North Asian countries.

Party domination of the government in Communist states is also limited by the manifestly strong part played by the bureaucracy within the Council of Ministers. Some commentators describe the Council of Ministers as being composed merely of 'technicians' and the position of minister as being therefore analogous to that of permanent civil servant in Western European countries. This view, as we saw in the previous Chapter, is at best an exaggeration and indeed by and large erroneous: the relative overlap between the Communist Party hierarchy and the administrative hierarchy at the top of the political structure of the Communist states makes it unrealistic to view the division as entirely clear-cut. But as the overlap is only partial, and as it does not altogether abolish the distinction between careers and approaches to government, it is not unrealistic to view Communist governments as being based on two types of pressures. Moreover, since the councils of ministers manage and even largely coordinate governmental matters, as we saw, given therefore that ministers, separately or collectively through the council or its Presidium, exercise important governmental functions, it is simply wrong to deny the bureaucracy an important part in the governmental machinery of Communist states. This makes single-party government in the Soviet Union somewhat different in character from that in, for instance, Atlantic states such as Britain, Canada or New Zealand. Admittedly, in the country at large, the role of the party in Communist states is much larger than is the role of the governmental party in a Western state, but, within the government, the role of the party is limited by the power of the bureaucracy in a Communist state while the influence of the bureaucracy is more indirect, and appreciably more covert in a Western European state. Thus, it is not altogether wrong to view government in Communist states as an alliance (a forced alliance to an extent) between party and bureaucracy and not, in the strict sense of the word, as full single-party government.

Single-party government in other single-party states: the predominance of Commonwealth countries. Communist systems form the majority of the single-party states which have controlled both government and nation continuously since the late 1940s or since independence. Only nine other countries have had full single-party rule throughout the period while in another three the party in power has exercised substantial dominance, but not total control; and only a further two countries have had single-party control continuously during the 1970s, while seven countries have been ruled by a single party for three-quarters of the time, but not continuously since 1945 (including one country, Cuba, which belongs to both groups). This means that, including Communist states, only twenty-five countries have always been ruled by a single party in the context of a single-party system and that less than thirty-five can be said to have been ruled predominantly in the same manner. This relatively small proportion shows the limitations of the single-party system as a permanent feature of modern government: outside Communist countries, single-party rule is rarely continuous, and it does not appear to be very durable since there have been more casualties (seven) than there have been recent 'successes' (three). Indeed, two of these three relatively recent 'successes' being Cuba and Afghanistan, the impression is reinforced that Communist rule is by far the most effective instrument in maintaining single-party government through single-party rule.[2]

Yet, while the Communist systems have been the most effective means so far of maintaining continuous single-party rule in a single-party system context, a group of Commonwealth countries comes fairly close behind. Four of the nine countries (Singapore, Kenya, Malawi, Tanzania) which have had a continuous single-party system and two of the three countries which have been continuously dominated by near single-party rule (Botswana and Trinidad) have been single-party systems from the Commonwealth while one other (South Yemen), was originally a British possession. The relationship between membership of the Commonwealth and continuous single-party rule is clearly not spurious, even though there are also other countries in the group. It is indeed reinforced negatively by the fact that, among the six countries which were dominated by a single-party government in a single-party system context but were no longer ruled in this manner by 1980, there is not one Commonwealth country (the six being Spain, Portugal, Chad, Liberia, Mauritania and Niger). Commonwealth countries which have had single-party rule from the start have been better able than other countries to maintain the hold of the single party (in contrast, while three formerly French controlled countries were ruled continuously by a single party since independence, three were not). This state of affairs suggests that in British possessions, parties were established fairly strongly before independence, often to fight British rule, as nationalist leaders felt the need to put pressure through a party organization, and this organization, though often harrassed, was not altogether destroyed. This ideology of the party varies markedly since the group includes Kenya, Malawi and Singapore, as well as Tanzania; it varies occasionally over time. But the strength of the single-party systems in a number of Commonwealth countries and their consequential ability to withstand the erosion of power (coupled with the seemingly lesser part played by the army) do account for the disproportionately large number of Commonwealth countries in the group of single-party governments based on a single-party system.

The non-Commonwealth countries in the group are three former French possessions (Tunisia, Guinea and the Ivory Coast), Taiwan, Mexico and South Yemen. This set of single-party governments is very different in character and ideology, as they range from Latin America to Asia, have a very different type of party organization, and span across the ideological spectrum from conservative to socialist and from very authoritarian to mildly liberal. The outstanding country in the group is Mexico, which is perhaps the best example of a successful non-Communist single-party system and in which a stable succession of governments contrasts with a long preceding period of civil strife and ineffective administration. The single Mexican party, the Partido Revolucionario Institutional (PRI), has kept a hold on the government by clever manipulation, by a careful socialization of political elites and by the integration of a number of groups in the organization.

Yet, while the rule of the PRI in Mexico is a clear success, which shows that single-party rule can provide a stable form of government outside the Communist system, it is also exceptional. There are no other examples in Latin America, and there are few similar examples outside Latin America, especially since, in the three African cases at least, the charismatic role of the leader has also played a major part. By and large, the desire or ability to engineer a party stemming from and accommodating various social groups and thus able to control the government in a relatively pluralistic manner has been almost non-existent outside the Commonwealth. Perhaps, the relative paucity of such examples stems from the fact that most Third World countries have only had a short independent life; and perhaps some of the current military regimes, as we shall see, will move in a similar direction. But it does remain the case that the Mexican 'model' has not so far been successfully imitated outside the Commonwealth, and especially not in that part of the world — Latin America — which had both the time and the need to establish a strong basis for its government through the development of an effective party.

Single-party government in a majority system. The predominance of Commonwealth countries. Twenty-five countries experienced continuous single-party government in the context of single-party rule; only fifteen countries experienced continuous single-party government (not necessarily of the same party) in the context of a competitive party system; and eleven of these countries belong to the Commonwealth, while another (South Africa) was previously in the Commonwealth. Only three non-Commonwealth countries, the United States, Costa Rica and Japan, have had continuous (or near-continuous) single-party rule in a competitive party context.

This suggests that the role played by Britain in introducing single-party government has been very large, but it has not been merely of a 'cultural' kind: the role of the electoral system (itself, of course, a consequence of British influence) is also clear. Four of the six Western countries which have consistently had single-party government since the war have also had the 'British' first-past-the-post system, while a fifth, Australia, has had the alternative vote; seven of the nine Third World countries which fall in the same category also adopted the British electoral system, while Japan has the single non-transferable system, a system which also exaggerates majorities though not to the same extent as the British system. Only two countries of the group (Malta and Costa Rica) adopted proportional representation. Since the first-past-the-post system, and indeed the majority system, are rare outside the Commonwealth, the relationship between single-party rule, majority system and membership of the Commonwealth is also very strong.[3]

Without the majority system, a substantial number of countries which have had single-party government would have been often, if not always, faced either with the need to build coalitions or to be ruled by minority governments. While minority governments, as we shall see, occur occasionally among Western countries, they rarely last for long periods; indeed, in countries which have adopted the majority system, minority governments occur occasionally (as in Britain or Canada). But, by boosting the support for the largest party, the majority system makes these occurrences of minority government relatively rare, and the principle of majority can therefore be seen to be 'workable' and become a 'norm' of the operation of government.

But the electoral system is only a booster, or a net. It is a booster in that it places in orbit one or two large parties, and it is a net in that it prevents these parties from declining as fast in terms of seats as they would in the context of proportional representation. But the effect of the majority system will only be marked if general sociopolitical conditions also favour a two- or near two-party system.

For, while it has sometimes been argued that the first-past-the-post system leads to a two-party system, it is also remarkable to note how few two-party systems exist outside the Commonwealth. Former British possessions may be among the few countries which have a solid single-party system, but they are also among the only group of countries where the two-party system has flourished and seems to constitute the stuff of political life. This makes for a reciprocal influence of the electoral system on the party system: two-party systems are maintained by the electoral system and politicians therefore prefer to maintain that system — and indeed in many cases do not even question its validity. And parliamentary government, which exists everywhere in this group except in the United States and Costa Rica, makes it necessary for the government to endeavour to have solid majority support.

Admittedly, some of the countries of the group have had a somewhat 'impure' form of single-party government. In three countries, the government has occasionally or even very frequently had some of the characteristics of a coalition (Australia, India, Malaysia) while in a fourth, Japan, the party in power has resulted from the merger of previously distinct parties and has displayed a high dose of factionalism. It could be claimed with some justification in these cases that the situation is not entirely different from that which prevails where coalitions control the government. But the permanence of the arrangement in Australia and Malaysia, as well as in India during the relatively short period of rule of the Janata Party in the 1970s, makes for a situation which is also not altogether different from that of 'catch-all' parties which include a large number of groups staying together primarily for electoral purposes. Moreover, these four countries are the only 'borderline' cases; in the other parliamentary countries which have been ruled by single-party government, the party which comes to power is a single party, even if it is not always wholly united.

Indeed, what characterizes the majority of these governments is that they are, in the strong sense of the word, party governments. The competition is marked, occasionally fierce, at election times, and the party which wins the election then takes all the available positions in the government. By and large, the constitution of the government is a rapid operation, and one which occurs as a result of, and immediately after a general election. Changes of leader within the government party are relatively rare, and follow an internal party procedure; they are more often due to old age and to the desire to retire than to political circumstances although, occasionally, age or illness are excuses and hide a political dismissal (though the fact that age or illness is given as an excuse by itself makes the situation very different from that which tends to obtain in coalition governments). Single-party governments of the competitive party system variety are thus not intrinsically different internally from those of Communist Party systems, and they are perhaps even more exclusively party-based than the single-party governments of Communist systems where, as we saw, the bureaucracy plays a prominent part.

There are some exceptions to this situation. In some of the African countries of the group (Botswana and Lesotho) the weight of parties is rather limited. In Japan, the factionalism of the Liberal Democratic Party has led to a tradition by which ministers are very often replaced, and prime ministers also change fairly regularly outside the context of a general election; indeed, ministers are often less clearly 'party men' than they are in other parliamentary systems: they are recruited in substantial numbers from among the civil service with the result that the overall role of the bureaucracy is somewhat closer to that which prevails in Communist governments. Finally, in the United States and to a lesser extent in Costa Rica (the only two presidential systems in the group), the weight of parties is less noticeable than in parliamentary countries. The United States government is a 'segmented' government where some party men are included, but more because they are friends of the president than because they are party men, as we saw in the previous Chapter. Yet it remains true that the government as a whole broadly represents the interests of the president's party, even if it is especially the president's wing of the party, and to that extent the United States government is a 'party' government.

As the United States, and even Costa Rica and Japan, constitute modified and somewhat less clear-cut forms of single-party rule, the predominance of Commonwealth countries in the group becomes more overwhelming. Britain can, therefore, truly be said to have invented and exported a form of government (in the sociopolitical and not merely institutional and constitutional sense), and this form of government has flourished in countries in which British influence has been marked. The dozen or so countries which have consistently had single-party government and electoral competition are the clearest evidence of this British influence. And, although in a less clear-cut fashion, Britain has also contributed to the implantation of strong parties in the large majority of non-Communist states which have operated under a single-party system. This is a clear achievement: it is therefore ironical that it should be in Britain itself that doubts began to be raised in the 1960s and 1970s about the validity of the form of single-party government in a competitive context which Britain invented and passed on to various parts of the world. Whether the disillusionment with this form of government will be strong enough in Britain and, consequently, in Commonwealth countries in the closing years of the century is therefore an intriguing and important question for the future of government across the world.

The fate of single-party governments across the world. Single-party governments of the single-party system or pluralistic party system varieties have been implanted in forty countries only (thirteen Communist, six Atlantic and twenty-one from the Third World); in six further Third World countries (Philippines, Cameroon, Gabon, Zambia, Senegal and Zimbabwe) there has usually been single-party government, but in either the context of a single-party system or in that of a competitive party system. Thus, the large majority of Third World countries have experienced party government, but, in most cases, the experience was only temporary: twenty-four Third World countries have never been ruled by one party, but only twenty-seven have been ruled permanently by a party government; no less than than fifty have oscillated between party rule and other forms of government.

The main challenge has come from military rule, and this challenge resulted not merely in oscillations between military and party rule, but in the overall decline, in the course of the period, in the number of countries ruled by a government controlled by one party. But this decline is limited in four ways. First, it particularly affected single-party systems, and competitive party systems only to a lesser extent: outside the Communist world there were seventeen single-party systems at the beginning of the period, but only six at the end, as against thirteen competitive party systems at the beginning of the period and ten at the end.

Second, the whole of the 'loss' of single-party systems is ostensibly due to changes among African countries: no less than eleven of the countries of sub-Saharan Africa which had a single-party system at the time of independence were ruled by a non-party government in 1980 (eight former French territories, two former

Belgian, and only one from among the Commonwealth countries). Elsewhere, on the other hand, the five single-party system countries had become six by 1980.

But, and this is the third point, four of these single-party system countries were controlled by a Communist Party in 1980, while a fifth country (Haiti) was a single-party system in name only and the role of the party in the governmental decision-making process was clearly very small. Thus single-party systems are, on the whole, in decline, especially outside the Commonwealth, and only with the armed intervention of Communist forces have new ones been set up in the postwar period. Single-party government based on a single-party system seems to depend on charismatic leadership or an armed rebellion to emerge, not a particularly propitious state of affairs for that type of government.

Fourth, on the contrary, although the number of single-party governments emerging in a competitive context has somewhat diminished, not only has it diminished less than the number of single-party governments based on a single-party system, and not only had two out of thirteen countries returned to this form of rule by the early 1980s (Senegal and Ghana), but 'gains' were made among countries which had been ruled in the early postwar period by non-party governments (four) and from among single-party systems (two). Thus, competitive systems are better able to sustain a single-party government than single-party systems; this is particularly noticeable in Latin America where single-party government and military rule seem to follow each other in an almost regular manner.

Thus, the examination of the 'pathology' of single-party government confirms negatively the broad conclusions which were drawn from the examination of countries which have remained under single-party rule. Single-party government remains stable either when there is a near two-party government or when there is a single-party system in a Commonwealth or Communist country: elsewhere, single-party governments are rarely a durable form of government. Single-party government occupies a middle position between coalition government — which results from highly fractionalized systems — and 'mixed' single-party and military government — which results from the fact that, in practice, outside the Commonwealth and Communist countries, the single party does not appear, on the whole, to be sufficiently implanted to withstand the opposition of outside forces, and especially the military. Although single-party government is the most common form of government, it has, in many countries, a transitional character — a situation which has to be related to the relative weaknesses of parties in the contemporary world in terms of ideology and programmes, and, almost certainly, of leadership as well.

(b) Coalition Governments

Coalition governments have given rise to an abundant analytical and polemical literature. Polemics have centred on the alleged potential 'dangers' stemming from coalitions, as well as from proportional representation, with which coalitions have been associated, because coalition governments were often described as weak, short-lived and ineffective. This view has since been altered, and some have come to praise coalitions for their role in bringing about consensus and in ensuring greater continuity of policies than single-party governments on the British model.[4] Meanwhile, the analytical interest in coalitions has also been intense, as they have been viewed as instances where techniques of rational-choice analysis could be applied to determine which coalition was likely to succeed.

But this substantial work on coalition governments has been almost entirely confined to Atlantic systems. This is, to be sure, where most coalitions have occurred: overall, since 1945, sixteen out of twenty-three Atlantic countries have had coalitions; in five of these countries, there was a coalition government continuously throughout the 1945-80 period; and, for the whole group, coalitions prevailed for about half the time.

But coalitions did not occur only in Atlantic countries. Although they are appreciably less common elsewhere than single-party governments, they have occurred in thirty countries of the Third World since 1945, and they did occur between 1945 and 1949 in four Eastern European countries which subsequently became Communist. Admittedly, in the Third World, coalitions are less widespread than in Western Europe: they are also less durable; while about two-thirds of the Atlantic countries were ruled by coalitions, on average, about half the time, only one-third of Third World countries were ruled by a coalition government, and this was, on average, for 9 percent of the time. While not unknown in the world at large, coalition government is therefore markedly more common, and more successful, in Europe. But this situation in itself needs to be explained: is it that coalitions are rarer outside

TABLE 4
Duration of coalitions in Atlantic countries
(1946-1971)
(years)

	Single-party	Two-party	Three-party	Four or more parties
Austria	4	21	—	—
Belgium	4	19	2	—
Denmark	11	10	4	—
Finland	2	3	3	15 (also non-
France	—	1	11	13 party)
West Germany				
(1949-74)	—	17	4	4
Iceland	7	13	5	—
Ireland	19	3	—	4
Italy	6	4	6	9
Luxembourg	—	24	1	1
Netherlands	—	3	2	20
Norway	19	—	6	—
Sweden	19	6	—	—

Six countries (Australia, Canada, Malta, New Zealand, the United Kingdom and the United States) had only single-party government; one country (Switzerland) had a permanent coalition of three or four parties. Spain, Portugal and Greece did not have a continuous period of competitive party rule.

Western Europe because there are fewer countries in which there is a competitive party system? Or is it that coalitions have a different character? And, if coalitions are viewed in the West as a 'normal' and effective form of government, does the same view prevail in the Third World?

The varied character of coalitions. There is no doubt that coalitions, in the Western European context at least, can be as effective as single-party governments. Specifically, coalition governments are not appreciably much shorter in duration, on average, than single-party governments. Earlier criticisms associating coalitions with a rapid turnover of the executive were simply ill-informed: they were often based exclusively on France, Weimar Germany or pre-fascist Italy; in other countries, coalitions have been stable and governments long-lasting. Admittedly, on average and overall, coalition governments last somewhat less time than single-party governments: for the 1945-71 period, and for seventeen countries of the Atlantic area (i.e. all the continuous parliamentary systems except Malta, which became independent only in 1965), the average duration of single-party governments was 4.6 years, while the average duration of coalition governments was a little under three years.[5] But, first, three-year governments are not 'short-lived': this is a 'respectable' duration. Second, in countries which experience both single-party government and coalitions, single-party governments are also shorter (3.3 years): there may be a different 'cultural' attitude towards the duration of governments. And, third, there is a vast difference in duration between types of coalitions: for the 1945-71 period, two-party governments lasted on average 3.3 years, three-party governments 3.0 years, four-party governments 2.4 years and governments of five parties less than one year. The unstable governments are therefore the governments of five parties: even governments of four parties are relatively stable. But there are few examples of governments of five parties: they were exclusively confined to pre-1958 France and to Finland. Elsewhere, the duration of coalitions was somewhat shorter than that of a single-party governments, but it was 'respectable'.

Coalition governments are therefore not normally 'volatile'; they cannot be treated as one group either. Indeed, they vary between two poles. One consists of stable governments set up for the duration of a Parliament, and lasting sometimes beyond, as in West Germany, Austria before 1966, the Netherlands often; indeed, in Switzerland, the coalition system is so embedded in the structure of politics that there is almost no turnover of parties or men. At the other extreme, there are shifting arrangements, liable to change frequently at the whim of party leaders or even backbench parliamentarians: this was the case in France before 1958 where there was, as in Greece before 1952, 'hyper-instability'; this is to a lesser extent the case of governments in Italy, Belgium, Finland, and, in the 1970s, Denmark. Between these two extremes, countries such as Ireland, Norway and Iceland mostly have long-lasting coalitions, but occasionally have shorter ones.

This disparity in the character of coalitions and in their duration suggests that the problem of the origin and composition of coalitions needs to be examined with care. The theoretical and analytical literature of the 1960s and 1970s endeavoured to approach this problem in terms of the 'logic' of a majority situation which appears to force parties, first, into a coalition, and, second, into the particular coalition which is least 'costly' in terms of their own programmes and the spread of patronage to other political groupings. So far, while rational-choice analysis has opened up avenues of inquiry, it has not succeeded in accounting in a truly convincing manner for the occurrence and specific character of coalitions.[6]

The first point which needs to be analysed relates to the circumstances in which coalitions occur. This might at first sight seem unnecessary as one might conclude that coalitions occur because of the requirement of parliamentary systems that governments must command a majority in the chamber. As a matter of fact, the situation is much less clear-cut. Admittedly, coalitions tend to occur in parliamentary systems, and they tend to occur when no party has an absolute majority in Parliament. But this is only a broad trend. First, coalitions do not occur only in parliamentary systems, even if one adopts a rather loose definition of parliamentary systems and includes 'modified' parliamentary and semi-presidential or dual systems on the French model. Coalitions have occurred since 1945, not merely in a country such as Switzerland which is not parliamentary although the chamber elects the Federal Council, but in a number of 'pure' presidential systems, such as Venezuela, Colombia, Peru or Brazil. Overall, there is a clear preponderance of parliamentary or modified parliamentary systems among those countries which have experienced coalition governments (fifteen out of sixteen in Western Europe and twenty out of thirty in the Third World); in the Third World at least, the number of exceptions is sufficiently large to cast some doubt on the linkage between the parliamentary structure of government and coalitions.

Second, even in parliamentary systems, coalitions do not necessarily occur when no party has a majority in Parliament; nor do they occur only when there is no majority party. There are many cases of minority governments, and some of these coalitions seem 'unnecessary'. V. Herman and J. Pope showed that, out of 207 administrations which were formed in twelve Western European governments between 1945 and 1971, seventy-four (over a third) were of a minority character. These governments were on average shorter in duration than majority governments: a majority government is 'safer' than a minority government, but some minority governments have lasted for long periods.[7] Coalitions set up although a single party commanded a majority in the chamber are rarer, but notable: they are common in wartime as between 1940 and 1945, but they also occur in other circumstances, for instance in Britain between 1931 and at least 1935, in Germany between 1953 and 1957 or in France between 1968 and 1973 and in 1981; outside Europe, they occurred for instance in Venezuela in 1958 and in Colombia for the bulk of the post-1958 period. Even if these cases are somewhat exceptional, they have to be accounted for; they undermine the view that coalition government is directly related to a parliamentary majority.

Two types of 'special' explanations can be put forward to account for the existence of 'minority' governments and 'unnecessary' coalitions. Minority governments can be explained as being merely transitional, especially in countries in which there is normally a majority party: the minority Canadian administrations and the 1974 British Labour minority administration could be explained in this way. 'Unnecessary coalitions' could be explained as being coalitions of a rather different type, corresponding to crisis situations rather than to the normal management of the affairs of the country: this might account for wartime coalitions, as well as for cases such as the 1931 British 'National' Government, which claimed to have been elected to deal with the 'extraordinary' character of the depression.

Yet neither of these explanations can account for all the cases. It may be true that 'England does not love coalitions'[8] and that, perhaps as a result, Canada does not like them either, but minority governments also occur in countries which are reputed to 'like' coalitions. As a matter of fact, only four Western European parliamentary democracies continuously had coalitions and five — all in the Commonwealth — never had coalitions at all. In the other nine parliamentary countries, coalitions ruled for three-fifths of the time during the 1945-71 period, while there were single-party governments for two-fifths of the time. These single-party governments were 'majority' governments in a majority of cases, but there were minority governments in Denmark, Iceland, Italy, Sweden, Ireland and Finland. Minority governments are relatively rare, but they are not exceptional, and they are not confined to countries in which the idea of coalition is not 'liked'.

There is in fact no single explanation for minority governments. The analysis conducted by Herman and Pope shows that many minority governments have tended to be found where one party obtained a near-majority of seats and could count (or at least could hope to count) on the support of 'independents' or of very small parties (Communists in Sweden for instance). But many minority governments exist without being based on such a large party: about a third (twenty-five) of the minority governments were based on parties with 40 percent or less of the seats in the chamber. Thus, coalitions are one solution, but only one solution to the problem of building a government in a situation in which there is no majority, while coalitions may exist even when there is a majority party.

The existence of minority governments and of 'unnecessary' coalitions is only surprising if it is believed that the majority, and only the majority, has to be represented in a parliamentary government. This view is an oversimplification. There was no such assumption in the past: parliamentary government started from the principle that it was up to the government and its head, appointed by the head of state, to find a majority. This could be achieved by a variety of means, including rather dubious ones: efforts were made to give rewards to those who supported the government, and these rewards ranged from personal favours to policy concessions. It could, for instance, be agreed (as happened in Britain in 1977-78) that certain Bills would be introduced and others would not be; the government might also be prepared to allow free votes and not to resign even if parts of its legislative programme or of its budget were not adopted. It became, admittedly, increasingly felt during the nineteenth and twentieth centuries that it was sensible to associate with the government those groups and parties that might otherwise be inclined to vote systematically against the executive. But this was a thumb rule, an ad hoc development, not a prerequisite of the parliamentary system. And it is still not a requirement to this day, as is shown by examples such as those of the British cabinet of the late 1970s, by the Swedish governments of 1978-79 and of 1981 or by the Italian government of the mid-1970s.

It does remain true, however, that coalitions have become 'normal' or 'expected' when there is no majority in Parliament, despite the large number of minority governments. It is therefore legitimate to ask: if there is to be a coalition when there is no majority party, what is this coalition likely to be? Can any 'rules' be found which will help to predict the types of coalitions which will probably occur in a given configuration of parties in Parliament?

The answer which was first given by those who analysed the problem empirically and analytically was rather mechanical: it was argued that, on 'rational' grounds, coalitions would tend to be 'minimum winning', as this would be the most 'economic' way for a set of parties to maximize their rewards both in terms of the share of portfolios and in policy terms.[9] This hypothesis proved to have a relatively weak explanatory value, however, not just because it could not account for minority governments and 'unnecessary' coalitions, but because it could not account for the many instances of 'surplus' coalitions which have occurred in Western Europe. There were indeed almost as many 'surplus' coalitions in the 1945-71 period (fifty-three) as there were minority governments (seventy-three).[10]

It was then suggested that the explanatory value of the hypothesis would be increased if, to the condition that coalitions should be 'minimum winning' was added the rider that they should include parties which were ideologically contiguous.[11] But even this improvement does not account for many cases of surplus governments, and it has the further drawback of not providing a solution when there is a choice between ideologically contiguous parties. For the concept of ideological contiguity is not very clear, at least in the post-1945 European context where parties are often close to the centre and resemble each other on some points while being distant from each other on others. Ideological contiguity may explain why a coalition between Communists and conservatives is unlikely to occur unless centre parties are also included, but it does not explain whether a coalition between socialists and liberals should occur in preference to a coalition between socialists and Christians or Christians and liberals.

Efforts to provide an overriding — and somewhat mechanical — explanation of coalition formation have therefore to be superseded by a broader attempt at accounting for the various types of coalition. For in the widest possible interpretation, coalitions range from what might be termed a 'technical' or purely 'parliamentary' pole to a societal pole. Even in the first case, coalitions may or may not take place, depending on political traditions, or a calculus of short-term versus long-term costs and benefits. Clearly one consideration will be that of building a 'minimum winning' coalition, as there are some pay-offs in such a strategy, but another consideration may be to associate others with the government because these might otherwise damage the government in the country, while a contrary consideration may be that it is possible to ride the parliamentary storm and to try out a more united, minority government which is easier to build. At the other extreme, coalitions may be built in order to meet a particular societal situation: the government may need the support of all the forces in the nation in order to ride a crisis, or to build up a new regime. Only by a gradual examination of types of coalition falling into one or the other of these categories — and indeed sharpening some of the characteristics of both these extreme positions — will a truly satisfactory empirical theory of the development of coalitions be developed.

'Parliamentary' and 'societal' coalitions. Between 1945 and 1980, there was no coalition government in the United Kingdom, but, during the previous thirty-five years, Britain was ruled for almost half the time by a coalition: from 1916 to 1922, from 1931 to 1935, and from 1940 to 1945. Yet, even during the pre-1945 period, coalition government was viewed as exceptional in Britain in terms of the circumstances in which it did occur, such as war, postwar reconstruction or the Great Depression. Similar 'crisis' situations can be found in which coalitions are set up in other countries: governments of the late 1970s in El Salvador and Nicaragua were coalitions; in Venezuela, in 1958, the leaders of Accion Democratica decided to form a coalition with the Comité de Organisacion Politica Electoral Independiente (Social Christian Party, COPEI) in order to reconstruct the liberal regime after the downfall of Jimenez and in order to avoid the political squabbles which had occurred thirteen years earlier and had, in their opinion, made the fall of democracy possible; a similar attitude prevailed in Austria in 1945 and led to the 'grand coalition' which remained in power until 1966.

Coalitions of this type may be 'exceptional' in that they correspond to crisis situations — or to situations which are perceived as such — but they are not necessarily exceptional in terms of their duration. The Austrian coalition lasted twenty-one years for instance, and as we noted, coalitions prevailed in Britain for about half the 1916-45 period. At the limit, these 'exceptional' situations may last indefinitely. This is indeed what occurred in two of the seven countries in which all post-1945 governments were coalitions, Switzerland and Lebanon, as well as in two of the countries in which there were long periods of coalition, Uruguay and Colombia. In these four countries, coalitions are or were set up because it is or was felt that the country could best avoid political and social difficulties if a 'permanent' coalition was organized: the point becomes one of trying to minimize potential problems, by anticipation, through the setting up of a coalition. Clearly, Switzerland has succeeded in this way in being the one outstanding example of a country in which ethnic-linguistic differences do not lead to political unrest. Lebanon may not have avoided the civil war of the 1970s, but the impact of the Israeli-Arab conflict on the country has been such that no political arrangement could have been expected to avoid major difficulties. In Colombia, where the coalition between Conservatives and Liberals has been maintained throughout the whole of the period following the demise of the dictator Rojas Pinilla, the government has been able to proceed within the context of the legal institutions, despite major threats coming from a variety of groups anxious to 'destabilize' the regime. And, on the contrary, the abandonment of the two-party coalition in Uruguay in 1967 and the return to majority presidentialism was soon followed by gradual army influence and the replacement of the civilian government.[12]

In the large majority of Western European countries, on the other hand, as well as in about half the countries of the Third World, coalition governments are set up primarily to meet the requirements of a 'parliamentary' situation. Yet, even in this context, one can distinguish three types of coalitions which correspond to sharply distinct views about the purpose or meaning of coalitions. First, there are coalitions which are set up within the broader division between Right and Left, when either the Left or the Right is divided into a number of parties: the 'bourgeois coalitions' which have occurred in Norway, Sweden and France between 1958 and 1981 as well as the Fine Gael-Labour Party coalitions in Ireland are of this type; the left-wing coalitions in Sri Lanka have also been of this type, as well as the Right and Left coalitions in Israel. Second, there are coalitions organized around a dominant party of the Right or Left and which may have to extend into the centre: the Swedish Social-Democratic-Agrarian coalitions, as well as some similar coalitions in Denmark and the groupings which are organized around the Christian Democracy in Italy are of this type; for a while, in the early part of the Bonn Republic, coalitions organized by Adenauer around the Christliche Demokratische Union (CDU) also had this character; Turkish coalitions have often followed this pattern, when the two major parties were short of an absolute majority. Third, there are situations in which many, if not all permutations are possible, either because there are only three significant parties (Germany from about 1957 to 1969, when the Sozialdemokratische Partei Deutschlands (SDP)-Frei Demokratische Partei (FDP) coalition became 'solidified', Belgium before the linguistic break-up in the 1960s, Luxembourg), or because, as in the

Netherlands, Finland and to a lesser extent Iceland, the four or more significant parties vary in the extent to which they feel 'distant' from each other. It is only in the last situation that the idea of a 'rational' calculus truly arises, and even in these circumstances the objective of a 'minimum winning' coalition, coupled or not with the requirement of ideological contiguity, is only one of the considerations of the politicians. In fact, cycles of permutations seem to occur, as if coalition partners become, after a while, tired of any given arrangement and look for possible greater pay-offs and a more 'congenial' association by embarking on a different type of coalition.

Coalition governments and the formula of coalition government.
The formula of coalition government has been manifestly successful in Western Europe: it has been adopted more frequently than the formula of single-party government, and it has nowhere led to a collapse of the parliamentary system (the military coup in Greece occurred after a period of manipulation by the king himself following a period of single-party government). Coalition governments seem ostensibly to have contributed to the general success of Western European democracies.

In the Third World, on the contrary, the formula of coalition government, although adopted to a substantial extent, has not been successful. Coalitions have lasted for substantial periods in only seven countries and in only five of these did the coalition government system resist military pressure. In twenty-three other countries, coalitions have been set up during a relatively short period, and in most cases only once; among the thirteen countries which began as independent states under a coalition, these coalitions were abolished after a few years in ten of them and were later reestablished in only three of these ten. It cannot be said that starting with a coalition helps to create a favourable 'political culture' in favour of coalitions.

Whether in its 'parliamentary' or in its 'societal' form, coalition government has been relatively unsuccessful outside Western Europe, except, to some extent, in South East Asia (Sri Lanka). This is perhaps because the parties have in general been too inchoate or too tribal. Alliances have therefore been fluid: instead of showing to the population, and to the army, that the politicians were able to work together towards the gradual strengthening of democracy (as occurred in Venezuela and to a more limited extent in Colombia) they have demonstrated that the government was both ineffective and riddled with internal disunity. 'Parliamentary' coalitions have seemed to lack roots in the population and to correspond merely to personal arrangements (as in Upper Volta or Zaire); societal coalitions have rarely appeared truly 'credible': the proclaimed desire to bring everyone into the government seemed more formal than real; disagreement within the government often led quickly to resignations and to the loss of authority of its members.

Thus, neither the coalition formula nor that of the single party has proved able to form a durable base for large numbers of governments outside Western and Eastern countries: only Commonwealth countries appear to have overcome some of these difficulties as they, alone or almost alone, seem to have been characterized by a political structure based on solidly implanted parties. Clearly, the political composition of Third World governments has so far been based only to a limited extent on political parties. Various forms of non-party government have played a substantial part, although these, too, have often proved unsuccessful.

2. Traditional, Military and Mixed Governments

Almost a third of the governments of the world, both in 1945 and in 1980, were not ruled directly, principally or even at all, by political parties. But, while the conception of what constitutes party government is fairly clear, the types and characteristics of governments which are not primarily based on parties are many, and they are even becoming more diverse. There is, admittedly, a basic distinction between two broad groups of non-party government, the traditional or patrimonial government and the military government. But there are also combinations of traditional and military regimes, as well as an increasingly common tendency for military governments, not just to become more 'civilianized' and to give way to party government, but to transform themselves into combined military-cum-party governments in which it is unclear, at least for a period, whether the 'party' aspect of the government is more than a convenient facade. Thus the analytical distinction between traditional, military, and party government, though unquestionably useful, needs to be qualified in practice as 'mixed' governments become a common feature of contemporary regimes.

Traditional Patrimonial Governments

Traditional patrimonial governments have become rare in the contemporary world; they are indeed the only form of government
which is being slowly but regularly depleted. In 1980, twelve countries were still ruled by a traditional government; most of these
were located in the Arabian peninsula, while the others were in the
Himalayas, the Pacific and Southern Africa. This number is about
half the size of the group of traditional governments in 1945 or at
the time of the independence of new countries.

Strong monarchical systems have always constituted a large
majority of traditional regimes, but, in the early postwar period, a
number of republics could be described as traditional, especially in
the Caribbean and in Central and Latin America. Probably because
the authority of ruling families has been seriously undermined,
these traditional governments all came gradually to have a mixed
composition, in which the army and occasionally parties were
represented in order to buttress the declining legitimacy of the
patrimonial groups. Thus, except in Western Samoa, only
monarchies remained at the end of the 1970s as examples of 'pure'
traditional government.

Indeed, even in the traditional monarchies which have been
maintained, the composition of governments has changed appreciably in the course of the 1960s and 1970s. The very small, almost
embryonic cabinets of the 1950s were composed almost entirely of
the monarch's relatives and friends; these cabinets have increased
dramatically in size in the subsequent decades as we shall see in
Chapter 6, and, consequently, although members of the ruling
families still constituted a significant proportion of the ministers in
many traditional regimes in the late 1970s, they have been joined by
members of a newly created bureaucracy, drawn admittedly in
large part from the elite, but appointed on grounds of technical
competence as well as on grounds of family connections. In almost
every traditional government, the cabinet has been comparable in
size and administrative structure to that of 'single' all-purpose
cabinets in other parts of the world.

But these governments remain traditional in that, apart from
elements of the bureaucracy, they do not include members of other
groups. The military plays a limited and subordinate part; in the
majority of countries, parties are banned and political activities
outside the government have a very limited scope. Even in Kuwait,

during the period of constitutional government, parties were not allowed; they were allowed in Nepal for a very short period and subsequently banned; the king of Jordan set up a single party, only to abolish it a few years later. Morocco is the only traditional country in which, in several instances, and in particular at the end of the 1970s, parties were given a significant place in the government; yet, even there, their position has so far remained shaky. As a matter of fact, except in Morocco and perhaps in Nepal and Kuwait, political parties are very weak in the country at large: their presence in the government might therefore have very little meaning. Thus, in the majority of traditional regimes, the pressure to open government to parties does not exist; the enlargement of the government to include civil servants is a result of the technical and economic development of these countries and can therefore be kept largely under control.

Traditional monarchies survive only, however, in small and isolated countries, many of which have become extremely wealthy as a result of oil and in which the traditional government can therefore provide considerable welfare benefits which may deflect demands for political change. But, in the larger traditional governments which existed earlier in the post-1945 period as well as in some of the smaller ones, the system was unsuccessful: six monarchies were deposed by military coups between 1952 and 1974 and at least five of these (Afghanistan, Iraq, Ethiopia, Libya and Yemen) were ruled by 'traditional' governments, while in Egypt the party system was weak and based primarily on a small number of influential families. A seventh monarchy disappeared as a result of the Communist take-over in Laos in 1975: this was a country in which the government had been controlled by a small number of members of the king's entourage. In Iran the Shah reversed the policy of banning parties and of ruling primarily with friends and members of the bureaucratic elite only relatively late in his reign: yet even the setting up of, first, a single-party system and, in the very last years, a form of controlled pluralism did not prevent his downfall. On past experience, it will be difficult for the remaining monarchies to be maintained unless changes lead to a gradual replacement of the traditional groups which controlled the government up to the 1980s, despite the oil wealth of many of these regimes and despite the apparent political calm which characterizes some — and indeed not all — of these traditional systems.

Pure Military Government

Traditional governments are in manifest decline: their numbers dwindle; they have been forced to associate members of the bureaucracy with the decision-making process; and they may even have to consider introducing parties or to rely on the military, if they are not to be overwhelmed. The fate of pure military rule, however, is not so simple: military governments are periodically set up in reaction to almost all (all except Communist single-party systems, in fact) types of government, but the new experiments are often inconclusive and short-lived. On the one hand, fifty-one countries (including two in Western Europe, Greece and, for a short period, Portugal) had, at least for a time, a government based purely on the military or to which the bureaucracy alone was linked and neither traditional groups nor parties associated. Thus, over a third of the countries of the world had at least a taste of pure military government: these included nearly half (forty-nine out of 102) of the countries of the Third World. On the other hand, in 1980, only twelve countries were run by a 'pure' military government: military rule had therefore been abolished in four-fifths of the countries in which it had occurred. This is a rate of growth and of decline which surpasses that of any other form of governmental rule: traditional regimes have been appreciably less numerous; they have declined steadily, but the rate of decline has been slow; party governments have been in power in the large majority of countries and have fluctuated appreciably, but the majority of countries have always been ruled by one or more party. Pure military rule is a common phenomenon, but one which does not last.

The spread of pure military government is not uniform across the Third World, but the transient character of this rule is a common phenomenon. Middle Eastern and South Asian countries are less likely to be controlled by a pure military government (about a third) than black African and Latin American countries (nearly 60 percent), but in all four regions pure military governments declined in the late 1970s. These included one in the Middle East, one in South East Asia, and five in each of black Africa and Latin America in 1980. On average, the military controlled the government in Latin America for 9.3 years during the postwar period, for 7.4 years in the Middle East, and for less than six years in South East Asia and in Africa South of the Sahara (but most countries of black Africa became independent only in the 1960s).

The transient character of pure military rule appears even more clearly if one considers, not the overall length of pure military government, but the duration of each of these governments, for in eleven countries (three of which were in Latin America), there were two separate instances of pure military rule, and in a further three countries (all of which were in Latin America), there were three. The duration of military government is on average of less than six years, and this average is almost exactly the same for each of the four regions of the Third World (5.77 years for the Middle East, 5.60 years for South East Asia, 5.95 years for Africa South of the Sahara and 5.65 years for Latin America).[13]

Nor are the variations above the average very marked. The military ruled alone in forty-nine countries of the Third World for sixty-six separate periods between 1945 and 1980, but in only nine cases did pure military rule last more than eight years and in only four did it last more than a decade (but in two cases having lasted nine years the military was still in control of the government in 1980). The longest cases of pure military rule were those of the Ayub Khan government (followed by the Yahya Khan government) in Pakistan (fifteen years), of the military rule in Bolivia between 1964 and 1977, in Nigeria between 1966 and 1979, in Peru between 1968 and 1978; somewhat shorter continuous pure military rule occurred in Uganda, North Yemen, Honduras and Panama in the 1970s and in Venezuela between 1948 and 1957. Conversely, in thirteen cases pure military rule lasted two years or less, in eighteen cases between three and four years and in twenty-six cases between five and eight years. The military is certainly unable, in contrast to traditional groups where they are still strong or political parties in the majority of countries, to alone provide the basis for contemporary governments for more than a very short period.

Indeed, even when the military controls the government without the help of traditional groups or parties, it has to rely markedly and often directly on the help of the bureaucracy. This was the case for instance in Pakistan and in Nigeria where the government was largely in the hands of civil servants although members of the military kept a firm control over broad policy decisions. Especially in larger countries under military rule, reliance on the bureaucracy is such that it is often questionable as to whether 'pure' military rule tends to prevail: the degree of influence of the bureaucracy is at least comparable in these countries to that which occurs in Communist countries.

Mixed Governments

The importance of traditional and pure military governments has thus diminished gradually in the course of the postwar period, despite the evident role of the army in politics, especially since the 1960s: increasingly the gap is being filled by 'mixed' governments. Over the whole period, 19 percent of Third World governments were of a traditional character and 12 percent were of a 'pure' military type, while another 12 percent were of a mixed character. In the second half of the 1970s, however, traditional governments accounted for only 12 percent of the total number of years of rule, while military government accounted for 14 percent — a small increase which conceals the fact that military rule peaked in 1975 with 20 percent of the governments in that year — while during the same period 'mixed' governments accounted for 22 percent of all the Third World governments.

Governments of a 'mixed' composition have thus been on the increase since the 1950s, but they have also appreciably altered. In the early postwar period, at a time when the majority of independent countries of the Third World were in Latin America, mixed governments took essentially two forms. There were governments to which the military belonged in association with traditional groups: in such a situation the military is either invited or at least allowed to participate in the government, but more to buttress the power of the (declining) ruling families than in order to replace them. Governments of this kind occurred in some of the Central American and Caribbean republics, as well as in some of the smaller South American states.

But the military was even more frequently associated with a political party, a facade of constitutional structure being maintained and giving a semblance of competition. This second form of association between traditional ruling families, a dominant political party, and the military was in existence up to the 1970s in Nicaragua, El Salvador and Paraguay, with traditional groups being more prominent in the first two of these countries, and the military more influential in the third. This system was replaced for a while in the late 1970s by a coalition of opposition groupings in both Nicaragua and El Salvador, but with only limited success.

In South East Asia, a similar example is that of Thailand, where the combination of traditional groups, the military and, occasionally, political parties, has been most durable: in Thailand, military coups tend to occur within the context of a broad equilibrium involving traditional groups and the military, with the monarch giving an appearance of legitimacy to the governmental structure.

Governments based on a loose association between the military and one or more parties have gradually changed in character in the course of the 1960s and 1970s, in part because of the emergence of mixed governments in countries where traditional groups were not prominent or had ceased to collectively play a major part. In Indonesia and Brazil, for instance, the military exercised almost full control for some years, parties being relegated to either ineffective support or token opposition; in Korea, the party facade of the government was reasserted more quickly, but there, too, the military dominated the government for a number of years. Similarly, in Madagascar, although the military has been in effective control, the government neither abolished parties nor did it rely entirely on a single party: an effort has been made to bring about a regrouping under a 'national front' formula, but the single-party system was not adopted by the late 1970s and elements of political pluralism remained. In all four countries, therefore, the military leadership was unwilling or unable to abolish party life or even to set up a full single-party system. Thus, the governments became characterized by an alliance between the military and one party in the context of some competition.

Mixed military-party governments in a semi-competitive context have always been relatively few, but their existence, especially in Latin America and in South East Asia, suggests that the military finds it difficult to abolish parties or even to set up a single-party system where traditions of pluralism are relatively strong. In the Middle East and in Africa, on the contrary, the military has been associated, in the main, with a single-party system. But, by and large, mixed governments have taken two broad forms, one where the party is at least as strong as the military and another where the party is a dependency of the army and serves to some extent as a legitimizing 'facade' for the military rulers.

In the Middle East and in certain parts of North Africa, military interventions have taken place within a single party, and usually in order to support one wing of the party against another. This is especially the case in Iraq and Syria where the army has operated within the context of the Baath Party, which has provided the overall framework to the government for at least a decade: both military and civilian members of the government tend to belong to the party. Similarly, in Algeria, the 1965 coup led by Boummedienne took place within the context of the Front de Libération Nationale (FLN) and left the organization of the party intact. Indeed, after Boummedienne's death, and although his successor was a member of the military, the part played by the army diminished to such an extent that the Algerian government has once more become party government, of the single-party variety, rather than mixed party-military.

The majority of mixed army-party governments are different, however, for they constitute efforts by military leaders to resort to a degree of civilianization which military regimes seem obliged to achieve if they are to avoid being overthrown. Thus, parties are set up, often entirely de novo, occasionally on the basis of previously existing organizations (in Rwanda for instance) as a conscious endeavour to extend the political base of the leader. It is, therefore, questionable as to whether, in particular in the early years, these governments are genuinely 'mixed', except in as much as the bureaucracy plays a substantial part as in other military regimes. Over time, however, ministers come to be appointed who are genuine party members. In Zaire, for instance, where the Mouvement Populaire de la Liberation (MPR) was created by President Mobutu in an almost wholly artificial manner, the endeavour to attract a few of the politicians of the previous competitive party period has resulted, after a decade of existence of the party, in a gradual blend of party and military in the government. The case is even clearer in Egypt where the military element had declined to such an extent that, by the late 1970s, and with the introduction of a semi-competitive party system, the Egyptian government could no longer be classified as even 'mixed': it was less influenced by the military than the Korean or Indonesian governments, although President Sadat was originally a military leader.

The role of the party in mixed governments appears also to have increased in the late 1970s in some African states (Congo, Benin, Ethiopia) because the military leadership has in some countries declared itself 'socialist' and not, as in some other states, ostensibly 'a-political' or even anti-party. The stress being on a highly ideological goal for the government and the country, the model entails reliance on the party as an instrument of political and social development at least as much as, if not more than, on the army. Consequently, the governments of these countries bear some resemblance to the Baath governments of Iraq or Syria. But, while the Baath is an old organization, partly controlled by civilians, the party-military governments of the 'socialist' states of black Africa still appear to rely more heavily on the military, and military leaders are deeply in control.

Whether set up to reinforce the power of a single military ruler or in order to help the 'transition towards socialism', single parties which emerged in the context of army dominance appear to have been broadly successful in their task. In the course of the post-1945 period, governments of this type were established in about two dozen countries: there has been only one clear collapse, that of the Central African Empire, where it was apparent, however, that the single party, created a few years earlier, was extremely weak and almost wholly nominal. Elsewhere, there have occasionally been oscillations between mixed government and pure military rule (as in Honduras) or a gradual decline of the role of the army (in Algeria, or Egypt, as we saw). But, in the main, mixed army and party governments have remained in existence. By 1980, they had lasted on average eight years in the twelve African states South of the Sahara where they had been introduced, while in four of the five Middle Eastern and North African countries where the arrangement had existed, it had lasted fourteen years or more and in the fifth, Libya, the experiment only began in the second half of the 1970s.[14] The blend between army and party at the top of the power structure appears, at least ostensibly, to be one of the more stable forms of government, one which is already arguably more stable than pure military rule.

But this stability has to be viewed in the context of the apparent limitations of the geographical and cultural scope of this form of government. Very few Latin American or South East Asian countries adopted this form of rule, while, as we saw, a number of countries adopted, with a limited amount of success, admittedly, a form of government which brought together the army, traditional groups, and a party embodiment of this group structure. Over half the experiments in mixed single-party and military rule have taken place in black Africa and a quarter in the Middle East and North Africa. Both these regions, and in particular black Africa, had earlier been characterized by single-party rule rather than by forms of pluralism. The development of the mixed army-single-party government therefore seems an attempt at finding a compromise between the very marked role of the military in the late 1960s and the earlier strength (or at least apparent strength) of a single party. One might even suggest that the experiment in military-single-party government constitutes a synthesis which 'resolves' the opposition between the single party and the military: this form of government has undoubtedly been a way, in many cases, for politicians of the earlier ruling party to be associated with military leaders in the government. As in parts of black Africa the single party and the army have constituted the only two forces which could pretend to run the government, the mixed military-single-party governments of the 1970s to some extent constitute 'coalitions' of a different type from the party coalitions which we examined earlier. But these arrangements are coalitions in so far as, in the same way as 'grand coalitions' in Western countries, they draw — or attempt to draw or perhaps pretend to draw — on the two main political forces existing in the nation.

In Latin America and in South East Asia, on the other hand, where the tradition of competitive politics has been stronger, but where, especially in Latin America, the reality of party government is often hampered by the weakness of the grass roots structure and the magnitude of the policy problems, the military is not often in a position to bring about a 'coalition' of the type which we have just described for black Africa. It cannot do so through a single-party system, because of the relative strength of the pluralistic tradition; it can attempt to do so by relying on a dominant, rather than on a single party, but the government which results does not have the appearance of a full coalition; it seems to depend on military might and to wish to usurp constitutional status through a facade of pluralism. This is perhaps why the military, especially in Latin America, is condemned to form the government on its own in a large majority of cases. While it can count on the collaboration of some sectors of the bureaucracy, it finds little support among the politicians and can rarely enlist them in government. Thus, governments in Latin America have a pendulum character: they swing between military and civilian rule — the latter usually being run by a single party but occasionally based on a coalition of parties in the context of a pluralistic party system. In Africa South of the Sahara, on the contrary, second generation leaders have often been able to practice forms of conciliation between the army and the politicians, largely because the single-party, rather than a pluralistic party system, had earlier been the norm. As a result, they have also been able to form governments which in the main have been more stable than those of Latin America; further, Africa South of the Sahara seems to be developing a viable alternative model for the political composition of governments.

Admittedly, the mixed military-party governments of many African countries are perhaps a transitional phase; they perhaps suggest a gradual return to single-party government, as has already been the case in Algeria and in Egypt; the mixed military-party government is perhaps a way of closing the 'parenthesis' of military government which had become seemingly 'unstoppable' in the late 1960s but lost much of its appeal in the following decade. And the decline of military government may be due to the fact that, in Africa at least, the military men themselves often give precedence to political ideologies and to political parties, unlike more 'traditional' military leaders, in Latin America in particular, but elsewhere as well. It is this heavy reliance of many African military leaders on parties as instruments of government which makes the military-single-party governments of black Africa genuinely mixed, but paradoxically, this state of affairs also helps the demise of the military in government, as, by emphasizing the role of ideologies and of parties, these military men show little real belief in the right of the military as such to govern.

We began this survey of the political composition of contemporary governments by noting that political parties had not fully succeeded in taking over governments, and that military rule did not provide a major challenge to parties. But we also noted that military government was essentially the result of protest and discontent with party rule, not truly a form of government which could present a positive alternative. The detailed examination of party government has shown the weaknesses of various forms of party systems in taking over and holding on to government. Only Communist states (helped by Soviet might) and states of the British Commonwealth can be said to have been, in the main, able to establish a durable form of single-party government; coalition governments and single-party governments compete on the Continent of Western Europe with neither form being truly in control except in a minority of these countries.

Elsewhere, there is competition too, but between party government and other forms of government, these latter being not so much, any longer, traditional groups but, and for a while increasingly, governments in which the military, helped by the bureaucracy, played a large part. This competition between party and military government is particularly marked in Latin America, where, except in a small number of the non-Commonwealth countries, party government has not really taken root and where the military comes periodically to power as compensation for or as a counter to the weaknesses of these parties. Elsewhere in the Third World, while parties are often weak, the pendulum movement from party to military rule is not so marked: in South East Asia, party government has in the main been better maintained, except when, as in the Middle East, traditional groups are still able to control the government. But perhaps one of the most interesting developments of the late 1970s occurred in black Africa, where, for a while, the incidence of military government seemed to be as high as it has customarily been, albeit cyclically, in Latin America; this is the development of the mixed form of government through which the military sets up and fosters a single party (while in the Middle East and North Africa, the military occasionally works through an existing single-party structure). The association between military and single party has had, to begin with, the effect of stabilizing governments in black Africa: the short-term duration of pure military government does not apply to these mixed governments. But, more importantly, mixed military-party government may also gradually bring about a return to party government, as it did in the distant past in Turkey (though with further difficulties) and in Mexico and in the more recent past in Egypt or Algeria. We are thus perhaps witnessing a movement towards a genuine increase in the proportion of countries under party rule, unless this development is merely an upward trend in a general cyclical pattern: this could be the case if parties were fundamentally unable to cater satisfactorily for the needs of contemporary societies and especially those societies undergoing a process of development.

Notes

1. These thirty countries are the Commonwealth countries which were independent before 1970.

2. Haiti is the third country in this category — not a very marked success for single-party government!

3. There is no intention here to enter the long and tortuous debate on the relationship between electoral systems and party systems. The point is merely to state that the majority systems, membership of the Commonwealth and single-party government are often associated.

4. There is no intention here either to examine the controversy of the alleged effects of proportional representation on the stability of governments. It is sufficient to note that the traditional view of the dangers of coalitions has been challenged in the 1970s, for instance by S.E. Finer in *Adversary Politics and Electoral Reform* (Wigram, 1975). The dangers of one-party government are presented as being as serious as, or more serious than, those of coalition government. See also A. Lijphart, *Democracy in Plural Societies* (Yale University Press, 1977).

5. 'Government' is defined as an administration headed by one or more leaders and composed of a given set of parties. Changes of government occur either when leaders change or when the parties in the government change or both (but not when individual ministers are replaced without a change of party composition). For a discussion of this definition see my *Introduction to Comparative Government* (Weidenfeld, 1969), p. 340 and V. Herman and J. Pope, 'Minority Governments in Western Democracies', *British Journal of Political Science*, Vol. 3 (1973), p. 192.

6. Among the vast literature on the 'rational-choice' approach to coalitions, the most important books are those of W. Riker, *A Theory of Political Coalitions* (Yale University Press, 1962), A. De Swaan, *Coalition Theories and Cabinet Formations* (Elsevier, 1973) and L.C. Dodd, *Coalitions in Parliamentary Government* (Princeton University Press, 1976).

7. V. Herman and J. Pope, op. cit., p. 194.

8. Quoted from Disraeli by V. Herman and J. Pope, op. cit., p. 195.

9. This was Riker's main thesis. See his *Theory of Political Coalitions*, especially at pp. 32 and following.

10. V. Herman and J. Pope, op. cit., p. 194.

11. This was A. De Swaan's main contribution. See his *Coalition Theories and Cabinet Formations*, especially at pp. 88 and following.

12. 'Societal' coalitions can be said to have occurred since 1945 permanently in Switzerland and Lebanon and more or less episodically in Venezuela, Colombia, Uruguay, Ecuador, the Dominican Republic, El Salvador, Nicaragua, the Central African Republic, Uganda, Togo and Zimbabwe.

13. 'Pure' military rule is here defined as government based exclusively on the military (with the help of the bureaucracy). Most long-duration military leaders have stayed in power through the partial or even complete 'civilianization' of their regime, as we shall shortly see.

14. In Africa South of the Sahara, mixed party-military governments have been set up in the 1970s in Benin, Burundi, the Central African Republic, Congo, Ethiopia, Madagascar, Mali, Rwanda, Somalia, Sudan, Togo and Zaire. In the Middle East and North Africa, they once existed in Egypt and Algeria and have remained in existence for substantial periods in Iraq, Syria and Libya.

5. PATTERNS OF POLICY-MAKING AND COORDINATION IN CONTEMPORARY GOVERNMENTS

It is commonly asserted that governments are now confronted with problems of such magnitude that they are, in many cases at least, 'overloaded'. This conclusion has so far been drawn mainly from the examination of Western governments, but this is probably not just because these alone are faced with economic, technical, industrial and social questions of an unparalleled complexity: the reason is surely also that, in the present state of our knowledge about governments and political decision-making, our awareness of difficulties in the West is appreciably larger than it is of similar difficulties in other countries. Clearly, at least in relation to the problems which societies faced two or three decades ago, the questions which all governments have to solve are strikingly more complex: the time-scale between policy elaboration and implementation has become very long, and the interconnection between policies has become more subtle.

In these circumstances, one would expect governments to have changed or at least attempted to change drastically the decision-making arrangements which characterized them in the past. In particular, it would seem logical to see them give considerable priority to the streamlining of the processes of policy-making and coordination which they had inherited or which new countries had imitated. This, however, has not happened on a major scale: there has been some noticeable change in the size of governments, which has often increased as new departments have been set up; we shall examine this point in the next Chapter. But the manner in which policies are elaborated and brought together has not been drastically altered; on the whole, most governments have followed the same patterns of decision-making as previously and the machinery of government itself has been little modified.

The most obvious reform is that which led some Third World governments, mostly ruled by the military and resulting from a coup, to set up a military or revolutionary council distinct from the 'regular' government. This development, as we saw in Chapter 3, has taken place on a rapid scale from the second half of the 1960s, although it still affects only a minority of Third World countries, most of them located in Africa and in the Middle East. But, while in some cases the setting up of these councils may have corresponded to a desire to sharpen the distinction between broad policy-making and management, the most common reason for the emergence of 'two-tier' governments does not seem administrative. Admittedly, very few of the countries affected by the change had a large working modern bureaucracy prior to the new arrangements; but, beyond the point that it is still difficult to assess whether, in practice, the effective impact of the change on policy-making and coordination is substantial, it must be noted that, by and large, the setting up of a distinct decision-making body has been motivated primarily by the need to offset the low level of credibility of new leaders. Thus, many revolutionary or military councils exist at least in part to increase the legitimacy of the executive among the groups on which it is attempting to impose its will.

These countries have to some extent modelled their new arrangements on those of Communist states where the government is also composed of a number of distinct bodies and where the overall structure is most complex. The result is an attempt, unusual outside Communist countries, at dividing the various functions of the government among separate bodies. This is not, however, an entirely new development of post-1945 Communist structures: the complex machinery of the Soviet government existed, on paper at least, before the Second World War and it was quickly extended to the countries where the Communist system was introduced. Nor did the development result from the desire to cope with an exclusively administrative problem. Admittedly, the marked increase in the size of the Soviet bureaucracy resulting from the takeover by the state of all aspects of commerce and industry led to a need, greater than in the West, to supervise bureaucratic decisions. But it was not bureaucratic overload as such which led to the division of the government into a number of parts, for what was more crucial was the fear that the bureaucracy might take over. Hence, the ideological point according to which party organizations have to be kept distinct from state organizations. And the distinction in turn owes much to the lack of legitimacy of Communist regimes and at any rate to their inability or unwillingness to allow for the free development of political groups. The party superstructure had to be imposed on the administration and on the population: the consequence on policy-making was merely an administrative side-effect, albeit, as it turned out, an important and indeed increasingly important one.

In the rest of the world, policy-making and coordination arrangements have remained appreciably more informal and changes have been, on the whole, limited. The one major exception is the United States where the staff around the president has markedly expanded at the expense of coordinating mechanisms among other members of the executive. This development constitutes an extreme way of tackling the problem of the increasing gap between what may be viewed as the political realities of the governmental system and its administrative needs. But the American solution could be envisaged only because, in the United States, the combination of a weak and decentralized party system, of a strong presidency and of a very large federal bureaucracy reduced the ability of ministers to oppose the development of a vast presidential office. And the experiment has had considerable drawbacks and may not ultimately have provided the desired co-ordination.

In other countries, both European and non-European, cabinet-type structures have broadly been maintained, both in relatively collective and in relatively hierarchical situations. At most there has been a certain tampering at the edges: what is remarkable is that, despite repeated warnings that cabinet government is unworkable and inefficient, it has changed so little. Whether this means inefficiency is, of course, more than a possibility, but it is interesting to note that the ill-effects have not so far been felt to be so obvious that they warranted a major overhaul of the system: the clamour for the restructuring of cabinet government has yet to be heard loud and clear.

1. The Limited Changes
in the Structure of Cabinets

The Pressure to Maintain Traditional Arrangements

One reason, perhaps the main reason, why so little change occurred in the basic structure of cabinets in Europe and elsewhere was that the system seemed to have served the interests of modern government well. The nineteenth century saw the emergence of a semi-representative, semi-administrative cabinet based on parties all over Northern and Western Europe; Latin American countries gradually adopted an analogous formula, although they were constitutionally presidential countries. Perhaps most importantly, the cabinet system had proved sufficiently flexible over time to enable governments to move from a hierarchical and bureaucratic structure depending on a monarch to a more open or pluralistic arrangement. For instance, the French Napoleonic system was gradually transformed during the monarchical period from 1815 to 1848 into a more egalitarian and collective decision-making organ, although, ostensibly at least, the formal structure of the government remained unchanged. By 1914 in Italy, by 1918 in Germany, cabinet-type structures had emerged out of the bureaucratic hierarchies which governments had previously been in these countries. Thus, not surprisingly, the impression grew that the cabinet system was the natural end-state of a universal evolution and that it was the governmental formula best adapted to the requirements of modern societies.

Indeed, there was much evidence for this conclusion, for the cabinet system had been particularly well-suited to the developing party systems of the early twentieth century and in particular to party government, whether of the single-party or of the coalition variety. At a time when parties provided a recruitment mechanism for a group of colleagues accustomed to work together in Parliament or in the decision-making bodies of the organization, cabinet government replicated the arrangement. It also made it possible for 'specialists' anxious to introduce reforms in a particular field (education or welfare, for instance) to find a place alongside 'generalists' who wished to have a say in the overall governmental policy. And, through the meetings of the cabinet, those who wanted to be more involved in the life of the government as a whole could participate more fully: the coordination of the machinery of the administration could thus occur smoothly, while a mechanism was provided to ensure an effective supervision of the civil service. The pace of decision-making may have been leisurely, as has often been pointed out in the case of British cabinets under Balfour or even Baldwin, but what needed to be done was done smoothly. And, if the decision-making role of the prime minister and of some of the top ministers was preponderant, this occurred without establishing formal status distinctions within the cabinet. The prime minister and his senior colleagues could rely on their moral authority to have their way, and meetings of the cabinet gave to all members at least an opportunity to be kept informed and voice their disagreements. As decisions at the ministerial level rarely required a technical background in economics, science, or social administration, ministers could address themselves to the whole range of cabinet decisions and make sure that these decisions were not incompatible or inconsistent.[1]

Finally, even well into the twentieth century, the size and structure of cabinets were such that there was little incentive to bring about drastic reforms. Most cabinets were relatively small. As late as 1945, the average number of departmental ministers in the Atlantic countries was only about a dozen and it was even smaller on the Continent of Europe; it was also rather small in Latin America.[2] Most governments of the late 1940s more closely resembled the Swiss government of the 1980s than the cabinets of the late twentieth century. There was therefore little incentive to alter the structure fundamentally, as the prime minister felt that he could keep in touch with all the ministers and as the ministers could keep in touch with each other. Consequently, there was little pressure to increase the size of the office of the prime minister: matters of coordination could be dealt with informally. Moreover, the prime minister often had a status similar to his colleagues' by virtue of the fact that he was often a departmental minister in his own right as well. His role as leader was therefore deemphasized, and he was necessarily prevented from devoting too much of his own time to matters of intergovernmental coordination and policy-making. Indeed, up to the 1980s, in a substantial minority of Atlantic countries, mostly smaller ones admittedly, the prime minister continued to hold a departmental post. In 1976, the head of the government was also a minister in six Atlantic countries: Ireland, Luxembourg, Malta, New Zealand, Switzerland and France.

However, in both parliamentary and non-parliamentary cabinets, the pressure to bring about some change gradually increased in the post-1945 decades. And, throughout the period, the reforms tended to take one or both of two forms. On the one hand, the idea of building an office around the prime minister acquired momentum; this was often viewed as being due to the leader's desire to increase his influence within the government, and, no doubt, in many cases, leaders have had such a desire. But there have also been administrative and organizational reasons, in that general problems of decision-making have seemed naturally to fall within the province of the leader, be he monarch, president or prime minister. On the other hand, the idea of increasing coordination by using senior ministers also gained ground, although it stopped short of a full reorganization based on 'superministers'. Slowly, non-departmental ministers with various titles were appointed. By so doing, leaders probably expected to defuse some of the opposition which the increase in their own staff tended to create, but they were also groping for a formula which would lead to better coordination by entrusting some of their colleagues with positions of broader responsibility, albeit within the context of a cabinet structure which remained ostensibly collective.

Prime Ministerial Staffs and Ministers in the Prime Minister's Office

Much has been said about the growth of prime ministerial offices, usually to criticize these for the part which they play in modern government in extolling the role of the leaders.[3] And prime ministerial offices have increased in size in the course of the post-1945 period. Yet, even in the 1980s it is a manifest exaggeration to claim that this increase amounts to a genuine transformation of the nature of governments, and it is even more of an exaggeration to hold the view that the functions of coordination and policy-making have thereby been transferred to the staff of the prime minister. Admittedly, prime ministers now have a sizeable group of civil servants and political aides at their disposal; these prepare the agenda of cabinet meetings and therefore, at a minimum, steer the activities of the departments at least to the extent that they help to decide the matters which are to be discussed in the cabinet, and the order in which these questions will come up. Moreover, a number of governmental services are occasionally attached to the prime minister's office — such as civil service administration, supervision of the media, long- and medium-term planning.[4]

But in most countries these developments have not been on a scale which could fundamentally alter the nature of the cabinet. It has been pointed out repeatedly in Britain that the prime ministerial office is very small and does not give the leader of the government more than the opportunity to steer cabinet decisions.[5] Even those who, like Crossman, have claimed that the British system has become 'prime ministerial' have not argued that this new situation was due to the part played by the prime minister's office.[6] In Northern Europe generally, the prime minister's position remains close to the traditional description. And, even in continental Europe, the role of the prime minister's office in buttressing the leader can be overstressed. In Germany and Austria, the chancellor has a special constitutional position, and the office of the German federal chancellor is large and well-staffed: yet, despite an attempt in the early 1970s to markedly increase the role of the chancellor's office, the effect was not very marked over the years and the office was unable to establish itself as the real policy-maker and coordinator. R. Mayntz states for instance: 'Schmidt uses the office to-day [1979] as a secretariat and a source of advice and information on various policy matters, but he definitely reserves for himself the leader's function and for his Cabinet the function of government-wide coordination'.[7] Even in France, where the dual leadership system of the Fifth Republic has led to the creation of a substantial presidential office alongside that of the prime minister, the outcome is still that the presidential staff does not truly supervise, let alone by-pass the departmental heads. S. Cohen concludes his investigation of the staff by stating categorically: 'The councillors of the President are not an indispensable element in the workings of the government'.[8] In fact, it is perhaps in Spain, at any rate under A. Suarez, that the office of the prime minister appeared to be the strongest, in part because of the tradition of leadership inherited from Franco, but almost certainly also because of the many fundamental problems of state which the new Spanish democracy had to confront and solve. These included the drafting of many fundamental laws, a constitution, regional laws, labour laws, etc., as well as the gradual build-up of practices of party collaboration in social and economic affairs which required top level negotiations between the leader of the government or his nominees and the leaders of the main political parties. Moreover, in the late 1970s the government party was in practice a coalition of groups, and representation of these groups had to be included in the prime ministerial office.[9]

While the growth of prime ministerial or presidential offices is viewed with suspicion, another method of increasing the influence of the leader on policy-making and coordination processes has consisted in appointing ministers directly under the leader and directly accountable to him. This practice occurs in a substantial minority of countries and it is on the increase. In 1966, these positions existed in forty-two governments: by 1976, they existed in fifty-four countries. There were in all sixty-five different persons occupying a post of this kind in 1966: these had increased to eighty-eight in 1976.

But this development is of only limited importance in relation to policy-making and coordination. First, some of these appointments have been made because the leader wished to keep for himself one or more departmental posts but could not genuinely administer them: the reason may be fear of competition from other ministers, for instance in the field of defence. Moreover, and perhaps more significantly, these positions have been set up primarily in governments whose leaders are already rather powerful and in which the tradition of collective government is weak. In fact, the distribution of the fifty-four governments which had these positions in 1976 shows that they have tended to exist in united governments which are intermediate between being hierarchical and being collective. On the other hand, they are rare in 'absolute' presidential systems where the leaders are truly very strong; they are also rare in countries which have a divided government: only two Communist countries, Albania and Vietnam, had ministers subordinated to the leader in 1976; not one of the nine African countries which had a military or revolutionary council in 1976 had ministers in positions subordinate to the leader. On the other hand, these posts are also rare in parliamentary countries, especially in the older parliamentary countries of Western Europe. They existed in only six parliamentary systems in 1976, Austria, Greece, Japan, Gambia, Guyana and Trinidad, less than a sixth of the total. But they were proportionately very numerous in dual systems (three-quarters of the cases) and in constitutional and semi-constitutional presidential regimes: in Latin America, for instance, the position of minister-secretary general to the presidency is very common. Thus, while

TABLE 5
Distribution of ministers at large and ministers subordinated to prime ministers or parliaments (countries)

	Number of countries	Ministers to leaders		Ministers at large		Deputy P.M. (not in post)	
		1966	1976	1966	1976	1966	1975
Atlantic	23	4	5	6	5	3	2
Communist	13	1	2	1	4	13	13
Middle East and North Africa	21	8	10	5	6	4	4
South and South East Asia	19	5	6	5	5	4	5
Africa South of the Sahara	38	12	15	5	7	6	5
Latin America	24	13	16	3	5	8	6
		43	54	25	32	38	35

probably reinforcing somewhat the position of relatively strong leaders, ministers subordinated to the leader are not appointed where they could be most crucial for the preparation of policies and the development of coordination, namely in strongly entrenched cabinet governments. And, finally, as ministers subordinated to the leader are often relatively junior, even when they are given a formally ministerial title, they constitute overall a very limited means of achieving an effective change in the decision-making processes of governments.

The Slow Growth of Non-Departmental Ministers

Meanwhile, cabinets and other types of single governments saw an increase in the number of non-departmental ministers, but this is far from being an entirely new development of the post-1945 period. Indeed, in Britain these positions had existed for a long time, but with a different purpose.[10] Originally, these 'sinecures' were filled to meet a political requirement: the Lord Privy Seal or the chancellor of the Duchy of Lancaster were appointed to give to cabinet meetings the benefit of their wisdom or of their influence. From the interwar period, the purpose became increasingly administrative: holders of 'sinecures' were expected to cover an area of government which any one department could not cover. After 1945, it also became the practice to give some of the holders of these 'sinecures' the task of chairing sub-committees of the cabinet dealing with a number of departments.

Similar developments occurred in other Atlantic countries, though not quite in the same regular manner as in Britain. Indeed, on the Continent of Europe, two types of special ministers of this kind began to be appointed, sometimes simultaneously, in a number of cabinets. Some ministers were given the title of deputy prime minister or of ministers of state, but with a function going beyond the purely political reasons which had led to their creation in the past. For instance, it was expected that these ministers of state would have sufficient status to coordinate the activities of a number of departments or that their department would acquire such prestige as a result of the position of the minister that its views would take precedence over those of other ministries. Alternatively, the ministers of state would be given a special task — of administrative reform, or of coordination of the public services —

although they were not given a substantial department in the strict sense of the word.

In this case, ministers of state exercise a function which is not altogether different from that which came to be characteristic of another type of minister, the minister without portfolio. These started to be appointed in the interwar period to cover special fields which could not be handled easily by one department, or they were concerned with a problem which covered more than one department; for instance, it became common practice in Italy in the 1950s to appoint a minister without portfolio with special responsibility for the *Mezzogiorno*.

The existence — and growth — of the position of ministers at large is an indication of the development of what might be called a 'buffer group' between the leader and the great bulk of ministers. In 1976, there were deputy leaders in about half the countries of the world, and other forms of ministers at large in a quarter of the countries. There was more resistance to the development in strict parliamentary systems, which is not surprising, and in the presidential systems of the absolute variety, which is more surprising, but is perhaps an indication that, in these countries, the leader is reluctant to divest himself of powers of policy-making and coordination which he may have acquired through a coup. The 'buffer' group of ministers at large suggests that the need for coordination and policy-making is felt to be strong and that the structures of government have to take this need into account, but the method remains a compromise, which does not in fact lead to a genuine transformation of governments. Many countries were not affected, since they did not have posts of this kind, or, if they had one deputy prime minister, this minister often occupied a departmental position as well and his status was exalted for political reasons only. In the second place, there is rarely more than one, or at the most three holders of non-departmental posts. Third, these positions are usually not permanent, for they may be abolished when a new government is set up. The case of the Italian non-portfolio ministers with special responsibility for the *Mezzogiorno* is the exception rather than the rule and it corresponds to the perennial importance of the problem; and Britain is also quite exceptional in having a substantial number of non-portfolio ministers established, so to speak, because they are embedded in the traditional structure of the cabinet. Clearly, the setting up of non-departmental positions does not provide more than a partial answer to problems of coordination and policy-making faced by cabinets and other united governments. In fact, they are to some extent merely a residuum of a much larger idea, prominent in some circles in Western European countries in particular, the idea of setting up genuine super-ministers to fill the gap between leader and departmental ministers.

2. The Idea of 'Superministers'

The idea of organizing an intermediate group of superministers within the government is a fairly old one, which was formally canvassed in Britain by L.S. Amery in his *Thoughts on the Constitution*, published in 1946.[11] But Amery's idea stemmed from the practice of the war cabinet of Lloyd George which was set up in 1916 in very special circumstances and for a definite and rather simple purpose, that of coordinating the British drive towards victory. The concept of the war cabinet was abandoned when peace returned and, presumably, single-mindedness in government ceased to be the order of the day. When Churchill again set up a war cabinet in 1940, the practice was therefore also viewed as a temporary expedient.

Yet, by 1940, the idea may have begun to be regarded by some as more than just a passing solution. Interestingly enough, the Vichy regime which was installed in France came to have a cabinet which was partly reorganized on the basis of a small number of super-ministers, with the rest of the government subordinated to them. In the Darlan government of 1941, for instance, it could be said by one author that 'Within the government there is a strict hierarchy...To each minister are in principle subordinated a number of 'state Secretaries' (junior ministers in the French nomenclature).[12] For a period after 1945, the needs of postwar reconstruction and the aura of planning or at least of a general state supervision of the economy seemed to suggest that superministers were the answer to the problem of the organization of modern government. For, it seemed that the only rational way of structuring the government was to see it as being concerned with a number of broad sectors — defence, economic affairs, social affairs, general administration — so as to ensure that the interconnected problems of industry, transport and agriculture, for instance, or of housing, education and labour, be properly considered. Moreover, it also seemed more rational that the problems of coordination at the top should be handled by a very small group of men who could see each other frequently and thus be constantly aware of each other's thinking and actions. And, finally, broad policy-making would be dealt with more satisfactorily, since it would be the responsibility of a very small group.

However, despite the support for the idea of superministers which prevailed in the aftermath of the Second World War, no postwar government was structured on the basis of a small number of men supervising a larger number of ministers: specifically, the idea was not put firmly to the test in either Britain or France which were the two countries in which the suggestion had been formulated most forcefully and had indeed been partially implemented during the war. Instead, it was attempted in practice in two fields only, defence and the economy. In the defence area, in the late 1940s, the three service departments were rapidly demoted to effectively become only sub-organizations, run by junior ministers, while a grand ministry of defence was set up. The three service ministers quickly lost their cabinet status and the defence minister became the spokesmen for the services in the cabinet. Interestingly enough, this development spread rapidly across a large number of countries: by the 1970s, there was scarcely any government where there were still service ministers in the cabinet and where there was no minister of defence; indeed, in many countries, there were no longer any service ministers at all — senior or junior — responsible for each of the services.

The fate of the 'grand ministries' of the economy was very different: after some enthusiasm, the concept was quickly abandoned — both in France and in Britain, among the European countries which had shown most interest in it. In France, the idea was jettisoned by De Gaulle soon after he came back to Paris in 1945: Mendes-France, who was such a minister, resigned in protest. In Britain, Cripps ceased to see any virtue in the concept when he became chancellor of the exchequer. For the idea of a ministry of the economy was subjected to a two-pronged attack: on the one hand, other economic ministers, for instance the ministers of industry or transport, were unwilling to see their position reduced to one of subordination to a grand economic supremo; on the other hand, the fundamental question of whether the minister of the economy or the minister of finance should have the final say was never fully settled. In both France and Britain, and almost at the same time, the minister of finance won the day: the ministry of the economy became reduced to a ministry of economic affairs without effective powers or even became a section of the ministry of finance with only a junior minister at its head.

By then the major battle for the setting up of superministers was truly lost, since the minister of finance was everywhere anxious to continue to control the various spending ministries individually: clearly, treasuries have more influence over a large number of relatively small departments than over a small number of large ones. With hindsight, it may have been a mistake to start implementing the idea of reorganizing cabinets so drastically by a confrontation between the treasury and the ministry of the economy; indeed, it may have been a mistake to proceed by stages and not to have restructured the cabinets fully, in one clean sweep, in the rather more favourable conditions of postwar reconstruction. Perhaps, even then, such a major reform was politically and administratively impossible, but, clearly, despite a number of attempts in subsequent decades, in Britain and France in particular, the endeavour has become a Sisyphean effort.

There were indeed three further waves of governmental reorganization in Britain. The first was the highly publicized suggestion of appointing 'overlords' in 1951 when the Conservative administration was returned to power. Probably in order to follow through the suggestions of Amery, Churchill stated that he would appoint a number of prestigious men to overview various sectors of government: in the event, only three 'overlords' were appointed, and these were each concerned with limited fields; they resigned after a few years without having made a significant impact, either on policy, or on the structure of government. The idea of appointing superministers was discredited for a period and it was only a decade later, in 1964, that it was taken up again by Wilson, in his first administration, when a new attempt was made to launch a grand ministry of economic affairs at a time when the prevailing mood in Britain was one of planning and rationalization. But the experiment collapsed, as in the 1940s, because the ministry of economic affairs never had any real supervisory powers, while the emphasis on economic development was replaced by considerations of financial orthodoxy: the defence of the pound led to a reemergence of the treasury's role. The only result of this second wave of enthusiasm for superministers was the merger of the foreign and commonwealth affairs departments and the abolition of the Colonial Office, but, in this respect, it is not clear whether political considerations — namely the desire to show that the period of colonialism was over — were not more important than ideas of administrative efficiency.

In the late 1960s and early 1970s, however, a third wave of efforts designed to set up superministers began to be noticeable, and the movement this time spread beyond Britain, to France and a number of other countries. It concerned social departments and to a more limited extent some of the specialized economic departments. The idea of bringing together the various aspects of social security, such as health and pensions, was probably due in large part to the escalating costs of public medicine. The 'social wage' became recognized as a large element in both national consumption and in the incomes of individuals. Thus, 'grand' ministries of social security emerged in a number of countries and, for instance in Britain, led to the demotion of departments such as health. Meanwhile, the need to coordinate various aspects of the 'productive' side of the economy led to the setting up of 'grand ministries' of industry to which more specialized departments such as transport would be subordinated.

Yet, even this third wave of social and industrial coordination by superministers had only a limited success. In Western Europe, the French Socialist government of 1981 has gone furthest in its attempt to undertake coordination at the top by appointing a number of 'ministers of state' in charge of whole sections, and especially in the field of 'social security'. But earlier attempts at giving superministers a truly coordinating role have been unsuccessful, except by and large when whole ministries have purely and simply been abolished and merged within a single department. For the stumbling blocks which have repeatedly been viewed as the causes of failure can seemingly be fully overcome only by the disappearance of the structures which should be coordinated. The presence of ministers, with or even without cabinet status, means that there are politicians who wish to exercise influence, and they normally have enough leverage in the government party to be able to have some effect; they are at least typically unwilling to abide on the nod with the decisions of any superminister who is a colleague and who may not have really high status within the party. The result is that 'subordinated' ministers may wish to carry out among a larger circle the battles which they have with the superministers. Thus, politically, the conditions of parliamentary government, which is based on collaboration among a number of colleagues, make it very difficult to implement the idea of superministers. This is perhaps why, in a mixed presidential-cum-parliamentary context, the experiment with superministers may be somewhat more successful in the French Socialist government of the 1980s.

Yet, the strength of the 'subordinate' minister is increased by the character of the administrative structure of the departments. These wish collectively to have their way as often as possible and they therefore resent the demotion to which they are subjected if there is a superminister above 'their' minister. If, in order to avoid duplication, the staff of the superministry remains limited in size and if, in consequence, the superminister needs the good will of the 'subordinate' departments to elaborate proposals and eventually to implement them, he or she is in fact wholly dependent on the departments which he or she is deemed to control. It is very unlikely that these will readily provide information and generally go out of their way to be helpful to a superminister who might then exert pressure to achieve policies which the department does not want.

This is why, in the final analysis, departments have to be abolished if superministers are truly to coordinate the activities of a broad sector of government. Otherwise, coordination occurs, whether there are superministers or not, by the traditional method of consultation and committee decision-making. In the same way as ministers at large or deputy prime ministers, superministers become essentially chairmen of committees on which the 'subordinated' ministers sit and in which coordination is achieved through consensus. Whether this mode of operation is ultimately less efficient than one in which superministers could command ordinary ministers is clearly difficult to tell, especially in view of the absence of clear-cut and working experiments in appointing superministers. But it does seem prima facie permissible to suggest that both coordination and, perhaps even more, global policy-making are likely to suffer as a result.

Atlantic countries have thus implemented the idea of 'superministers' only to a limited extent. Perhaps even more surprisingly, since leaders are stronger outside Western Europe, the idea of a fully hierarchical government has not spread in countries where the constraints of parliamentary governments do not apply. By the late 1970s, there had been only three clear-cut examples of a total restructuring of the government on the basis of a number of superministers between the leader and the rest of the government, and these experiments had been unsuccessful. In Indonesia, at the end of the Soekarno regime the government was based on a small number of superministers and a large number of ministers; the experiment was ended by Suharto. In Guinea, the government was restructured in this manner for a few years; there is little evidence of the way in which the arrangement altered decision-making patterns, but it was abolished. In Mauritania, the government was restructured after a coup in the later 1970s, but the experiment with superministers did not survive another military coup. The idea of organizing the government in this manner is thus essentially an idea, a suggestion, rather than a reality. It may appear to be the only practical way of significantly altering decision-making processes in semi-collective governments in which attention has to be paid to the susceptibilities of ministers, but it may simply be too radical, or unworkable. So far, it seems that the burden of policy-making and coordination is not felt to be so vast that cabinets cannot share it with the leader and yet be able to manage the departments.

3. Policy-Making and Coordination by and around the Leader: The Case of the United States

While most Western governments and a substantial number of Third World governments have introduced minor changes in the structure of the executive, the evolution of the United States government deserves special consideration because almost all the effort has consisted in giving a major say to the presidential staff; whereas various centrifugal pressures, including congressional pressures, resulted in the departments of the United States government acquiring a large dose of autonomy, attempts have been made since F.D. Roosevelt to establish the principle that policy-making and coordination should be located primarily within a newly 'institutionalized' presidency.

On the surface, this division of labour may be viewed as sensible, indeed rational: the president is the only elected official within the executive branch; he, therefore, is the only member of the executive who has presented a programme to the nation and it must be assumed that, to an extent at least, and at any rate more than any other member of the executive, he is anxious to see that this programme is implemented. Moreover, again by virtue of his election, the president is clearly expected to have views on and responsibility for the whole range of problems which face the executive. While cabinet secretaries should be good administrators, the president should be the one to lead and coordinate.

Such functions cannot be fulfilled, however, unless the president has around him a substantial staff of great talent. Thus, the tasks of policy-making and coordination could not be expected to be accomplished as long as the Executive Office of the president was small, indeed, almost non-existent. It is, therefore, quite logical to argue that, until Roosevelt, the President of the United States did not wholly fulfil the policy-making and coordination functions; but it is not certain that, even with a large Executive Office and in particular with the White House Office, the president, by himself and through his staff, has the capacity to exercise these functions.

The consensus of opinion seems to be that this is not really the case and that ultimately, there is relatively little that the Executive Office can do if departments are adamant in not following its leadership. This is despite the fact that efforts have repeatedly been made, both in order to activate the departments, as under Kennedy and Johnson, or to restrain them, as under Nixon. The staff of the Executive Office has increased in truly vast proportions to help achieve this task: the White House Office alone jumped from a mere thirty-seven under F.D. Roosevelt to 510 in 1973; the Executive Office as a whole increased by 50 percent between 1965 and 1973.[13] Moreover, the number of agencies multiplied in the postwar period and were subjected to periodic and drastic reorganizations. The first agency was the Bureau of the Budget, created in 1921: it was first placed within the Department of the Treasury, but was later placed directly under the president; the White House Office was set up in the 1930s; and the National Security Council and the Council of Economic Advisers were set up at the time of or immediately after the Second World War. Various new bodies were created in the 1950s and 1960s, until Nixon reorganized the whole structure by instituting a Domestic Council, paralleling the National Security Council, by transforming the Bureau of the Budget into an Office of Management and Budget and by placing this office as well as the many organizations set up under Kennedy and Johnson under the Domestic Council.

The multiplication of the new agencies was an indication of the extent to which the Executive Office was viewed as being the place where policy-making and even more coordination were deemed to occur. In the Kennedy and Johnson eras, in particular, there seemed to be a widely held belief in the usefulness of setting up new agencies, outside the regular departments, to undertake the programmes to which the president gave high priority and which cut across the province of the regular departments; this was the case for instance with the Office of Science and Technology, set up in 1962, the Office of Consumer Affairs or the Office of Economic Opportunity, both set up in 1964.

Consequently, the Executive Office has a staff which can follow up the activities of the various departments. It can even be argued that there are now two 'rings' in the office. The Executive Office constitutes the outer ring, with the members of the various agencies — and the members of the Office of Management and Budget in particular — being concerned with the supervision of activities of departments or acting as a spur to the departments. The White House Office, meanwhile, constitutes the inner ring, with the special aides being entrusted with the presentation of ideas and with helping the president to control and supervise the activities of the rest of the Executive Office and of the government in general. As N.C. Thomas points out: 'White House Office staff fall into two general categories. First, there are the experts and intellectuals whose skills, knowledge and experience make them valuable as idea generators and as evaluators of policy alternatives...The second basic category of White House advisers include close political associates and personal friends of the President'.[14]

Thus, the United States structure has gone as far as seems possible in setting up a special machinery designed to help the elaboration of policy and its overall coordination. Yet, the result does not seem to have produced effective coordination or more than occasional bouts of involvement in policy-making. There are examples of policy-making by the White House Office, admittedly, the clearest cases being provided by the activities of H. Kissinger before he became secretary of state. Indeed, at the time, the situation in the United States government closely resembled the Soviet practice with two parallel, and occasionally inconsistent, sources of decision — a situation which was sometimes repeated under Carter with Z. Brzezinski. But there are many more examples of ineffectiveness on the part of the White House aides and of the Executive Office.

To begin with, the White House Office suffers from being composed too ostensibly of friends of the president who tend often not to have many contacts within the federal civil service; this is sometimes compounded by the numerous comments made about the arrogance and self-importance of the presidential aides. The result is a situation of conflict, which has been documented for instance by T.E. Cronin in a survey of White House officials designed to examine the relationship between the White House and the departments: two-thirds of the forty-three White House aides stated that there was considerable conflict, not a situation likely to lead to satisfactory results in terms of the ability of these men to coordinate policy or to develop new policies which the departments will then follow.[15] The result, on the contrary, is an attitude of 'guerrilla warfare', or resistance by the departments, not of acceptance of the guidance of the White House staff.

Indeed, conflict and divisions seem to exist within the Executive Office itself, and in particular between the members of the 'outer ring' and the members of the White House staff who constitute the 'inner ring'. In the early period of development of the Executive Office, during and after the Second World War, the Bureau of the Budget was undertaking and coordinating activities and the president used the Bureau for this purpose. But, gradually, under Truman and even more in the 1960s, the role of the Bureau of the Budget was reduced. As R.S. Gilmour says: 'The opinion is widespread that the White House has taken over from Management and Budget on legislative matters of any real importance'.[16] And A. Shick continues: 'As it became the institutionalised presidency, the Bureau became separated from the President'.[17] The Budget Bureau had become an office servicing every president: the result was that the White House Office had taken over the most sensitive functions and that it had come, so to speak, to control the Bureau of the Budget and the whole Executive Office.

One reason for this development was naturally the size of the Executive Office, and, to begin with, of the Bureau of the Budget which grew to 600 and more in the 1970s. As A. Shick points out: 'with a 500-man complement, the Bureau was just too large and too remote to be the President's own'.[18] Hence, the dilemma: if any organization in the White House is to be in a position to control or at any rate supervise adequately the activities of the departments, it must be relatively large; but, when it becomes large, it is no longer a body which the president can effectively trust, in all senses of the word, to carry out his own ideas of policy-making and coordination. The history of the Bureau of the Budget (now Office of Management and Budget) is most revealing in this respect, as it shows an almost linear relationship between the size of the Bureau and the extent to which its whole procedure became 'routinized'.

'Over a period of decades, the Bureau had become a rigidified institution, suffering from what Herbert Kaufman has termed "the
natural history of organisations".'[19] But the president could no
longer have his way and make his mark on the activities of the
Bureau, he could no longer change the personnel composition of
the Bureau, which had become so large that a change would have
been a total revolution; and, by then the president no longer had
authority to appoint more than a 'handful of Bureau policy
leaders'.[20] Indeed, as the Bureau grew larger, it came to be more
closely in touch with the departments, a development which might
seem to justify further the increased presidential reliance on the
White House Office.

Yet, despite their increased size, neither the Executive Office nor
the inner circle of the White House Office were large enough to be
able to control the administration effectively. A staff of several
hundred in the White House Office may look very large — and
indeed is very large by the standards of presidential or prime
ministerial offices elsewhere, even if one takes into account the
relative size of the United States and of other Western democracies
— but this size is small by comparison with the size of the
bureaucracy of the federal government, which is over three million
strong. Consequently, all the White House Office seems able to do
is to push for a few of the ideas of the president. As a Kennedy
White House aide quoted in T.E. Cronin ('White House-Depart-
mental Relations') said: 'In retrospect, I don't think you can coordinate much from the White House. You just don't have the people
and the numbers...and you can't evaluate all that much'.[21] And,
as M. Comarow, executive director of the Presidential Advisory
Council on Executive Organization said: '[The President] doesn't
have an evaluation system; he doesn't know how his programmes
are doing...The President don't have a group of people who
understand and who focus all their time on organisation questions...The President does not have a coordination mechanism'.[22]

The argument was that the new Office of Management and
Budget would provide the mechanism. It is not clear that it has
done so, any more than the earlier Bureau of the Budget did, and
the reason is the same: the president cannot rely on organized,
'institutionalized' bodies, but the informal bodies are too small.
Ultimately, there seems to be no solution, since, if the bodies increase in size, they will lose their informality and clear dependence
on the president.

Finally, it is arguable as to whether policy-making and coordination can be affected by a body of transient aides and presidential friends when the rest of the machinery of government is staffed by a permanent career civil service. We noted that departmental secretaries came to take the point of view of the staff because this is organizationally and psychologically the only way for them to have a hold over their departments;[23] to expect outsiders, even covered by the aura of the president's authority, to make more than an occasional impact on the administration process is quite unrealistic. What the White House Office and the Executive Office can do is to try and 'sell' the ideas which are closest to their hearts: they cannot impose them, nor can they have much leverage beyond the relatively small number of matters in which the president has a truly active interest. Perhaps it was the recognition of this situation which led to the setting up of the Domestic Council which includes, alongside presidential aides, representatives from the cabinet on lines analogous to those on which the National Security Council was set up.

Policy-making and coordination thus take place only to a limited extent through the Executive Office in the United States. It is not the case that the concentration of these institutions around the president can solve the basic problem of the division of the executive branch into a 'collection of badly separated principalities'.[24] This does not mean that, in another context, one for instance in which there was not such a long tradition of autonomy among the departments, a body such as the Executive Office would not be able to be more effective: moreover, the size of the American bureaucracy perhaps makes it impossible to expect genuine coordination to occur and the policy-making process to be smooth. Indeed, it may well be that, without the White House Office, the American bureaucracy would have split up completely into autonomous agencies without any common purpose. But it does remain that an institutional distinction between 'managerial' and 'coordinating' or 'policy-making' bodies seems unable to solve the problems posed by the complexity of these policy-making and coordination problems in the contemporary world.

4. Governments with Two Parallel Councils

It is clear that, potentially at least, the American Executive Office exercises many functions of policy-making and coordination. It is much less easy to ascribe precise functions to the revolutionary or military councils which have been set up in Third World states from the mid-1960s. When the Burmese Revolutionary Council was set up in 1962, such a development naturally could not be viewed as a significant change in the structure of Third World governments; where relatively small new councils were set up, as in the two Yemens, the arrangement could be viewed as an extension of the 'junta' principle. Moreover, it was, of course, uncertain as to whether these developments would merely be temporary and designed to meet a transitional situation as had often been the case in the past in Latin America, simply in order to help a new military leader to establish his influence. Indeed, the abolition of the Libyan Military Command in 1976 and the reduction in size of the Sudanese council seemed to constitute a return to more traditional governmental structures. But, by the 1980s, there have been too many revolutionary or military councils, and they have lasted too long in a number of countries not to suggest that they have become, by way of imitation of Communist states in large part, an important element in the organization of governments in the contemporary world; this is especially the case in black Africa where they are in existence in a quarter of the countries and where the growth has been rapid.

It is still too early to be able to state with assurance what part these councils play in the executives to which they belong. Clearly, moreover, their influence varies over time and from country to country. When they are very small, and are akin to a traditional Latin American junta, they are likely to act, for a while at least, as a collective leadership group, though, more than occasionally, one leader emerges from the group and reduces the other members of the council to a secondary position. When the council is large — with twenty or more members — it is likely to have a primarily symbolic or legitimizing function, akin to that fulfilled by some legislatures of single-party systems. But, in many cases, the council has an intermediate position: it probably plays a substantial part in the governmental process, especially in the early period, though it does not have a monopoly of policy-making and even less of co-ordination. For it is in competition with the 'regular' government, a competition which the leader probably fosters as he is likely to wish to play one body against the other in order to establish his own power: councils which have lasted longer than the original leader of

a coup are relatively rare.[25] Moreover, the regular government is
likely to exercise considerable influence in view of the fact that the
ministers, being in charge of the departments, have the civil service
machine at their disposal, which the military or revolutionary councils do not have. Thus, except where there is considerable overlap in
membership between the two bodies, which is rare (Mali being
exceptional in having almost the same men in the two bodies), military or revolutionary councils are likely to be occasional sources of
policy-making in conjunction with, and perhaps often in opposition to, the regular government.

The cases of the Portuguese and Nigerian councils, which have
been better detailed, help to give an idea of the role of these bodies
and of the evolution of this role over time. The Portuguese military
council can be said to have been really powerful, and to have been
the true policy-making body, for about two years. The military
governments of the mid-1970s were subordinated to the Revolutionary Council: indeed, the clash between the council and Spinola
and the eventual resignation of the latter strengthened the power of
the council for a time. Thus, the council could for instance decide
on substantial measures of nationalization as well as on the relationship between the state and various 'private' bodies — from the
Church to political parties and to the mass media. At that time, the
Revolutionary Council viewed itself, albeit temporarily, as the
repository of the new Portuguese legitimacy and it took over the
functions of representation and legislation as well as of government
in the stricter sense (but the large role played by many parliamentary governments in effectively deciding on legislation before
sending it to Parliament makes the position of a revolutionary
council such as that of the early Portuguese council not structurally
different from the that of an 'ordinary' parliamentary executive).
Only in 1976, when parliamentary elections led to the emergence of
an alternative source of legitimacy, did the Revolutionary Council
begin to lose power and influence, although it did not disappear
and it still played a limited — but somewhat negative — part in the
early 1980s.

The dominance of the Portuguese council was short, if very
intense and heated. The Nigerian council had a more sustained
influence over a longer period, although its role did seem to vary
markedly. In 1966, when the military government was instored, the
Nigerian executive structure was formally viewed as being based on
two layers with a distinction between a Supreme Military Council

(SMC) and a Federal Executive Council, composed of 'commissioners'. But the division never quite followed 'functional' lines. There seems little doubt that, originally, the new military leaders wished to give the Supreme Military Council the major policy-making powers while the 'commissioners' would be confined to administration: attempts were made to introduce civil servants in the government. This move was successful in Northern Nigeria where the Executive Council was composed of top civil servants as early as January 1966.[26] At the federal level, however, civil servants refused to become heads of the departments[27] and the commissioners had therefore to be drawn mainly from among the military. Meanwhile, as the Nigerian military needed the support of civilians, and especially of politicians, in the context of the civil war effort, more and more civilians were gradually drawn into the government, while the Supreme Military Council remained composed of military men. To an extent, the distinction between the two councils seemed therefore to be designed more to help Gowon to benefit from both civilian and military legitimacy than to be based on a division of administrative responsibility. After the departure of Gowon, in 1975, however, it seemed that the new leaders, Mohammed and Obasanjo, relied more on the Military Council, in part because of divisions among the civilians.[28] Indeed, the representative character of the Executive Council declined at the time: thus, the SMC determined policy over the allocation of revenues from the regions and it made many amendments to the draft constitution.[29]

Thus, in Nigeria at least, there was no clear-cut division of power between the two segments of the government: depending on the issue and the political situation leaders relied more heavily on one or the other of the two bodies to achieve their aims. The 'regular' government has clearly been concerned with management, while the Military Council has determined a number of policies; but the 'regular' government has determined others, a situation not unlike that of Portugal in the first two years after the return to democracy. The 'model' of the two-layer government in the Third World is thus likely to be in a state of flux. Much depends on the extent to which the leader succeeds in establishing his own position; much also depends on the extent to which the regular government, which the leader is more likely to be able to control, is able to erode the power of the military council by its clear hold on day-to-day affairs. Yet, it would be wrong to dismiss military councils as merely being stepping stones enabling leaders to establish their position. Many military leaders are also likely to distrust the civil servants and politicians whom they have to appoint to the 'regular' government: because they lack both prestige and technical competence, these leaders are likely to continue to rely more than occasionally on the military council to counter-balance the strength of the other segment of the executive (as the Nigerian example shows); consequently, the military councils are likely to be involved in policy-making and in coordination.

This seems to be particularly the case in certain of the 'Marxist' regimes which have taken over some of the African governments from the middle of the 1970s. In Ethiopia, for instance, the revolutionary council is not merely a means for the leader to legitimize his power: it is also the place where many battles, both ideological and personal, occur among the ruling group. Political tension has remained high for a number of years, and the device of the revolutionary council, as in Communist states, has enabled the factions to propose and alter policies. If these factions succeed in both organizing and mobilizing support within the country, the members of the revolutionary council thus have a political base, and their views cannot therefore be ignored. The dilemma which faces the leadership is thus one of either having to accept that much policy is determined within the revolutionary council or to forcibly eliminate opponents. So far, both strategies have been adopted successively or, indeed, concurrently. It may, therefore, be concluded that the tensions within revolutionary councils will gradually lead these bodies to impotence, but it may also be that a modus vivendi will emerge by which they maintain at least a substantial element of policy-making and coordination, as has happened in Communist states, to which we shall now turn.

5. Policy-Making and Coordination in Communist Governments

The structure of Communist governments is intriguing: it is highly complex, heavy, and consequently perhaps burdensome. But, probably more by accident than by design, it addresses itself to the functional division between policy-making, coordination and management. Indeed, some of the organs of Communist governments seem specifically devoted to policy-making, others to coordination, and yet others to management.

The general secrecy surrounding the activities of Communist governments is a major difficulty in determining the precise functions of each of the organs of these governments, and the assessment of the value of the arrangements is consequently necessarily vague. But, at a time when there is a pressing need to find satisfactory solutions to the problems of policy-making and coordination in government, the examination of the way in which the Communist executive operates is a clear imperative.

The origin of the distinction between the Politburo, on the one hand, and the Council of Ministers, on the other, is, of course, due to the general division of the political process in Communist states between a 'party half' and a 'state half'. The role of party organs being generally to ensure that the administration strictly follows the 'socialist path', the main emphasis is on a distinction between supervision and implementation, the party being as much concerned with detailed oversight as with a general overview. Thus the party organs may be regarded as interfering with detailed management as well as providing the main lines of policy: it may indeed be that efficiency is reduced as a result. Moreover, the role of party organs is also to organize and control the life of the party, which is a vast structure in all the Communist states: as a result, top party bodies are concerned with the management of the activities of the lower echelons as well as with the supervision of the state administration. Thus it would be wrong to view the division of Communist governments into a number of components as a straight division between policy-making and coordination, on the one hand, and management, on the other. There is a considerable degree of overlap of functions and a degree of vagueness in the activities.

Yet it remains the case that, by a gradual process of specialization which occurred over decades, the division of Communist governments into a number of bodies has led to an emphasis on functional differentiation in the activities of the executive. And, in this regard, the division between the Politburo and the Council of Ministers has been only one aspect of the distinction. We pointed out in Chapter 3 that Communist governments had come to be composed of three or four bodies 'above' the group of departmental ministers. There is everywhere a Politburo, a Party Secretariat, and a Presidium of the Council of Ministers, although there is some doubt as to whether the last of these bodies is effective everywhere; and there is also in many Communist states a State Council or a

State Presidium. Thus, the articulation of the government has to take into account, not merely the party 'half' but the state 'half', as the Council of Ministers is led by men whose role is to ensure that the activities of the council as a whole are united and presumably follow the required line.

Politburos

It is tempting to describe the Politburo or the Communist Party in a Communist state as the 'real' government, as the equivalent of the cabinet in a Western European country. It is, indeed, manifest that Politburos resemble cabinets in parliamentary systems in a number of important respects. First, as we pointed out in Chapter 3, they have become, if they were not during the period of Stalinist hegemony, relatively collective. They constitute teams which remain together for very long periods. In the course of the postwar period the membership of Politburos changed very slowly: up to the late 1970s, China and Czechoslovakia were the only countries in which there had been a complete change in the composition of the Politburo; Poland was to be a further case in 1981. But, in other cases, on the contrary (the Soviet Union, East Germany, Hungary and, above all, Albania), there was never an abrupt change in membership, merely a very gradual and slow replacement: only two of the fourteen-strong Albanian Politburo of 1965 were no longer members of that body in 1976. The increase in the size of Politburos may indeed be explained in part by the difficulty of dismissing members: new blood had therefore to come by additions to the membership.

Thus, whatever influence some individuals may have over the others, there is no doubt that, as bodies, Politburos constitute organizations whose members have as much, if not more in common as the members of parliamentary cabinets in Western countries. Moreover, members of Politburos work more closely together than ministers in Western European governments: instead of being spread across the various departments in the governmental section of the capital city, members of Politburos tend to have their offices on the same floor of the party headquarters building and can therefore thrash out problems informally by seeing each other on many occasions during the day.

TABLE 6
Membership of Politburos of Communist Parties in
Communist states

	1955	1965	1976
Albania	9	14	18
Bulgaria	10 (1953)	11	15
China	10	24	24
Czechoslovakia	8	13	14
East Germany	14	22	28
Hungary	11	19	15
North Korea	15 (1962)	15	25
Mongolia	9 (1962)	10	8
Poland	15	15	16
Romania	12	14	35
USSR	12	19	23
North Vietnam	13 (1962)	13	—
Yugoslavia	14	14	13
Average	11.6	14.6	18.9

Second, Politburos resemble cabinets in terms of their size. While Communist governments are all large, and the Soviet government is particularly large, the Politburos have about the size of an average Western cabinet. They have markedly increased in the course of the post-1945 period, admittedly: they had eleven members and alternatives, on average, in the mid-1950s, but by the mid-1970s, this average had almost doubled to about twenty members. There were indeed appreciable differences from country to country: Yugoslavia, Poland and Hungary are the countries where the increase in size was the smallest, while Romania, China and East Germany are those where it was largest. But, despite these differences, Politburos remain 'manageably' small; they are still bodies where discussions can take place and, as in cabinets, where a collective spirit can emerge.

Finally, Politburos resemble cabinets in that there seems no doubt that they take the major governmental decisions relating to the country. The documentation is, of course, extremely patchy: except for some very special occasions, we do not know which decisions are taken by which body and, even then, to what extent the decision is in effect prepared by another body with the Politburo being perhaps involved only at the latest, and rather formal, stage. But, were this to be the case, this would not distinguish Politburos from parliamentary cabinets, as, there too, most important decisions are not merely prepared but, for all intents and purposes taken, by 'preparatory' bodies. One can therefore state with considerable assurance that, to the extent that a top political body takes major governmental decisions, Politburos are the bodies which do so in Communist states.

But these three characteristics are not sufficient to justify a claim that Politburos are the real equivalents of Western cabinets. First, Politburos are involved in party decisions as well, with which Western cabinets do not concern themselves. Politburos are not merely party organs on paper, although decisions are, of course, prepared by the Secretariats, for they are involved in the life of the party, and in particular in appointments within the party structure. Second, while Politburos are concerned with administrative matters beyond general policy decisions, they seem to be doing so only if a serious problem arises and not in a routine manner: the Council of Ministers and the state organs are concerned with the administration of the country. The Politburo intervenes only if there is a contentious issue or one on which party leaders feel strongly. The Politburo is thus an organ of 'spot checks' rather than a detailed supervisor of the administration. Admittedly, Western cabinets do not become very involved either in details of administration. But, at least, and as a matter of routine, administrative questions come to them to be discussed, would it only be because, on the Continent of Europe at least, decrees and regulations of the government have to be approved formally by the cabinet before they can be enforced.

Moreover, the composition of Politburos differs, and seems to differ increasingly, from that of Western parliamentary cabinets. This is in part because Communist governments are large and Politburos comparatively small, but this is not the sole reason. Politburos have always included only a small number of top ministers and of members of the government, and they have also always included a substantial number of non-governmental members. Indeed, during the 1960s and 1970s, the *proportion* of members of the government belonging to the Politburo declined overall, and, in a number of Communist countries, the *absolute* number of government members declined. In the early post-1945 period, Politburos tended to include all the heads of the most important departments, in particular foreign affairs, defence, internal security, and the plan. This was no longer always the case at the end of the 1970s: these were members of the Politburo in the Soviet Union and Poland, for instance, but not in Czechoslovakia. The only members of Councils of Ministers which Politburos normally included were the chairman and one or more vice-chairmen. As a result, members of the Council of Ministers no longer usually form the majority of the Politburo, while they used to do so in the early years after the Second World War.

The rest of the members of the Politburo are, first and foremost, members of the Secretariat: these are present in larger numbers than in the earlier period. In 1955, only one of the five party secretaries, Khruschev himself, was a member of the Soviet Politburo of twelve (including one candidate-member); in 1965, three of the ten secretaries were members of the Politburo of nineteen (including six candidate-members); and, in 1976, six of the eight secretaries were members of the Politburo of twenty-three (including six candidate-members). This must mean that the first secretary can count on a very solid group of supporters in the Politburo (but it may be suggested that this increase in numbers is now required because the first secretary can no longer count on the kind of automatic support, based on fear, of earlier years). And, beside the party secretaries, the Politburos include representatives of various sections of the party apparatus, such as regional secretaries, and of related groups, such as the trade union movement.

Thus Politburos of Communist states are not composed in the same manner as the British cabinet, for they are not the whole, or even the bulk of the 'regular' government. They are composed for a very large part of members of the party bureaucracy, with special emphasis on the national party apparatus. This, of course, should not be surprising if we deem the Politburos to be what they are formally, namely the highest organs of a political party; their composition resembles much more that of the executive of a political party in the West than that of a Western government. But it is normally accepted that the Politburos' area of intervention and decision-making extends well beyond, indeed, is entirely different from that of the executive of a Western political party, even where that party is in power, in part because the first secretaries are regarded as the top political leaders in Communist states and in part because the organizational ideology of these states is one which stresses that the party is the vanguard of political life in the country. Thus one can conclude that Politburos do only a part of what cabinets do, that they are concerned with broad aspects of policy-making to be thrashed out in detail by the Council of Ministers (unless the Council of Ministers has presented the proposals in the first instance) under the influence and advice of the Secretariats which act, in this respect, as research bureaus and which are, as we saw, represented so well on the Politburos. These seem to be the outer circle — and perhaps in many cases the more formal part — of a policy-making process which seems to include, on the one hand, the Councils of Ministers, and, on the other, the Secretariats.

Party Secretariats

It is not possible to understand the role of Politburos without taking into account the influence of the Secretariat whose top members clearly form part of the governments of Communist states. At the time of Stalin, of course, it was argued that the whole government of the Soviet Union was concentrated in the Secretariat; indeed, Stalin's rise to power was due to his ability to control the apparatus of the party through the Secretariat. Thus, the Secretariats of Communist parties fulfil functions which go far beyond those of a government. Given that the party is in many ways a state within the state, and that the Secretariat is the ruling element in the party structure, its position vis-à-vis the Politburo bears some relationship to the position of the state administration vis-à-vis the party structure.

But the Politburos of ruling Communist parties belong to the government in a way which is not wholly dissimilar to that of the Executive Office of the president in the United States. In a sense, the Secretariat is at the disposal of the first secretary, and the other members of the Secretariat who belong to the Politburo can to some extent be regarded as 'aides' of the first secretary even more than as ministers subordinated to the prime minister in a cabinet or hierarchical government. The first secretary can rely, through the other secretaries, on the help of a very large body even though the Secretariat is nominally responsible to the Central Committee and not to the Politburo. In the Soviet Union, for instance, the Secretariat has seemingly a staff of about a thousand, divided into

a number of departments which duplicate, and therefore can supervise, the activities of the various departments of the government.
The Secretariat has indeed always been the means by which links
have been maintained with the other Communist parties, including
ruling Communist parties: it therefore plays an active part in
foreign affairs.

What the Secretariat precisely does in terms of the preparation of
governmental decisions or of supervision of the administration is,
of course, known only patchily. But it seems clear that the
Secretariat provides the leader and the rest of the Politburo with
background research and with forecasts. Specifically, the role of
the Secretariat in planning matters is wide, would it be only because
the plan is discussed at the grass-roots of the party before being formally adopted, according to the principles of democratic cen-
tralism. Khruschev's decision to modify agricultural policy was one
in which the Secretariat, rather than the regular government, seems
to have been markedly involved. Although the first secretary is not
quite as free to choose his subordinates in the Secretariat as an
American president is to choose his White House staff, the
Secretariat of the Communist Party does nevertheless play the part
of an informal 'second' (or for that matter 'third') government in
Communist systems.

Yet it would be wrong to exaggerate the influence of Secretariats,
especially by contrast with Politburos, but also with the government as a whole. To judge from the Secretariat of the Communist
Party of the Soviet Union (CPSU), the size of the staff in Moscow,
however substantial, does not allow for the possibility of developing new programmes in detail and of ensuring their implementation. The opportunities which members of the Secretariat have are
not, ultimately, appreciably greater than those of the presidential
staff in the United States. Interestingly enough, the size of the staff
is almost identical in the two countries, and it compares very un-
favourably to the size of the staff of the ministries in Moscow, let
alone throughout the Soviet Union. Clearly, the authoritarian
character of the Soviet system makes it easier for the Secretariat to
follow up its suggestions; clearly, too, the fact that the Secretariat
controls appointments across the Soviet Union, directly and indirectly, gives a leverage to the Moscow staff which the Washing-
ton presidential staff does not possess. But there are also marked
limits to the actions of the Secretariat, as government departments,
too, have in the Soviet Union a weight and an inertia which they

cannot have as easily in a more open political system such as that of the United States.

What is therefore perhaps most remarkable is the conjunction and osmosis between the Secretariat and the Politburo. The Secretariat provides a technical background basis for action, while the Politburo provides both a collective political basis, as well as a permanent link with the Council of Ministers. Thus the combination of the two organs leads to a greater grip on policy-making and on some coordination than does the American system, based as it is on a 'secretariat' (the presidential staff) depending exclusively on the president, which is somewhat isolated from the departments. One can therefore better understand the logic of associating department heads, in the United States, with the presidential staff, both in the National Security Council and in the more recent Domestic Council. But the Communist arrangement is more institutionalized, and it ultimately rests on the greater political importance of Politburo members. Thus, Secretariat and Politburo have an opportunity to exercise a substantial amount of policy-making and to see that it 'sticks', although even taken together, these bodies are not the equivalents of cabinets, since management but also much coordination and even some aspects of policy initiation are in the hands of the Council of Ministers and its leading organs.

State Councils and Presidiums
of Councils of Ministers

In the state 'half' of Communist governments, two bodies supervise the activities of the Councils of Ministers. These are the State Councils or State Presidiums which exist in most Communist countries, although there is none in Czechoslovakia where the presidency on the Western model has been retained, and the Presidiums of the Council of Ministers.

The State Council or State Presidium is sometimes described as a collective presidency; it does indeed have some of the formal powers of presidents, and it also has some legislative powers, for instance between sessions (which are short, of course!) of the Parliaments. Specialists do not believe on the whole that these bodies exercise real influence, however. It is not known how often they meet.[30] Yet it has been suggested that they were occasionally influential: it is for instance thought that the Council of State rivalled the Council of Ministers in influence (on coordination, presumably) in East Germany and in Romania.[31] But this seems to have been an exceptional situation. Overall, their role appears to be symbolic rather than effective.

The case of Yugoslavia is different, as the Executive Council was set up in 1953 to replace the Presidium in 'a deliberate effort to divide the executive function into the "political executive", involving action of a "creative or directive nature" and the "technical executive", involving day-to-day administration'.[32] Yugoslavia is therefore the Communist country which most clearly applies the distinction between policy-making and coordination, on the one hand, and management, on the other, within the organs of the state. In this, the Yugoslav arrangement most closely resembles those which have tended to spread in Third World countries where military councils have been set up. Almost certainly, however, the structure of the Executive Council in Yugoslavia is due to the need to take into account the regional character of Yugoslav politics; indeed, the paramount importance of regionalism led to some policy-making taking place in the state organs, and not being concentrated in the party. But the Yugoslav structure, with its Swiss-like Executive Council concentrating on policy-making and coordination, is one of the most interesting endeavours at a formal division of governmental powers in the contemporary world.

The second supervisory body of the Council of Ministers is the Presidium of the Council of Ministers. It is generally agreed that this body has substantial influence where it exists, but it is not clear that it exists formally everywhere nor, where it does, how often it meets. It is composed of the more senior members of the Council of Ministers, those who hold the titles of vice-chairmen or even first vice-chairmen as well, and of the chairman. These form a substantial group — from at least half a dozen to about a dozen — some having departmental functions, while others are 'at large'. Although the existence of the Presidium as a collective organ may be in doubt, it is clear that the vice-chairmen, individually or together, are the equivalents of the 'superministers' whom cabinet governments have occasionally attempted to appoint but who can rarely be given a genuine supervisory role in view of the customary equality of members in Western cabinets. Given a different tradition in Communist states, given also the larger size of Communist governments, given indeed the existence of Politburos and Secretariats, an overall hierarchy is easier to accept in these systems. It is therefore clear that vice-chairmen and Presidiums exercise de facto functions of coordination, under the supervision of the Politburos to which many belong, but above the ordinary members of the Council of Ministers who have essentially managerial functions. It may be an oversimplification to conclude that policy-making, coordination and management are neatly divided into the spheres of activity of Politburos and Secretariats, Presidiums, and ministers. There is some overlap of activities, as there is some overlap of membership. But the Communist structure is the one which most closely approximates the functional division of government, which thereby gives to each group a more 'manageable' task and which therefore has stumbled — largely by accident — on a formula which seems reasonably well adapted to the needs of modern government.

Policy-making and coordination are thus the object of experiments in modern government. Some of these appear to be expedients: they reflect for instance the instability of leaders and the fact that 'usurpers' constitute a sizeable proportion of current world leaders. But highly institutionalized systems, such as Communist systems, are now experiencing forms of government which are rather novel, based on three or more bodies: these seem to correspond to the exigencies of the times. And the American experiment, with its many difficulties and problems, also corresponds to a search for a solution to the problems posed by the place of policy-making and coordination in the structure of the executive. So far, cabinet governments have not found it necessary to change markedly their original arrangements. Yet, even though the process of change is very slow, it is taking place in a variety of ways. Gradually, the most established systems are circumventing some of the official structures, an indication that, despite the fact that the ideology of a collective government is strong, the cabinet arrangement is no longer wholly satisfactory in terms of the tasks which have to be performed. Cabinet governments seem increasingly unable to escape the logic of the trends which Amery discussed a third of a century ago. To say that the structure of government is in flux or in question is a banality; indeed, it is always in flux, even if it was not always, or even enough, consciously in question. But it seems increasingly the case that parliamentary systems are conducting a rearguard action against the long-term trend: for this reason alone, it seems high time that politicians and observers in these countries openly faced the problem of the need for a 'steering' policy-making group and perhaps even for what we have called a 'second' government.

Notes

1. See J.P. Mackintosh, *The British Cabinet* (Stevens, 1962), pp. 413-4, on Baldwin's leadership.

2. See Chapter 6.

3. The role of prime ministers' offices in extolling the importance of prime ministers has often been mentioned. See for instance A.H. King, *The British Prime Minister* (Macmillan, 1969), p. xii.

4. This has been the case, for instance, among Atlantic countries, in France and Spain.

5. See A.H. King, ed., *The British Prime Minister*, p. xii; see also, in this work, G.W. Jones, 'The Prime Minister's Power', pp. 188-9.

6. Crossman's analysis is based essentially on the transformation of the characteristics of society as a whole and of parties in particular. See his Introduction to Bagehot's *English Constitution* (Watts, 1964), pp. 37-57.

7. R. Mayntz, 'Executive Leadership in Germany', in R. Rose and E.N. Suleiman, eds, *Presidents and Prime Ministers* (American Enterprise Institute, 1980), p. 166.

8. S. Cohen, *Les conseillers du président* (Presses Universitaires de France, 1980), p. 178.

9. C.R. Alba, 'The Organisation of Authoritarian Leadership: Franco Spain' in R. Rose and E.N. Suleiman, op. cit., p. 283.

10. See Chapter 2 on the development of the cabinet in Britain.

11. L.S. Amery, *Thoughts on the Constitution* (Oxford University Press, 1964), pp. 88-95.

12. R. Aron, *Histoire de Vichy* (Fayard, 1954), p. 378.

13. R. Rose, *Managing Presidential Objectives* (Macmillan, 1977), p. 34.

14. N.C. Thomas, 'Presidential Advice and Information' in N.C. Thomas and H.W. Baade, eds, *The Institutionalised Presidency* (Oceana Publishers, Inc., 1972), p. 138.

15. T.E. Cronin, 'Everybody Believes in Democracy...' in N.C. Thomas and H.W. Baade, op. cit., pp. 151 and following.

16. R.S. Gilmour, 'Central Legislative Clearance', *Public Administration Review*, Vol. 31, 1956, p. 171.

17. A. Shick, 'The Budget Bureau', in N.C. Thomas and H. W. Baade, op. cit., p. 106.

18. Eod. loc.

19. Ibid., p. 107.

20. Eod. loc.
21. T.E. Cronin, op. cit., p. 160.
22. Eod. loc.
23. See Chapter 3.
24. T.E. Cronin, op. cit., p. 154.
25. Nigeria is an outstanding exception.
26. S.O. Olugbemi, 'The Civil Service; an Outsider's View' in O. Oyediran, ed., *Nigerian Politics under Military Rule, 1966-79* (Macmillan, 1979), p. 98.
27. P. Chiedo Asiodu, 'The Civil Service: an Insider's View' in O. Oyediran, op. cit., p. 82.
28. A.D. Yahaya, 'The Struggle for Power in Nigeria, 1966-79', in O. Oyediran, op. cit., p. 265.
29. O. Oyediran and O. Oloogunju, 'The Military and the Politics of Revenue Allocation', in O. Oyediran, op. cit., p. 208; see also J. Bayo Adekson, 'Dilemmas of Military Disengagement', ibid., p. 228.
30. L.G. Churchward, *Contemporary Soviet Government* (Routledge and Kegan Paul, 1968), p. 134.
31. H.G. Skilling, *The Governments of Communist Eastern Europe* (Croswell, 1966), p. 120.
32. H.G. Skilling, op. cit., p. 143.

6. MANAGEMENT AND THE DEPARTMENTAL MINISTRIES

The most exalted part of governmental activities may be broad policy-making and the coordination of services, but by far the most visible part of the governmental structure relates to the management of the ministries. Most members of governments control a department, and, in many administrations, all the ministers do so, including the leader himself. Not surprisingly, for members of the public, a government is essentially a collection of ministers with a specific portfolio.

Yet these ministries are far from constituting a universal and stable set which remains identical or even very similar over time and space. To begin with, departments as we know them have been constituted only comparatively recently, even in the West: eighteenth century governments were small — with four or five ministers in posts — and the attributions of the ministers were often vague or shifting; governments grew only slowly in the nineteenth century. In the rest of the world, the emergence of modern government is an even more recent affair. Basically, it is in the two or three decades after the Second World War that, for the first time in the life of the planet, there have been governments all over the world, composed of a significant number of bureaucratic agencies mostly staffed by indigenous civil servants and headed by ministers drawn from a national political hierarchy. As country after country became independent, colonial structures were transformed, occasionally overnight, into ministries on the model slowly arrived at in Europe

in the nineteenth century, while countries which had escaped colonialism because of their remote or primitive character also moved
away — mostly very rapidly as well — from traditional feudal
forms of rule and adopted 'modern' bureaucratic arrangements.
And these transformations occurred at a time when governmental
intervention in every country expanded in an unparalleled fashion
in order to cover economic, social, even cultural sectors of activity
to an extent which would have been thought impossible or indeed
repellent a century ago. Everywhere, whatever ideology was
officially proclaimed, governments began to have the resources and
the desire to become involved in almost all corners of the life of the
country which they ruled.

The combination of this spirit of intervention and of the
geographical spread of national bureaucratic agencies led to an un-
precedented rate of growth in the number of ministerial departments and in the number of ministries from the 1950s to the 1980s.
In about twenty-five years — from the late 1940s to the mid-1970s
— there was a trebling in the aggregate number of ministries which
were deployed across the world to look after our destinies. Around
1950, there were about 850 positions in the seventy-odd countries
which were independent at the time; around 1975, about 2,500
departmental ministers existed in the 140-odd countries which had
achieved independence. The larger part of the increase was due to
the doubling in the number of independent countries, but a
substantial part was the result of the multiplication of portfolios in
the large majority of countries, both old and new. Overall, this
expansion reached almost 50 percent, from about twelve posts per
government in the late 1940s to a little under eighteen posts in the
mid-1970s. Never before had there been such a rapid rise both in
the number of governments and in the number of positions in each
government, and, although the rise in the number of positions continued to occur in the 1970s, it is unlikely to take place at such a
quick pace in the coming years.

It is therefore interesting to monitor the rate at which this
increase occurred across the world and the forms which it took; but
it is also interesting to discover to what extent governments, at the
end of a period of such rapid expansion, have come to differ in size
and composition, below the universal and almost mechanical trend
which led almost every country to have more ministers in the 1980s
than in the 1940s. For some governments have remained rather
small, others have always been large, yet others have expanded

dramatically, while in a few cases periods of rapid increase have been followed by years of contraction. A number of distinct patterns have emerged, even though the underlying trend has been one of growth. Thus, the excursion into an analysis of ministerial departments in the post-1945 period is not due merely to a desire to record the unique expansion of governments at the time; it is also aimed at assessing how the growth took place and how large were the variations across countries and types of societies and therefore at discovering the lessons which can be drawn from these variations.

1. General Evolution of Governments since the Second World War

Variations in Government Size in the Mid-1970s

Even a first impression shows that variations are substantial. To begin with, there were important differences in the size of governments in the 1970s. On average, in 1976, governments had between seventeen and eighteen departmental ministers — that is to say, men in charge of a sector of activity and, in principle at least, responsible only to the leaders or to the whole government. But the range was substantial, between governments which had as few as five or six ministers, and, at the other extreme, the Soviet government which had no less than seventy-seven different ministers, the second largest government being that of Guinea, with thirty-nine posts. Both of these governments were based, formally or not, on a structure of coordinators and might therefore be viewed as exceptional as a result. Yet, even if they are excluded, ample variations in size still exist: for there were in the late 1970s an appreciable number of governments with twenty-five and indeed thirty or more ministers, while at the other end of the scale, some countries were ruled by governments with fewer than ten ministers.

A number of explanations appear to account for this state of affairs. First, the size of the population of the country plays a part. Countries with very small populations often had very small governments: in 1976, out of ten governments with ten portfolios or less, seven were ruling countries which had a population of under five million. But the explanation is only a partial one, as Table 7 shows:

TABLE 7
Population size and government size
(departmental ministers only)
(1976)

No. of departmental ministers	Under 5 million	5-20 million	Over 20 million
Under 10	8	1	2
10-14	28	10	2
15-19	15	18	11
20 or more	8	17	17
Total	59	46	32

The extent of state intervention is another partial explanatory factor. Communist countries had substantially larger governments than other countries. The fourteen countries ruled by a Communist party since the 1950s had on average thirty departmental ministers, and, even if the Soviet Union is excluded as its government was by far the largest, the average of twenty-three departmental ministers is substantially above the world average of eighteen. Only Albania, the smallest of the Communist countries in terms of population after Mongolia, had a government with fewer than fifteen departmental ministers, while the Cambodian and Laotian Communist governments were still recent and had not expanded their size. Outside the Communist group, however, the trend is less clear: the largest governments in 1976 were those of Guinea, Egypt, Libya, Syria, Gabon and Mauritania — not a group which had a common economic and social ideology.

Thus, neither population size nor economic and social 'interventionism' accounts for more than a proportion of the variation in the composition of governments: traditions and culture also clearly play a substantial part. Latin American governments, for instance, are smaller than other governments. In 1976, they had an average of 13.5 departmental ministers — four fewer than the world average. Indeed, Latin American countries were also clustered close to the average: of the Latin American countries proper, only Bolivia, Brazil, Mexico, Venezuela and Cuba had sixteen or more ministers. Other Third World governments tended to be appreciably larger, especially those of black Africa, while Atlantic governments were fairly close to the world average, but also included very small (Luxembourg) and very large governments (Britain, Australia, Canada).

Perhaps the clearest cultural difference, which we have already encountered at other points in the study of government, is the difference resulting from membership of the Commonwealth. Commonwealth governments formed five of the six largest Atlantic governments; Guyana and Jamaica had the largest governments in Latin America after Cuba; in South and South East Asia, four of the nine largest governments were those of countries belonging to the Commonwealth while a fifth, Burma, had been a British possession in the past. Only in Africa was the trend less marked, as some governments of French-speaking countries were large — indeed, constituted the three largest governments in the area in 1976. On average, Commonwealth governments had 19.3 ministers in 1976 — nearly two points more than the world average.

Thus, variations in the size of governments are the result of a number of distinct factors in which demographic, ideological and cultural elements play a complex part. Thus, too, a number of broad geographical patterns emerge, which help to summarize similarities and differences. Atlantic governments often have around fifteen departmental ministers; they have more (around twenty to twenty-three) if they belong to the Commonwealth; they have very few if they are very small (Luxembourg, Iceland), but usually only if they are very small. Communist governments usually have more than twenty members, and they sometimes have as many as thirty members or more. Latin American governments often have as few as ten to thirteen members, as have the governments of small South or South East Asian states, while the governments of other countries in South and South East Asia have about twenty ministers. Middle Eastern and African governments also frequently have around twenty ministers. It seems that, in these two areas, ideological considerations play a part: left-wing governments are on the whole larger than conservative governments, although this is no more than a general trend.

Evolution since 1945

The marked character of these geographical variations is sharpened if we examine the patterns of evolution which led to the situation of the 1970s. Overall, governments grew by about 50 percent during

the previous three decades — from somewhat over twelve posts in
1946 to somewhat under eighteen in 1976. Of course, this overall
average takes into account a much smaller number of countries in
the 1940s and 1950s, and by the 1970s the average size of the
governments of older countries was somewhat larger than the
average size of the governments in newer countries (by about two
posts), but the governments of new countries have tended to increase somewhat faster and the gap is thus gradually being closed.
Overall, one new post has been created in each government every
five years in the post-1945 period.

This average growth conceals marked variations, however. There
are indeed two types of variations. First, there is a remarkable difference between the 'low' growth governments of the Atlantic area,
Latin America and South East Asia and the 'high' growth governments of the other three areas. On average, the governments of the
Atlantic area and of Latin America gained only about three posts
over the three-decade period — one new ministry every ten years —
but the governments of South East Asia gained under five posts
during the same period — one and a half new ministries per decade.
In the other three geographical areas, on the other hand, the gains
were much larger — eight posts in the Communist countries, eleven
posts in Middle Eastern countries between 1946 and 1976 and six
between 1961 and 1976, while, in black African countries, the
governments gained nearly five posts between 1963 and 1976 (too
few countries were independent before 1960 to make the calcula-
tion at that time meaningful). Thus, in these three regions, the
gains were two or three times larger than they were in the Atlantic
area, Latin America and South East Asia.

But the evolution of the size of the government was also very different in the Communist world from what it was in the Middle East
and in Africa. In these two regions, the gains were regular over the
whole period, and almost from year to year. In the Communist
world, on the other hand, movements were more complex: periods
of rapid expansion were followed by periods of stagnation and even
contraction. Communist governments have evolved in a spiral-like
fashion in the course of the last three decades, the all-time high
being, however, not the mid- or late 1970s, but the late 1960s.

Thus, a general survey of the evolution of governments since the
Second World War shows that, while there was a substantial
increase in the number of departmental ministers in every region of
the world, this increase did not take place at the same rate

everywhere nor was the rate always regular. The result is that governments differ more from each other in the early 1980s than they did in the 1960s and early 1970s. By the mid-1970s, the average size of Communist governments was almost double that of Atlantic or Latin American governments (it was less than 50 percent larger in the early 1960s) and African and Middle Eastern governments had become about 50 percent larger than Latin American governments. This increased differentiation suggests a need to explore more fully the rates and the specific nature of the expansion which occurred from the 1950s to the 1970s.

2. Relative Stability of Governments in the Atlantic Area, Latin America and South and South East Asia

In the Atlantic area, in Latin America, and in South and South East Asia, the decades following the Second World War were marked by a slow and regular growth in the size of most governments. This trend was clearest in the first two of these geographical regions, which can be examined jointly. Despite the fact that the political instability of Latin American regimes contrasts sharply with the stability of parliamentary government in most of Western Europe and in the old Commonwealth, the ministerial structure in both regions followed a similar pattern characterized by relatively small governments increasing at a relatively slow rate and undergoing only minor reorganizations.

One seemingly important reason for this stability is the relative longevity of governmental structures in both the Atlantic area and Latin America: in the rest of the world, most governments were set up after 1945. There are some striking exceptions to this relative stability, admittedly, especially in the Atlantic area, but, in both regions, and in presidential as well as in parliamentary regimes, the nomenclature of ministries seems often to have acquired a status approaching constitutional rigidity. This has been particularly true in many Central American and in some South American states as well as in Scandinavia and indeed in the majority of small European democracies.

Most governments in the two areas started in 1945 with about ten departments — a few more in some, a few less in others, especially in the very small states. This number was made up of four to six 'law-and-order' departments and of a variable number of economic and social ministries, usually covering broad sectors. Thus, typically, a country had ministries of foreign affairs, interior, justice, finance as well as agriculture, commerce and industry (usually together), public works and transport (also often jointly), education, labour and health. The last two sometimes did not exist at all or were linked, and there were also three service departments — war, navy and airforce. A government which had all these departments as separate units would have been larger than average; in some cases, on the other hand, the same minister combined several departments.

Even in the 1940s, however, there were some large governments, all in the Atlantic area: these were, on the one hand, those of four continental countries — France, Belgium, Italy and Greece — and, on the other, those of the four Commonwealth countries of the area. It was, indeed, the existence of these eight relatively large governments which accounted for the average size difference between Atlantic and Latin American governments.

France, Belgium, Italy and Greece all had governments somewhat larger than the average in 1945, with between fifteen and twenty ministers. In all four cases, the size of the government in the early reconstruction period appeared to be due in large part to the need to build relatively large coalitions between three, four or even more parties. When these difficulties diminished in two of the countries, the government also decreased in size. In Belgium, after 1950s, when the royal question was settled, governments fell from about seventeen or eighteen departments to fifteen (they were to increase again when the linguistic question arose in the 1960s); in Greece, after 1952, when a majority party came to power, the size of the government was reduced from nineteen or twenty to fifteen or sixteen. In France and Italy, on the contrary, where coalition difficulties continued, the size of the government did not decrease — though it did not increase as much over the period as it did across the whole area.

But difficulties in building coalitions are not the only cause of 'oversized' governments in the Atlantic area for the largest governments of all have always been the governments of the Commonwealth countries. This is true of the British administration, which is huge if ministers of state and parliamentary secretaries are taken into account. Even if only departmental ministers (both within and outside the cabinet) are considered, British governments are among the largest, normally having around twenty-two positions. Australian and Canadian governments are also large, as are New Zealand governments, especially in view of the size of the country. This size was reached from as early as 1945 either because a number of economic or social ministries were split (for instance with the setting up of departments of health, pensions, national insurance, local government) or because special interests regarded as essential were catered for (fisheries, mines, immigration). The Commonwealth 'tradition' is thus different from that of most of continental Europe and of Latin America: governments are relatively large, almost certainly partly in order to give positions to members of the government party.

Elsewhere, governments started from a relatively small base of about ten to twelve departments, and the growth has been slow, as well as steady. A number of indicators help to monitor the character of the growth. If one lists all the departmental ministers in the Atlantic area, one finds that, on average, each country has had only twenty-two different departments — a relatively small number, given over three decades and given the economic and social changes which occurred during those decades. Of these twenty-two posts, eleven existed throughout, completely unchanged, with the same titles and broadly the same functions. As governments in the Atlantic area had about sixteen departmental ministers on average at the end of the period, this means that, in most countries, two-thirds of the departments which existed in the mid-1970s had existed continuously since the 1940s. And the situation was broadly similar in Latin America: out of about sixteen posts per country, slightly over half had existed throughout the period, and two-thirds of those existing in the mid-1970s had remained continuously since the early postwar period.

Gains and losses of departments are the result of a number of movements. Some ministries were set up some time during the period and remained in existence; others, which existed immediately after 1945, were abolished; yet others were created and were subsequently abolished; and some were created, abolished, and re-created again. Clearly, a stable ministerial structure is one in which no change at all occurs, but one of steady growth is one in which the new departments which are created are rarely abolished subsequently. Naturally, where abolitions occur on a large scale, the governmental structure shows marked instability.

By and large, as we saw, Atlantic and Latin American countries displayed a high propensity to maintain traditional departments; they also displayed a low propensity to abolish new departments once these were created. About a quarter of all the posts in existence throughout the period were constituted by new creations which were subsequently maintained: these creations were slightly less numerous in Latin America (4.4 posts on average) than in the Atlantic area (5.8 posts on average). These increases were due mainly to the setting up of departments in the social field and, but sometimes less frequently, in the primary or secondary sectors of the economy (ministries of mines in Latin America for instance).

Thus half the posts were maintained throughout the period and a quarter were 'successful' creations: the last quarter is composed almost equally of two groups — departments which were abolished and 'unsuccessful' innovations. The posts which were abolished were mainly the result of the reorganization of defence departments: ministries of war, navy and airforce ceased to exist in many countries, especially in the Atlantic area. A number of departments connected with the aftermath of the war were also abolished (reconstruction — usually transformed into a ministry of housing, however — as well as food and veterans). In all, abolitions of departments accounted for less than three posts on average in the Atlantic area, and only slightly over one post in Latin America (as traditional service departments were kept more often than in the Atlantic area).

'Failed' innovations — that is to say departments which were created and abolished a few years later — account for only about two and a half departments on average: only once every ten years, in each of these regions, was a ministry created which did not correspond to a perceived 'need' during the subsequent period. Indeed, there is more: the number of years in which 'unsuccessful' departments were in existence constitute only about 4 percent of the life of all the ministries throughout the postwar years in the forty-odd countries of the two geographical areas, as 'unsuccessful' experiments usually lasted for only a few years and therefore 'weighed' less overall than departments which were maintained.

Moreover, these 'failures' were heavily concentrated in a small number of countries. In the Atlantic area, two-thirds of them occurred in Belgium, France, Australia and New Zealand alone; in Latin America, they occurred primarily in Argentina, the Dominican Republic and Cuba, which together accounted for three-fifths of this form of ministerial 'instability'; and the Cuban case is rather special as it is analogous to that of other Communist countries which we shall examine in the next section.

In general, Commonwealth countries also displayed rather more instability of ministerial posts than most other countries of the Atlantic and Latin American areas. If both the posts which were maintained and new posts which were subsequently abolished are taken into account, France had the highest number of 'movements' (69), followed by Belgium (43), Australia (34), New Zealand (18), and Canada (17); in Latin America, Argentina comes first with 34, followed by Cuba (30), the Dominican Republic (21), Jamaica (20), Bolivia (19), Honduras (16), and Guyana (12). Jamaica and Guyana occupy the fourth and seventh positions respectively, although these two countries became independent only in the 1960s and therefore had less time than other countries to change their departmental structure. In both the Atlantic area and Latin America, the governments of Commonwealth countries are thus larger and more unstable in their composition than the governments of other countries — although the *political system* of Commonwealth countries, especially those of the Caribbean, has been more stable than those of surrounding nations. Only countries with very unstable forms of government (Argentina, Bolivia, the Dominican Republic in the late 1950s and 1960s) or which have had major political problems that were found difficult to handle (France, Belgium) displayed as much instability in their governmental composition as Commonwealth countries.

Yet, despite these cases, the ministerial structure of Atlantic and Latin American countries remained remarkably stable from 1945; it was indeed surprisingly stable, in view of the major social and economic changes which occurred during the period. An almost identical degree of stability of ministerial posts can be found in most countries of South and South East Asia. This high stability is perhaps due primarily to the fact that, although many South East Asian countries are new (only a few were never dependent on a European power — Japan, China, Thailand — a majority was created after 1945 and a near-majority in the 1950s), they are somewhat older as independent countries than African states and have generally had long traditions of administrative development under colonial rule. Moreover, South and South East Asian states have a higher degree of national identity: these were not countries which were suddenly created in an arbitrary manner and whose administrative structures were started almost entirely from scratch.

On average, countries of South and South East Asia had slightly under twenty-two different departments at one time or another during the 1946-76 period, five more than Latin American countries and about the same number as Atlantic states. Somewhat over eight of the portfolios remained the same throughout the postwar years, as many as in Latin America, but less than in the Atlantic area. Given that South East Asian countries had on average more departments than Latin American countries, the ratio of stable to changing ministries is lower in South East Asia — between a third and two-fifths — as against half in the other two areas, and the number of 'movements' is correspondingly higher. On average, five new departments were created and subsequently maintained, two were abolished, and six were set up but later abolished: this last figure is about double that for Latin America and the Atlantic area. Putting it differently, if 'failed' innovations are measured as a proportion of the total number of years during which all departments were in existence, they form between 7 and 8 percent of the total in South East Asia, against 4 percent in the other two areas.

There was thus more 'instability' in the composition of South and South East Asian governments than in the Atlantic area and in Latin America, but the difference is not vast. Moreover, a large part of the difference stems from governmental characteristics in four countries — Burma, India, Indonesia and South Vietnam — which are at variance from those of the other nations of the South and South East Asian group. Together, these four countries accounted for three-fifths of the 'failed' innovations in the area; if they were excluded, the pattern of evolution of the area would be almost identical to the pattern of evolution of ministries in the Atlantic or Latin American areas. The number of departments which were set up in the region falls from twenty-two to eighteen (sixteen in Latin America) with nearly eight departments remaining unchanged, five being new creations which lasted throughout the period, two abolitions of original departments, and only three 'failed' experiments.

New experiments and even ministerial instability were very marked, on the other hand, in Burma, India, Indonesia and South Vietnam. The size of governments changed fairly frequently, with the curious result, however, that there was little net growth over the period as a whole; and the nomenclature of ministries varied markedly over the years. In the four countries, on average, as many as thirty-five different departments were set up at some point during the period, almost double the number for the rest of the area (eighteen). While ten of these thirty-five posts remained unchanged, only four of the subsequent creations were maintained; three of the original departments were abolished; and no fewer than seventeen departments were set up and later abolished. Thus, half the total number of departments which existed at some point in these countries were 'failed innovations' — against one-sixth or less for the rest of the region, for the Atlantic area and for Latin America. With 170 movements for the four countries, there were twice as many changes as in the rest of the region.

The case of South Vietnam does not require detailed examination: the war and the various military coups led to an instability which is unparalleled in the rest of South and South East Asia. In Burma, the swelling of ministries in the late 1950s was followed by a sharp reduction as a result of the military takeover by General Ne Win in 1958; U Nu's return to power in the early 1960s was too short to lead to renewed growth. But, since the late 1960s, the government has increased slowly in size with the result that Burma had only five more departmental ministers in 1976 than in 1947 — the average for the region as a whole.

The evolution of Indonesia was broadly similar: the growth in the number of portfolios at the end of Soekarno's regime was followed by a drastic reduction when Suharto took over in 1965. This was subsequently followed by a further upsurge, a rapid decrease, and a slow growth of departments which led the Indonesian government to be twenty-four strong in 1976 — six more posts than in 1949. It was therefore appreciably larger than the average for the region as a whole, but remained within the range of some of the Commonwealth governments of the Atlantic area (Britain, Canada, Australia). The Indonesian experiment of a large government, with upwards of forty portfolios in the early 1960s, was coupled, however, with an attempt at building a hierarchical structure with a number of 'superministers'.

The Indian government has always been in part hierarchical: 'ministers of state' are appointed alongside and under the 'full' ministers and from time to time heads of departments are moved from the position of a 'full' minister to that of a minister of state. But this is not the only way in which changes in departmental structure have taken place in India. Substantial reorganizations and numerous experiments occurred, many of which appear to have failed, however, as the new departments were often subsequently

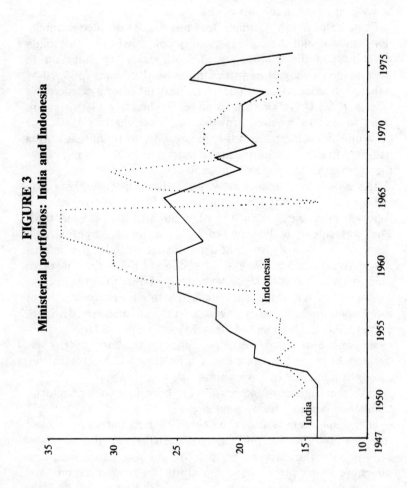

FIGURE 3

Ministerial portfolios: India and Indonesia

abolished. But the Indian government was never subjected to the very rapid movements which occurred in Burma and Indonesia. Indian governments never varied markedly in size: the maximum number of departments (including those led by ministers of state) was twenty-six in 1965. It is not change in size, but frequent, though gradual, alterations in departmental nomenclature which characterized the Indian government. There therefore seems to be some unease, or concern about the efficiency of the ministerial structure as well as perhaps, as in many Commonwealth countries, less of a belief in the almost constitutional status of departments. But it is not an unease which has so far led to a desire to entirely restructure the national government, as occurred in Indonesia or Burma.

Burma, Indonesia and South Vietnam therefore constitute a category of their own: the evolution of their governments is very different from that of almost all the other governments of South East Asia, Latin America and the Atlantic area. India, on the other hand, resembles other Commonwealth countries, although the movements are somewhat more marked. These are the countries which display the largest dose of 'instability' in ministerial nomenclature as well as the highest propensity to establish large governments. Elsewhere in the three areas, governments are very stable in composition and have had only a slow growth, except in a small number of continental countries in which coalitions are formed with difficulty and in a few politically very unstable Latin American countries.

3. The Instability of Communist Governments

The evolution of Communist governments since 1945 is very different. It is also rather paradoxical, since it is characterized by a very high degree of organizational instability, which contrasts with the stability of the leadership and indeed of the whole ministerial personnel.[1] For what is characteristic of Communist governments is not only that they are large — larger than those of almost all other countries, with seventy-seven different positions in the Soviet government and an average of twenty-three posts for all the other governments in the Communist world in 1976; they are also remarkable for a sizeable average growth over three decades following the Second World War; but they are even more remarkable because governmental growth in the Communist area was not the result of regular increases, nor even of one major boost occurring immediately after the Communist takeover. There were many ups and downs. At first, indeed, these governments on average *contracted* between 1946 and 1961, having first vastly increased — up to the mid-1950s — and subsequently sharply declined, and the reduction was indeed very pronounced in some countries (and especially in the Soviet Union). There was then a period of rapid expansion which resulted in an average gain of eight posts between 1961 and 1976, a net gain of one post every two years, while in the countries which we examined previously, the gain was of only one post per decade.

Yet, even between 1961 and 1976, the increase was not regular. There was considerable expansion in most Communist countries (though not in all) in the 1960s; there was then a contraction in the early part of the 1970s, which in turn was followed by renewed expansion in the mid-1970s. As a result of these see-sawing movements, the average size of the thirteen Communist governments of East Europe and North Asia (the only Communist governments in existence since the early 1950s) was still not as large in 1976 as it was in 1971, when it reached thirty departmental posts.

The developments which took place in Communist governments in the postwar period were thus appreciably more complex than in other governments. Communist administrations did not easily find an appropriate or efficient ministerial structure. There seem to have been two reasons for this state of affairs. First, East European and even North Asian countries often found it difficult to successfully imitate the Soviet structure of very large government with very specialized ministries for very long. These countries had frequently experienced more 'conventional' governments and a tradition had developed which ran counter to the Soviet structure. This is why, in a sense, the structure of the Soviet government is unique: it has been imitated in other Communist states, but only to an extent, and primarily by those countries which have been politically close to the Soviet Union. With sixty departmental ministers in 1946 and seventy-seven in 1976, the Soviet government has always been much larger than the governments of other Communist states. Even the Chinese government, which came closest to the Soviet government by number and type of departments, was always appreciably smaller; it has come to acquire a very different shape in the 1970s.

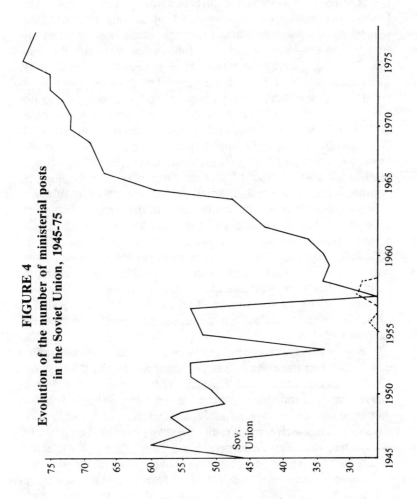

FIGURE 4
**Evolution of the number of ministerial posts
in the Soviet Union, 1945-75**

Yet even the Soviet government has not found it easy or even possible, at least until the late 1960s, to establish a firm ministerial structure. Reorganizations and changes in nomenclature have been frequent: they did not occur merely under Khruschev, who in the 1950s wished to impose a new 'functional' structure of departments, they also occurred before and afterwards. Overall, the Soviet government was characterized by a long and irregular tendency to decline slowly in size throughout the late 1940s and the first half of the 1950s. There then followed a very sharp drop, in 1957-58, as a result of the efforts at reorganization attempted by Khruschev, and for a few years the Soviet government was almost the size of an 'ordinary', though large, government elsewhere, with fewer than thirty-five departments — indeed, fewer than thirty in 1957. But, between 1961 and 1965, the Soviet government increased very rapidly in size to become larger than it had ever been; its growth was then much slower, yet significant, up to 1974, when it reached an all-time high of seventy-nine different portfolios. It declined a little afterwards to seventy-seven portfolios in 1976.

Movements in the size and composition of the Soviet government have thus had a major amplitude: gains or losses of several posts within a year have not been uncommon; there was a major dip in 1954 followed by an almost equal increase the following year. Not only were the increases and decreases considerable in absolute numbers, they were substantial in percentage as well, even despite the large size of the government. For instance, between 1960 and 1965, the government doubled in size, having been halved between 1956 and 1957.

Not surprisingly, these changes have meant considerable variation in the nomenclature of the departments. In the thirty years after the end of the Second World War, there were 246 different 'movements' or individual changes in departmental structure — that is to say an average of *eight changes per year*. The Soviet government is massive, but it is also massively modified on a yearly basis. Over the thirty year period, no fewer than 128 different departments were set up, but only fourteen of these were in existence continuously (11 percent of the total), while half or nearly half the admittedly much smaller number of ministries which had existed in the Atlantic area, Latin America, or South East Asia have remained in existence during the corresponding period. And even if we add the seventeen departments which have existed almost continuously throughout the period, only about a quarter of the ministries have remained relatively stable. Meanwhile, fifteen of the existing departments of the 1945 structure were abolished; eighty-two new ones were created, thirty-two of which were subsequently abolished, sometimes only a few years after their creation.

It is true, of course, as is often pointed out, that government departments in the Soviet Union are more numerous than elsewhere because they are more specialized: they might therefore seem to correspond to what are, in other countries, sections of ministries. Even the departments which have existed continuously throughout the postwar period are mostly different from, and appreciably more specialized than those which have remained continuously in existence in other countries. While defence, foreign affairs, finance and agriculture are departments equivalent to the 'basic' ministries which we found to form part of the core of other governments, the 'continuous' Soviet departments have included planning, foreign trade, merchant marine, railways or communications; they have also included such departments as higher education, light industry and building materials. Generally, social departments are much less numerous and more ephemeral, while the economic departments have been, occasionally at least, specialized to a degree which is totally unknown elsewhere. This situation is not altogether surprising, in view of the degree of economic interventionism which has characterized the Soviet Union: thus, not only heavy engineering, textiles or defence industries have a department, but also iron and steel, cotton, leather and oil — at least from time to time and depending on the reorganizations of the overall structure. But while it is true that this marked specialization indicates a major departure from the practice of the countries which we have so far examined, the size of the industry and the amount of governmental intervention suggests that the departments which are thus organized are not necessarily lighter or involved in fewer activities than the less specialized departments of other countries in which the volume of economic matters handled by the government is smaller. Only a detailed examination of the activities of government in various countries could give a precise answer to this question, but it seems at least reasonable to claim that the fifteen or so departments of a small country such as Denmark may not involve ministers in more problems than the seventy-five or so departments of the Soviet Union, which is fifty times larger in population and in which private activities are very limited.

The centralized organization of economic departments in the Soviet Union has obviously created problems of management and of control, some of which are indeed documented, in particular by the comments made by Khruschev who attempted to restructure the Soviet government on a different — and more 'rational' — functional model, only to find that his proposals were even less practical and effective than the more traditional practices. Hence the dip in the number of ministries and the almost immediate return to a more conventional arrangement. But, from the second half of the 1960s, a more acceptable solution seems to have been found to the question of the structure of the Soviet government since, for the first time since the Second World War, the number of yearly *movements* has fallen markedly, although it remains above the level which we found to exist in the three regions which we previously examined. Since the late 1960s, only a few departments have been set up, and very few have been abolished: of the almost 250 movements which occurred since 1945, only twenty-eight — scarcely more than a tenth — occurred in the course of the decade since the mid-1960s; the average number of yearly creations of departments was three, while in the previous two decades, eleven or twelve ministries were set up on average every year.

The Brezhnev-Kosygin period was therefore the first in the post-1945 period when the Soviet government appeared 'established' and the government seemed to move almost exclusively in the direction of steady growth, a development not unlike, as we shall see, the movements which were characteristic of many African and Middle Eastern governments. The Soviet Union may therefore have found a nomenclature of ministries acceptable to both the party and the bureaucracy. Whether such a nomenclature is — and is regarded as — effective is more difficult to say in view of the general tendency of the Brezhnev period to be one in which a premium was put on political stability at almost any cost. Indeed, in order to preserve stability, the Soviet government of the early 1970s has tended to solve problems of administrative structure by additions, rather than by reorganizations, and few departments have been abolished. But this solution cannot be adopted indefinitely, and, from 1974, the need to contract the massive government once more seemed to prevail; there may therefore be pressure in the future for a return to more radical organizations. But, for a decade at least, the Soviet government did enjoy a degree of stability which has been unparalleled in its history and indeed in that of the governments of other Communist countries.

For the instability of governmental structures is not merely a characteristic of the Soviet Union, it is a general feature of Communist states, both European and Asian. On average, the thirteen Communist countries of the European and North Asia group had fifty-five different posts throughout the post-1945 period, three times the average for Latin American countries and two and a half times the average for Atlantic and South East Asian countries. Albania, Hungary, North Vietnam and Mongolia had the four most stable Communist governments, yet all of them, except Albania, had a larger number of governmental posts than any Latin American country, Cuba being, significantly enough, the only one which came almost to the same level. Among Atlantic and South East Asian countries, only Belgium, France, Australia, Canada and the four 'unstable' South Asian countries which we analysed earlier created about the same number of departments during the period.

The number of ministerial departments which have existed in Communist states is in part the result of the comparatively larger size of all Communist governments, as we know: these governments usually had well over twenty ministries and indeed almost thirty ministries on average at the beginning of the 1960s and in the mid-1970s. Yet, although larger than the governments of other regions, Communist governments have never come very close to reaching the size of the Soviet government. On the whole, they have not attempted to cover branches of industry with the same degree of specialization, in part possibly because the level of industrialization is often lower than in the Soviet Union, and also because, even when it is higher (as in Czechoslovakia or East Germany), it has a narrower range of interests; industry is probably also, by tradition, comparatively more decentralized. By and large, Eastern European Communist governments have remained close to the Atlantic structure and seem to have adopted the Soviet arrangements only with some difficulty. Even by the mid-1970s, some Eastern European Communist governments remained very similar to their Atlantic counterparts, not merely those of Yugoslavia, which had nineteen members, and of Albania which had thirteen members, but those of Hungary (nineteen portfolios) and Czechoslovakia (sixteen portfolios). Indeed, the Czech government was no larger in 1976 than three decades earlier.

The case of Czechoslovakia is exceptional, admittedly, largely as a result of the adoption of a federal structure of government in the late 1960s. Elsewhere in Eastern Europe, governments were appreciably larger in the 1970s than they were in the 1940s, though only in two cases (East Germany and Romania) does one find an increase in size in the late 1960s and up to the 1970s paralleling that of the Soviet Union, with Bulgaria showing a tendency to follow suit, though at some distance. In the other Eastern European countries, the peak for the period was in the late 1950s: Poland thus had thirty-eight ministries in 1953-54, Hungary seventeen in 1957, Czechoslovakia twenty-nine in 1957.

The trends are not markedly different overall in the four North and East Asian Communist countries. China seemed for a time to be about to closely follow the Soviet Union both in the size of its government and in the specialized character of its ministries. The number of portfolios reached almost fifty in the late 1960s, after a long period of slow growth; the types of departments which were then in existence were broadly similar to those which had traditionally characterized the Soviet Union, one originality being the multiplication of ministries in charge of the engineering industry: there were up to eight such departments from the middle of the 1960s.

But, in 1972-73, the Chinese government underwent a major reform as a result of which the number of portfolios was cut to twenty; some new departments were subsequently created and the government reached thirty-one portfolios in 1976, but it no longer closely resembles the Soviet administration. In the late 1970s, its character was more similar to that of the North Korean government, which had never expanded to the size of the Chinese, although it experienced some growth up to the early 1970s and a contraction in 1973. Mongolia and North Vietnam, on the other hand, perhaps because of their closer ties with the Soviet Union, continued to increase the size of their governments in the 1970s, somewhat in the manner of the East German and Romanian governments.

Thus, nearly all Communist governments are larger than the governments of the Atlantic states, and nearly all have, nearly all the time, specialized departments covering in greater detail the various aspects of industrial activity. But only in the Soviet Union has this development so far led to the emergence of a mammoth government, the Chinese leadership having clearly felt that a government of the size which had been been reached was not 'manageable'. So far, other Communist governments have succeeded in containing growth within much lower limits: whether these governments are more effective as a result is a matter that only a detailed study of achievements can gradually resolve.

But, since the magnitude of the changes in the number and nomenclatures of departments is much larger in all Communist states than in Atlantic, Latin American and South East Asian states, it is valuable to examine more closely the history of the creation and abolition of departments, especially in Eastern Europe, where one can compare six countries (Albania and Yugoslavia having had a different evolution) which have followed with varying degrees of reticence the lead of the Soviet Union. By and large, there have been two big 'waves' of creations of departments. The first was in the first half of the 1950s, though it manifested itself earlier in Romania and Poland; indeed, in Bulgaria, Czechoslovakia and Hungary, this large wave was preceded by a first, smaller round of increases in the late 1940s. But, overall, the creation of departments in the 1952 to 1956 period was larger than that any time before or since in the six countries. Overall, a third of all the creations of departments which took place in the three postwar decades occurred during these five years. This was the period when, for instance, ministries of chemicals, coal, railways, forestry, were set up in Romania, or ministries of power, chemicals, paper, building materials, wood industry, were set up in Poland. By 1957, however, the impetus for the creation of new departments had waned; indeed, as early as 1956 the number of abolitions was larger than the number of creations to reach the all-time high for the six countries which we are examining here — a net decline of eleven departments in that year. The late 1950s were a period when governments declined in size in all six countries, with gains of one or two departments in 1958 and 1959 being more than offset by losses of nine departments in each of these years.

With the 1960s begins the second wave of gains in most, but this time not in all of the six Eastern European 'Soviet-inclined' Communist countries. Bulgarian governments had increased in almost every year between 1963 and 1974, but the main changes occurred between 1963 and 1968, especially in Czechoslovakia and East Germany, while 1966 to 1969 were the years of new creations in Romania, where for instance ministries of oil, electricity, machine-building, but also local government and youth were set up. These creations were to some extent compensated by losses at various points during the period, but, in general, these occurred primarily in the 1970s, especially in 1971 and 1973.

Poland and Hungary were markedly different in that they almost completely 'escaped' the second wave of changes, and it is this difference which accounts for the fact that, in Hungary in particular, the total number of movements is substantially smaller than in the other 'Soviet-oriented' Eastern European Communist states. Out of thirty-three creations of new departments which occurred in Poland during the three decades, only six occurred after 1957; and out of twenty-nine creations of new departments which occurred in Hungary during the same period, only three occurred after 1957, and none at all after 1964. In parallel, out of twenty abolitions of departments which occurred in Hungary during the three decades, only three occurred after 1957; in Poland, while the trend was not as marked since ten out of twenty-four abolitions occurred after 1957, there were none the less fewer abolitions in the last two decades than in the first.

Poland and Hungary seem therefore to have achieved from the late 1950s the kind of stability of governmental structure which the Soviet Union in turn achieved, as we saw, from the middle of the 1960s, but which no other 'Soviet-inclined' Eastern European Communist state has so far achieved. In Poland and Hungary, however, this relative stability of departments (especially in Hungary) has been obtained on the basis of a relatively small government — not very different from the type of governments which exist in Atlantic states. In particular, very specialized industrial ministries have not been set up in Hungary and only to a modest extent in Poland, some of the departments abolished in the late 1950s and early 1960s being among those which corresponded most closely to the Soviet model.

Instability in the structure of government is thus not universal in Communist states, but it is common and it seems to be associated with experiments in setting up highly specialized departments in the industrial, commercial and agricultural fields of the economy. These may not prove satisfactory after a few years or may no longer correspond to the direction in which the leadership wishes to see the country moving particularly fast. Only the Soviet Union has so far succeeded in having a very large government, with highly specialized ministries, and yet in maintaining, at least since the mid-1960s, a high degree of stability, which means slow growth, few creations of new departments and few abolitions of older ones.

The Soviet Union may have found an equilibrium for the structure of its departments. Meanwhile, except for Hungary and Poland which seem to have opted for a different — more Western — model, the other Communist countries continue to display growth and instability, indeed sometimes erratic movements in their ministerial arrangements. It therefore seems fair to conclude that because the Communist form of government has not by and large led to a stable ministerial structure, the need for a division of the overall governmental structure into two, or even three levels is more pressing; unless it is claimed that, on the contrary, since the Politburo and the Presidium of the Council of Ministers are most engaged in policy-making and coordination, changes in ministerial structure are less important and experimentation becomes a valuable instrument for improving the management of the public services.

4. Rapid Growth in the Middle East and Africa

In the course of the 1960s and 1970s, the size of governments in the Middle East and Africa increased substantially: departmental structures have tended to move away from a pattern characteristic of the Atlantic area or Latin America to one more resembling that of Communist states.

The development of ministries — indeed the setting up of ministries in many cases — is, in these two regions, a phenomenon of the 1960s. Only five African countries South of the Sahara were independent before 1960 and two of these, Sudan and Ghana, were independent from the mid-1950s only. Middle Eastern and North African countries are, in the main, somewhat older, but only half of them were or became independent immediately after the Second World War (eleven out of twenty-one). Some became independent in the 1950s (Libya, Morocco, Tunisia) while most of the states of the Arabian Peninsula emerged as independent nations with a government in the real sense of the word only in the 1960s. Thus, not only in the 1940s, but even in the late 1950s, the governmental structure was still inchoate or very new in many Middle Eastern countries. This accounts for the fact that the average size of governments in the region as a whole underestimates the real growth of Middle Eastern and North African governments. Calculated on the basis of countries which were independent in

1946, the average number of ministries in Middle Eastern governments increased from 10.3 to 15.4 between 1946 and 1961 and
reached 21.3 in 1976. Middle Eastern governments doubled in size
while those in Latin America and South East Asia increased by a
third; putting it differently, a departmental portfolio was added
every three years to Middle Eastern goverments, and a similar rate
of growth occurred in African governments from the 1960s.

The increase was large, but it was also regular and continuous.
From a mean of 12.7 positions in 1961-63, African governments
increased at the rate of 0.3 to 0.4 positions per year to 13.5 portfolios in 1966, 13.9 in 1968, 15.5 in 1971, 16.0 in 1973 and 17.6 in
1976. From about the same average in 1961, Middle Eastern and
North African governments advanced even faster to 14.0 in 1966,
16.5 in 1971, 17.6 in 1973 and 18.7 in 1976. By its regularity, the increase in the size of African and Middle Eastern governments differed from the growth patterns of Communist governments, but it
also differed by the fact that the net growth was almost equal to the
movements which occurred. New ministries were added throughout
the 1960s and 1970s — but few were abolished: there were seemingly few 'failed' experiments. This may be only a temporary state of
affairs, resulting from the fact that the countries are still new and
that many of them were still run by their original rulers in the
mid-1970s. Indeed, in a few cases, military coups have been followed by a reorganization of government and a reduction in the
number of ministerial posts; this was to some extent the case in
Ghana and Niger (in a manner resembling earlier developments in
Burma and Indonesia), but not in Nigeria or in many of the
French-speaking countries which were taken over by the military in
the late 1960s and 1970s.

The development was regular and based on periodic additions
because, by and large, Middle Eastern and African governments
started from a relatively small base corresponding to the structure
of Latin America or European governments, and added little to this
structure in their first few years as independent nations. Indeed, in
particular in the countries of the Arabian Peninsula, the base was
very small indeed and the government was altogether built from
scratch. This accounts in part for the greater yearly increase in the
size of the Middle Eastern governments than in that of African
governments. If three Arabian emirates in which the government
grew extremely rapidly between 1963 and the mid-1970s were excluded, the rate of growth of the rest of the countries of the Middle

East and North Africa is reduced by about one sixth (five departments instead of six) over the period.

This linear growth has resulted in the setting up of many specialized departments as in Communist states, but the character of the specialization differs from that of Communist countries and reflects the different economic basis of these states and the different economic goals of their governments. In African countries, in the early 1960s, governments included mainly traditional ministries. Three-quarters or more of the countries had departments of foreign affairs, finance, interior, justice, public works, agriculture, education and health, while two-thirds had an information ministry and about half departments of defence, economics, labour and trade. A scatter of departments — transport, local government posts, veterans — existed in a small number of countries: these were often drawn directly from the structure of the former 'mother-country' from which the new states emerged. Perhaps the most original of the departments which were created at the time was that of mines, which was set up in six African countries in the early 1960s.

By the mid-1970s, departments such as mines, water, planning, youth, tourism, had become appreciably more common: half the African countries had a ministry of mines, for instance. By examining the types and number of new departments set up in the 1960s and 1970s one can thus draw a picture of the concerns of African governments. One is 'social independence' — the recognition of authenticity — and this is shown by the setting up of ministries of culture and youth; another concern is that of communication development, which appears through departments such as transport and posts; and a third is related to the desire to develop the primary sector, shown by departments of mines, natural resources, power and water, as well as by departments dealing with agriculture, such as irrigation, livestock, etc. This pattern is repeated, with some differences, in the Middle East and North Africa, where, in particular in the Arabian Peninsula, departments of oil and water have been set up and where departments relating to the Arab or Moslem culture have also been created.

Although the growth has generally been large and indeed linear, it has naturally been more marked in some countries than in others. In some countries, the size of the government has become substantial, even by Communist standards. By 1976, a third of the African governments had twenty portfolios or more, and five of them had more than twenty-three (Ivory Coast, Nigeria, Gabon, Mauritania and Guinea); one country, Guinea, had the second largest government in the world. Nine — or nearly half of the Middle Eastern countries — had governments of twenty portfolios or more, three of which (Libya, Syria and Egypt), had over twenty-six ministries, with Egypt having thirty-six departments. It is among these countries that one finds those where experiments in setting up 'pyramidal' governments have taken place — without much success, as we saw in the previous Chapter.

The contemporary world is thus rather sharply divided into two groups of countries, those in which governments are relatively conventional and where the main offices of state are broadly the same as they were in the 1950s and those where there has been substantial growth and innovation in the 1960s and 1970s. The first category comprises by and large the countries of the Atlantic area, Latin America, and South and South East Asia: there has been some growth, though slow, and this growth has tended to be limited to the setting up of a few 'social' departments. The second group comprises the Communist world, Africa, and the Moslem world: in these three areas, governments are usually larger, and they are growing, often rapidly. The size of these governments reflects a substantial degree of specialization of the ministries. But, while the growth has been steady and indeed almost entirely regular in Africa and the Middle East, it has been chequered in the Communist world. Moreover, the field of growth has been different: in the Middle East and in Africa, expansion has taken place over the whole range of governmental activities, in education and social affairs, culture and 'guidance', as well as in the economy, although, in this respect, growth has been concentrated on the agricultural and energy sectors rather than on industry. In the Communist world, larger governments — and the Soviet government especially — have corresponded to a desire to give to industry maximum departmental coverage. But, as this growth has been accompanied by a substantial number of reorganizations, it seems that the leadership has found it difficult to achieve a truly acceptable solution. The paradox is that this chequered development of ministries has occurred in Communist states in the context of a very stable political system; in Africa and in the Middle East, the steady growth has occurred generally and to the same extent whether the leadership and the regime have or have not been stable.

Differences in the structure of government departments are thus remarkable. At the end of an evolution during which governments expanded rapidly and, indeed, in many cases, were created entirely from scratch, distinct patterns have emerged which correspond to the traditions and ideologies which characterize the contemporary world. The influence of 'constitutionalism' probably accounts for more 'traditional' governments in Europe and Latin America, although Commonwealth countries appear to be different because, there, the tradition is more strictly 'political' than constitutional, and the role of parties is essential. The desire for industrial development — but also the difficulties in applying this policy — has characterized Communist governments, although, in some cases, there seems to be a return to a more conventional ministerial structure. The aim is to press for cultural and social change in an economic environment dominated by primary production: this accounts for the nature and extent of governmental growth in Middle Eastern and African countries. These governments are thus very different from Latin American and South East Asian governments although these, too, nominally belong to the Third World, as the services on which governments wish to give emphasis are manifestly different. One matter is common to all countries, however; ministries are set up and ministers are given portfolios in order to be able to control, as efficiently as possible, the implementation of policies. This raises the question of the relationship between government and bureaucracy to which we need now to turn.

Note

1. *World Leaders*, pp. 172-5 and 234-7.

7. GOVERNMENT AND ADMINISTRATION

The questions 'Where does government end?' and 'Where does the administration begin?' have more often given rise to polemics than to systematic analyses. It seems that government and administration are engaged in trench warfare with frequent skirmishes and occasional major attacks. There is rancour and even anger on both sides: civil servants are often accused by politicians of wanting to take over the government; ministers are often accused by civil servants of being insufficiently competent, or perhaps even interested, to understand the technicalities of administration. Each group feels misunderstood and unlucky in having to operate with the other group.

This situation can perhaps be explained by the fact that, while the border between government and administration is usually well-marked in terms of personnel, it does not correspond to any clear difference in activity. Students of public administration have long pointed out that there is no distinction between politics and administration: the process of decision-making is the same. The old-fashioned view that the government initiates policy and the administration implements it has been replaced by one of interpenetration. There may be a hierarchy, but there is no substantive break and no real division of subject-matter on which to peg an institutional distinction between politicians and administrators.

Yet, even if there is no break in the chain between political and bureaucratic decisions, indeed if decisions are labelled administrative for reasons of convenience rather than substance or simply because some problems are relatively uncontentious, governments are usually distinct from the bureaucracy. First, they normally operate in the limelight while the administration remains in the shadows: they are endowed with an aura which civil servants do not have. But, more importantly, members of governments have different origins from civil servants: they are catapulted from outside over the heads of administrators who form corps in which careers start at the bottom or at least at the middle echelons. Thus the government leads the bureaucracy but ministers have not followed the bureaucratic line to the top. This state of affairs makes the matter of 'Where does the government end and the administration begin?' extremely relevant, especially since the division between government and administration has given rise to such polemics. Hence the questions: 'Where is the border to be?' 'How far should the government extend into the bureaucracy?' But hence, too, a more fundamental question: 'Has the division to be such that it necessarily leads to conflict?' Is it not possible to devise a formula whereby the two elements of the chain could truly cooperate rather than be engaged, overtly or covertly, in forms of antagonism? As there is no substantive distinction between administrative and political decisions, could the division between membership of the government and membership of the bureaucracy be blurred to such an extent that a merger between the two groups might even be envisaged?

Does Government Have to Have an End?

The most radical solution would obviously be for government and administration to belong to one and the same group. Western European systems have emphasized, indeed sharpened as much as possible, the distinction between politicians and administrators, and thereby created for themselves the conditions of a major conflict. Is it therefore realistic to look for an opposite arrangement by which the distinction would be less neat and at the limit disappear? For this to be the case, there seem to be three, and only three solutions. One would be for governments to be recruited from the civil service; the second would be for the civil service to be recruited from among politicians; and the third would be a subtle mix between political and civil service careers. These arrangements do occur, to some extent at least, in the contemporary world, but they are relatively rare and seem to depend on special circumstances.

The rarest case is that of the pure administrative state, of the state in which the whole government is made up of civil servants. There is then no end to the government in that the government resembles — is — purely and simply the top of the civil service pyramid. Orders flow from ministers to the lower echelons in exactly the same way as they flow, within the civil service of a Western European country, from the permanent secretary or director-general lower down the hierarchy.

But such a situation is rare for two reasons. First, it depends on the existence of a very strong, highly legitimate, almost unquestioned single ruler who can provide legitimacy on his own to the structure of the whole edifice. Instances of such arrangements have therefore existed only in monarchical systems where change or development is very limited. In most situations, on the contrary, the ruler simply does not have enough personal strength to dispense completely with men from outside who will give him support and buttress his strength, be they from the aristocracy, the army, or even from other groups. And second, even if the ruler can dispense with outside support, he is unlikely to rely entirely on the bureaucracy as an organization: he will want to rely on men whom he can trust, in whom he can confide. He may draw this entourage from among the civil service, but some of the appointees will pass over others or will be moved from one part of the service to another to fulfil some special functions which the leader wishes them to implement. In this way a government is constituted — that is to say the leader appoints a group of men on whom he can count, or thinks he can count. Although they may have been drawn originally from the civil service, the fact that they have received the leader's stamp of approval puts them in a different category from other civil servants. And, consequently, the question arises of the type of linkage between members of the government and the rest of the bureaucracy. If, in turn, members of the government do not find that they can fully trust those civil servants below them who have moved up the ladder according to the promotion rules of the civil service, they will want in turn to appoint some of their supporters to the positions directly under their own. Thus, the border between government and administration is constantly rolled back, and the occasions for conflict and jealousies are multiplied.

Governments of an entirely civil service character thus rarely exist: they are merely an extreme case which is approximated only in special circumstances. Nor do opposite extreme situations exist very frequently either: this is the case of a public sector structure in which there is, in effect, no regular civil service at all and where the totality of the personnel is political. The whole of the bureaucracy then belongs to the government, being appointed by the leader, the ministers, and by their subordinates with only one consideration, namely that they be part of the political group or faction which is in power and that they therefore share the goals, ideology or standpoints of this political group.

Such a situation is obviously rare in the contemporary world, since it is almost universally felt that the technical character of most questions precludes any government about to come to power from being rash enough to want to replace the whole of the existing bureaucracy with another group of men who would be more sympathetic to their views. Indeed, even if the new political group wished to operate such a 'clean-up', it would simply not find the trained personnel able to fill the required positions. Thus, an operation of this kind has to stop at some point, and cannot affect the totality of the civil service.

Yet, some practices have constituted somewhat watered down versions of this extreme model: the American spoils system arrangement was perhaps the closest approximation and the current American model still has more than a few traces of its early origins. This is why it is so difficult to state where the United States government ends. It is clearly not composed merely of the relatively small number of secretaries who head the various departments; it does not even stop at assistant secretaries, since many appointments below this level are made on the same basis as those of secretaries and assistant secretaries. There is genuine interpenetration between the 'political' personnel, appointed without tenure, and the 'civil service' personnel, whose career is defined by age and seniority rules. What the American practice has done has been to roll back the borders of the government and indeed to create a huge 'no man's land' into which the government extends. Government ends, in the United States, where the president and his entourage cease to be interested in the substance of the decision. And a very old tradition suggests that this point occurs at a relatively low level in the bureaucratic structure, although, periodically, critics have felt that the frontier should be brought upwards.

But the reason why critics sometimes raise the issue is that the

American government has to pay some price for extending itself so far down within the bureaucratic hierarchy; and the price is so high that compromises are constantly made, and regular civil servants indeed have increasingly come to occupy positions of 'responsibility'. The 'spoils system' and the 'merit system' do not work in unison. There is no real merger between 'political' appointments made by presidents or their secretaries and the civil service appointments which have a regular career. There is, in fact, opposition and one which cannot be suppressed because the bureaucracy is too large, and the federal government's activities too widespread, for the political personnel to be, despite their numbers, more than a small element above a huge structure. The situation might have been different had presidents less frequently alternated between the two parties and if new presidents had not therefore felt obliged to surround themselves with entirely new groups. When two presidents of the same party follow each other, there is more gradual change and therefore less of a sharp reminder to federal civil servants that they belong to a different circle. But as there is frequent change in both party and president, the result is a periodic emphasis on the need to draw the line between political personnel and civil service personnel. American governments may end somewhat lower down than Western European governments, and the frontier may be twisted and tortuous, but it nevertheless exists. It simply does not seem possible, in a large industrialized country, to turn the whole civil service into the government.

Hence a third, and markedly more frequent solution to the problem of the distinction between politicians and civil servants. This consists in trying to merge the political and administrative elements by giving a political 'colour' to the civil service while allowing it to operate according to 'normal' bureaucratic rules of career and tenure. This seems to be possible, however, only where a strong political party dominates the polity and is, and is known to be, permanently in power. Such is the situation in Communist states, as well as in single-party states where the party has strong tentacles within the population and is engaged in shaping the society according to its views. For the paradoxical outcome of the repeated distinction between party and state structure in the Communist states is an effective blending, though to a varying degree, of the party element and the state element.

In Communist states, members of the civil service 'half' — the technicians and other specialists — are able to move up the

bureaucratic ladder to the top echelons within the government: as
we saw, ministers, and especially deputy-chairmen of the Councils
of Ministers, have a say, not merely in management, but in coordination and even in policy-making. But these civil servants agree
to abide by party rules and their whole promotion prospects depend, and will continue to depend, on an association with the party
hierarchy. Thus there is osmosis, even if the party element is more
visible in some parts of the government than in others; indeed, this
osmosis can successfully take place because the party component is
never quite the same from one segment to the next, even from one
government member to another. The result is a structure in which
one can say only — as one can say, *mutatis mutandis*, for the
American structure — that the government extends very low down
into the civil service hierarchy: the distinctions which occur are
matters of degree, convenience, occasion. It is therefore irrelevant
to ask whether a vice-minister, in the Soviet Union, is or is not part
of the government; it would also be irrelevant to ask a similar question for men located even lower in the bureaucratic structure.
Where government ends is not just unclear in Communist states
and other single-party systems based on the same strict model; the
border is pushed back into a territory which extends so far away
that it is forever in an indefinite haze. There is, in truth, no end to
government, merely a difference in the mix between what is government and what is usually called, but carefully left undefined, the
administration.

Governments with Clearer Boundaries

It would be very neat to be able to contrast the case of these governments with 'no end' to an opposite group of countries in which, on
the contrary, the government has very sharp edges and there is a
clear cut-off point where government ends and the bureaucracy
begins. This is, admittedly, what the 'classical' theory of democratic government suggests should occur, by stating that the
ministers, responsible to the people in a direct or indirect manner,
should implement their policies by way of civil servants, neutral
and impartial, moving up the echelons of a career entirely distinct
from the political career. But, although it is the case in many countries that the list of members of the government constitutes only the
top echelons of the administrative machine, the frontier is often

much more vague. While the theory on which the system is based is one of separation and of clear recognition of the specific role of each group, the practical needs of management, coordination, and policy-making entail that there be close links between the politicians and the administrators. A variety of devices have therefore been invented to overcome the difficulty. Some of these are informal; others are more formal and constitute a clear break from the principle of a sharp division between the political and the administrative personnel.

Among the informal devices is the substantial infiltration of civil servants in many governments, including governments of the pure parliamentary type. This is usually done by the backdoor, however, and the extent of the phenomenon can be measured by considering in detail the occupational and career backgrounds of members of government in the various countries — a point which we shall examine in the coming volume. But another, and indeed essential device is provided by ministerial staffs, whose numbers have indeed multiplied in many countries. The *cabinets* which exist to help ministers are clear means of ensuring that the head of the department is not alone in his encounters with the bureaucracy; as a matter of fact, a final assessment of the effect of this development has become difficult to make, as members of the personal staffs of ministers are also often drawn, not merely from outsiders, but from members of the civil service on whom the minister knows or thinks he can rely but whose skills and knowledge of the bureaucracy he needs in order to implement his views. Ministerial *cabinets* constitute buffers which help to reduce the distance between what is the government and what is the administration. Whatever their well-known drawbacks (that they are too small to ensure that the ministers be obeyed throughout the department, that, since they are often in part composed of civil servants, they put the department's case to the minister rather than the minister's case to the department), they clearly constitute essential mechanisms which have been recognized as important, even by governments, such as the British government, which long resisted their development.

Meanwhile, in many countries, these informal devices are supplemented by formal arrangements whereby governments are composed of more than one level. In a minority of states — about a third — there are junior ministers with various titles who work with and under ministers in order to help them in their managerial tasks.

212 The Organization of Governments

Thus, it is still the case that in most countries, ministers do not find it necessary or possible to appoint subordinates drawn from the political circles; in these cases the immediate subordinates of ministers are in the top echelons of the civil service. But the fact that the posts exist in a third of the nations shows that in many governments, too, there is a recognized need for an intermediate level which will help the ministers to work with and influence the administrators.

It would be wrong to exaggerate the importance of this development. First, the countries in which these posts exist are a minority, although it is a minority which is spread across the world and includes some of the more traditional cabinet systems, and Britain to begin with, as well as countries which have leader-based governments which might naturally be expected to be 'hierarchical'. In 1976, out of thirty-seven countries outside the Communist world which had positions of junior ministers, eight were from the Atlantic area, among which Britain and France figured prominently; these posts also existed in almost half the black African states (sixteen out of thirty-eight). The area of the world in which they were least common was the Middle East (four countries out of twenty-one), perhaps because many governments in that part of the world, as we saw in the last Chapter, had been set up almost from scratch in the 1960s. Thus cabinet governments with long traditions of a strict distinction between government and administration were as likely to have posts of junior ministers as newly-independent countries.

Second, the development is also still limited because while a third of the countries of the world had junior ministers, only a small minority of ministers, in each government, were given help in this manner. There were about 200 junior ministers across the world in 1976, or about 4.5 posts for each government which had them — a much smaller number than there were ministers. Only in a few countries was the number of junior ministers approaching that of full ministers, and only in a few others was the number at least substantial. At the other end of the range, in eight countries, there was only one junior minister and, in another six, there were only two. In these fourteen countries, as well as in those where there were three, four or five junior ministers, the position remained exceptional. It was designed to handle the particular problems of a field of government; it was not a means of altering the governmental structure in general.

The countries in which large numbers of junior ministers are appointed included Britain (with two 'layers' — that of the ministers of state and that of the parliamentary secretaries, in all over forty), France (where there are about as many 'state secretaries' as there are ministers), and India (where positions vary rather frequently); the positions were also extensively used in countries as diverse as Gabon, Pakistan, Sudan, Belgium and Egypt. Taken together, these countries accounted for half the number of junior ministers in 1976: these were the countries where government truly had two or even three levels, and where the border between government and administration was extended markedly downwards within the bureaucracy.

Elsewhere, there was usually no systematic desire to 'cover', protect, or help ministers, by a second layer of 'official' members of the government. The device of 'junior ministers' thus does not correspond to a clear-cut theory of what government should be and how it should connect with the civil service. The technique seems to be used more to meet special needs in an 'empirical manner'. What appears to be the case is that, in some situations, governments leave to the civil service the whole of the running of affairs below one general layer of departmental ministers; in others, junior ministers are appointed in only some of the departments, yet elsewhere junior ministers are appointed nearly everywhere and constitute a fully developed layer of the governmental machine. Nor is this indeed all, as the junior ministers may not always be drawn from the political sector and civil servants may be appointed to help the ministers, although they may then come to acquire a governmental status.

In general matters, the appointment of junior ministers has also to be seen in connection with the development of the personal staff (the 'cabinets') of each of the ministers. Thus, the overall practice is one where some ministers are protected, so to speak, by an 'avant-garde' of junior ministers, while others may have at their disposal, not one or two men or women subordinated to them in a hierarchical manner, but a whole group of staff, whose role is to examine the civil service decisions and indeed occasionally to delve low down into the decisions taken by the departments. Formally, the functions fulfilled by junior ministers are somewhat different from those of the personal staff but, in reality, the difference is not always very marked. Indeed, some junior ministers are 'at large', in that the minister does not give them a specific sub-section of the department to direct personally, but uses them for general advice or for delicate tasks (a function which parliamentary secretaries often fulfil in Britain). Conversely, some members of the personal staff of ministers, when the staff is substantial, as in the ministerial *cabinets* of a French minister, may be somewhat specialized and cover only specific sub-segments of the minister's province. Indeed, in general, although they may theoretically be empowered to supervise the activities of civil servants down the line, the contacts of members of the personal staff of ministers are necessarily concentrated at the top echelons: their effective role is therefore not likely to be markedly different from the functions fulfilled by junior ministers.

Thus the question of the role of ministerial assistants — whether junior ministers or members of a personal office — can be analysed along a continuum ranging from a pure 'line' to a pure 'staff' position. At one extreme, ministerial assistants are a clearly recognizable echelon in the hierarchy of the department, and, when this hierarchical structure covers the whole range of activities of the department, it may be suggested that the department is organized along the lines of a 'grand' ministry with the minister being, in fact, a 'superminister' acting through assistants. This is what tended to happen in the defence field throughout the world when the various service ministers were demoted and became junior ministers. But this situation is rare in other governmental fields, as are instances of 'superministers'. Interestingly enough, in the case of defence departments, reorganizations have occurred in several countries, as a result of which the service departments have been altogether abolished and a new division sometimes introduced between 'personnel' and 'supply', while the heads of the three armed services — who are the equivalents of the top echelons of the bureaucracy in other fields — report directly to the defence minister. A 'super-ministry' has been created, but the effect is that the 'fluctuating border' between politics and administration has moved upwards and the movement has benefited the bureaucracy.

If one moves away from this extreme, but rare, hierarchical structure in which departments are subdivided into sections each of which is headed by a junior minister, one finds the relatively more frequent occurrence of departments in which one or two sections only are given a political head, while the rest of the department is directly dependent on the minister. This occurs for instance when a department was previously autonomous and is incorporated in a

larger ministry: some recognition is given to the newly amalga-
mated section, as conflicts are anticipated or it is expected that the
merger will only be accepted with difficulty by civil servants and
groups lobbying the department. Although the junior minister in
charge of the section is formally in a 'line' relationship with the
minister, he has in reality a somewhat ambivalent role. On the one
hand, he administers the sub-section of the department 'for' the
minister, while presumably representing this section of the department against other interests; on the other, he is the agent of the
minister in order to achieve a greater degree of centralization and at
least greater loyalty to the department overall. Thus, the situation
of these junior ministers bears some similarity to the case of
ministers without portfolio who are subordinated to the prime
minister. The junior minister, like the minister without portfolio,
may have a special responsibility, but he is also appointed to ensure
that, as a result, the section concerned is better integrated with the
whole department.

A third type of junior minister is fully 'at large': the case often
occurs in treasury departments, although 'second' ministers of
finance are sometimes in charge of a special section, for instance,
that of the budget. Junior ministers 'at large' can also be found in
other departments, when these are so vast that the minister needs
an overall subordinate. The minister may informally ask the
'second' minister to take special responsibility for a particular section, but the division of responsibility may not always be clearly
defined and the junior minister may simply be assigned tasks as
these arise in order to relieve the minister.

The members of ministerial *cabinets* constitute a fourth group,
somewhat, but only somewhat, different from those of junior
ministers. Of course, members of the staff of ministers have no formal responsibility: they are not in the line of 'command' in the
department. However, as, in practice, they acquire some authority
as a result of their position close to the minister, and as civil servants down the line are often unable to have more than occasional
personal contacts with the minister himself, the role of the staff
members is not very different from that of junior ministers who are
appointed at large: there is here only a variation in degree. If the
staff of the minister is composed of very junior men and if their
views are not felt to be often accepted by the minister, they are
likely to do little more than give advice to their political 'master',
but if they are senior and widely respected, their power may be as

large as and not markedly distinct from that of junior ministers.

The question of 'Where government ends' is both difficult to answer in practice and theoretically intriguing. It is cloaked in mystery and even humbug, largely because it seems that no serious analysis has been made as to what could be a sensible, rational, and indeed workable answer. There is no theory of the linkage between government and administration taking into account the psychological and organizational problems posed by the linkage; there is merely a hope that the problem will not arise in the form of major confrontations, as the conflict between civilian and military power has so often exploded. Since civil servants do not possess arms, they are unlikely to overthrow governments forcibly, but there has been much comment about their real or imagined power to undermine both the decisions of governments and the confidence of ministers. Such a situation should not be allowed to continue without a major overhaul, as it results in serious lack of trust, probable if not certain loss of efficiency, and the introduction of palliatives which obscure, rather than clarify, the role of officeholders.

The simplest solution is, of course, that which has been adopted in Communist states and followed in some other single-party systems, but it begs the question altogether since it seems predicated on there never being any change in the ideological colour of the political personnel. It is therefore, in truth, not a solution. Although wasteful in resources and energy, the American solution is probably the one which at least approximates the greatest honesty; it has the advantage of ensuring rotation at the top of the bureaucracy to a greater extent than other systems, and it restores the political function to its true importance. Yet it does not seem to avoid altogether the danger of 'undercover' rule by the civil service; indeed, it has not suppressed the conflict between the government and the bureaucracy, and its real or perceived administrative costs are such that it is unlikely to be adopted by more than a few countries — and especially not by those which give great prominence to the technical competence of the civil service. The question, therefore, is open, and will perhaps remain without solution for a substantial period. Meanwhile, members of bureaucracies will continue to feel both threatened and worried by their political masters; they are likely often to undermine them or even conspire in overthrowing them, as has frequently occurred in Third World countries, while they display elsewhere, in some cases at least, a tendency to stay on the sidelines instead of binding their energies to help governments to carry out their tasks.

8. CONCLUSION

The reasons why structures of government need to be studied are simple but overriding: these structures have to provide the acceptable and efficient mechanisms whereby governments can cope with both the political and the administrative problems which they face. There was a time when cabinet systems were thought to be the natural end-states of the evolution of these structures; there has since been a suggestion that cabinet government is about to disappear — indeed is disappearing before our very eyes. Neither conclusion is warranted by the facts of the evolution of government over the last few decades: cabinet governments exist, but they are only one among a number of types of governments. These types have become more numerous and more complex, and yet none of them seems to meet the overall requirement of solving both the political and administrative problems of our societies.

There are five broad types of governmental arrangements in the contemporary world. This is a simplification because governmental structures do not fit easily into types, but are spread along two dimensions of hierarchy *v.* equality and of unity *v.* differentiation. If we consider these five types, however, we have a reasonable approximation of the ways in which governments are currently organized. One of these arrangements remains so far relatively inchoate: this is the one, recently adopted in many Third World states, by which governments are divided into two separate bodies, a revolutionary or military council and a 'regular' government.

Although the formula probably has much to commend it from a policy-making and managerial point of view, it still corresponds mainly to the desire to buttress the political strength of leaders emerging after a coup and not to an administrative preoccupation with the nature and speed of public decision-making. It needs to be more rigorously applied before it becomes a genuinely effective form of government. Another type, probably the most common, and certainly common in much of the Third World, is the hierarchical government in which ministers and their subordinates depend wholly on the leader and where essential decisions are made by the leader. In contrast, cabinet government maintains a reciprocal relationship of power and influence between leaders and ministers while the overall structure of government remains profoundly united. In Communist countries, on the other hand, there are at least three bodies and levels among which the government is divided, while the American structure forms a category of its own by displaying a unique degree of decentralization only partly compensated by the personal staff of the president increasingly attempting to bring more closely together the many agencies of the executive.

Hierarchical Governments

Hierarchical governments are numerous, but their origins have little in common. They are, in some ways, a residual category, comprising as they do traditional monarchies and some regular presidential systems, governments led by charismatic founders of the state and executives run ruthlessly by 'usurpers'. They are the least elaborate of the forms of contemporary executives and consequently the least likely to be the basis of future governments. For they depend primarily for their maintenance on a relatively unsophisticated political system and society. First, hierarchical governments require the firm control of one man over the society, for the leader has to be able, not just to appoint and dismiss his subordinates, but to appoint them without fear of criticism from among any group from which he chooses to select them: ministers have to be without a political constituency; they must not even be viewed as possessing the kind of technical skills which, sooner or later, would make them indispensable. Nor should there be a large bureaucracy below the ministers, as power and inertia within this bureaucracy constitute limitations on the leader's initiatives and ministers might correspondingly acquire much influence. Hierarchical government has to be, to become more than just a passing phenomenon in a society, very small government. Because they pressed for large governments, the enlightened despots of the past, as we saw, came to form governments led by bureaucracies; these in turn constituted major obstacles for the leaders and their governments ceased to be, in truth, hierarchical. For complex governments, the hierarchical model is not a stable form of executive structure. On occasion, a military leader will attempt to rule hierarchically after coming to power in the wake of a revulsion against a discredited regime, but the government will not remain hierarchical for more than a short period unless the country is so small and isolated, and demands for change are so minute, that the system can, so to speak, be immune from the 'contagion' of more complex forms of government elsewhere in the world.

Cabinet Government:
Its Resilience and its Problems

By and large, hierarchical governments tend to move either towards a two-level, semi-collective set of arrangements relatively close to the Communist pattern or towards a cabinet form of executive. Meanwhile, the cabinet system, despite the many internal and external pressures to which it has been subjected, has so far survived better than some had predicted in the 1960s, although there is some doubt about its future strength and spread. In the 1980s, cabinet government exists in about fifty countries, in Western Europe, in the Commonwealth, and among a number of presidential systems of the constitutional or near-constitutional variety. In these governments, the leader is helped by a group of men and women who have been in politics together for a substantial period and who are therefore jointly and continuously involved in affairs of state (even if they are, for substantial periods, in the opposition). This is clearly a sophisticated and complex form of government as it depends on the maintenance and strength of a balanced relationship within the political groups.

For cabinet government to thrive, a number of conditions have therefore to be met; these are currently mainly the result of a strong and lively party system, preferably neither single-party nor very divided, although the cabinet system can and does survive, for a while at least, under both these extremes. Western European countries have, by and large, party structures of this type even if, in the French case at least, but also in Finland, constitutional arrangements have had to provide some reinforcement to strengthen the party structures. Many Commonwealth countries have inherited from Britain a markedly strong tendency to organize cleavages around political parties and thus to build parties which have solid roots. And a few presidential systems have maintained or recently developed, despite the built-in tendency of the constitutional arrangements to break the party structures and to develop factions, a strong party basis on which the government is built.

Cabinet government needs to have a closely-knit group at the top. In the contemporary world, parties have become the only way in which this can practically be achieved. In the past, interconnected ruling families did occasionally provide such a group base for governments; here and there traces of this occurrence subsist in more isolated countries of the world. But monarchs have often broken the basis for such a development, because they wished, or felt the need to promote social and economic change and therefore, like the enlightened despots of the eighteenth century, worried lest aristocratic or other ruling families might want to slow down or indeed prevent change: thus, monarchical systems more commonly set up hierarchical and bureaucratic governments than cabinet systems on a 'non-party' basis.

Parties create teams at the top, on the contrary, because where parties are solidly implanted there is in truth no one who has enough political strength to run the country alone. Only in extreme circumstances, of war, of total political reconstruction, does a leader emerge who is so much above the rest of his party that he can dispense with the support of colleagues and organize at will the governmental machine; and, even in such cases, the hegemony of the leader only lasts a few years. Party then reemerges on a collective basis, with little oligarchies gradually climbing the ladder by helping each other inside the organization and against other forces. Parties are thus the central elements in the characteristic structure of cabinet government, and so long as parties remain firm structures in the political systems of the contemporary world, cabinet government also has a strong chance of remaining one of the main arrangements by which countries are ruled.

Yet, cabinet government is clearly ill-suited to the requirements of modern administration in a number of ways. First, it simply does not solve the difficult problem of decision-making in complex societies, because it is better equipped for short-term, on-the-spot decisions than for long-term planning. It is too egalitarian, at least within the oligarchies which run political parties; it is also too 'political' in its overall conception. The semi-egalitarian groups which lead the countries where cabinet government prevails dissipate on consensus-building a large segment of their time and energy; policies cannot be imposed from above, as leaders have to take into account, except for very short periods, the views of their colleagues. The whole decision-making arrangements are based on agreements, arrived at gradually, not on order and commands passed on to subordinates. There may be some incentive to follow the leader when an election victory creates a 'state of grace' or simply the feeling that, without the leader, the party would be lost, but this sentiment soon fades out. Given the pressure from each ministerial department to make suggestions or to propose ideas which do not correspond to those which other departments are making, cabinet government quickly settles for its main decision-making mode, the committee of relatively equal members discussing together the basis for a compromise between opposite standpoints. It may be that collective decisions are relatively infrequent in the rather large context of the full cabinet, but the cabinet's existence is the raison d'être for the committees in which decisions are taken collectively. Cabinet government is government arrived at by discussion, one in which what is embarrassing may be kept undecided for a very long period.

However, perhaps the major reason why cabinet government is ill-suited to the needs of long-term policy-making is not because decision-making is egalitarian or consensual: an even more serious problem results from the fact that cabinet government is in essence too 'political' to be sufficiently concerned with 'administrative' or 'managerial' matters. There is, in truth, some incongruity in a system which trains men to become decision-makers in an administrative field by giving them primarily the tools of the coalition-makers, the 'conspirators', or the public orators. Cabinet members may be able to convince a group or a crowd to follow a policy: they are not, by training and probably by temperament, men or women who are primarily interested in developing ideas and proposing programmes. Within political parties, research and analysis has a low priority, at any rate in the main, and research is not usually conducted by truly active politicians at the top of their party. Understandably enough, from the point of view of the immediate individual or group priorities of the party leaders, public campaigning and internal struggles occupy the front of the scene: consequently, even when they started as engineers, planners, economists, social scientists, those who come to the top of their party can rarely continue to address themselves to policy-making in the manner of those who stayed in these occupations. This situation, coupled with the relatively short careers as ministers which we shall examine in the coming volume, has the effect of tilting the interest of the men at the top of parties in the direction of what have to be called 'purely political' problems (what is in French called *la politique politicienne*) rather than in the direction of policy-making or administrative questions. It has often been pointed out that many cabinet leaders and ministers are concerned with short-term questions and that cabinet members have a two-dimensional, rather than three-dimensional view of political life. This disease is endemic: it stems from the nature of decision-making and from habits developed during a pre-ministerial career. But it naturally has the effect of making cabinet government ill-equipped for the requirements of complex modern societies.

This situation is not corrected by the increasing part played by the bureaucracy, for politicians find it correspondingly more difficult to relate psychologically to the concerns of civil servants. And the more these are competent to solve policy problems, the more difficulties arise in terms of claims of disloyalty, on the one hand, and counter-claims of ineffectiveness or even ineptitude on the other. In reality, cabinet government is based on the existence of a yawning gap between politicians and administrators. The system can only work if the two groups are fundamentally different, and yet the two have to cooperate, indeed understand each other. Hence, the perpetuation of a number of myths, whereby civil servants are induced to be loyal to the political masters. But these, in turn, can only realistically be maintained if politicians accept that civil servants should benefit from a number of sought-after measures which reduce the inefficiency of the bureaucracy (tenure, size of staff, etc.) and which lower the general reputation of the administration with the public as a whole. There is not, and in truth cannot be, a real 'understanding' between government and bureaucracy in the context of cabinet government: and policy-making, coordination, and indeed management must ultimately suffer.

Admittedly, in practice, many types of cabinet government reach some kind of compromise. Perhaps the most important of these comes from the fact that the distinction between politicians and administrators is often reduced as a result of a number of accidents. One of these is that ministers and governments generally operate as if they were purely formal elements in the decision-making process: this was the case in France in the 1946 to 1958 period of the Fourth Republic; this is almost certainly the case in countries where coalitions are weak and transient; and this is to some extent the case in Japan, where ministers rotate posts so quickly that their hold is likely to be minimal. But another form of 'accidental' solution results from the other extreme situation. When the same party stays in power for long periods, there comes to be an osmosis between the leaders of the party and the civil service and the careers of the two groups become almost indissolubly linked: this type of situation occurred in France between 1958 and 1981 as well as in a number of presidential systems outside Europe (Mexico for instance). Even if the osmosis is not complete, there is at least an interpenetration of ideas which has the effect of eroding the barriers between cabinet government and administration: Sweden before 1976 was an example of this state of affairs. It has been the misfortune of Britain since the 1960s that, at the very time when she badly needed long-term policy planning in order to reconstruct her economy and indeed to reform a number of out-moded aspects of her social life, the changes of party hold of the government have been so frequent that the association between civil servants and politicians has never had time to become strong.

Thus, while cabinet government is manifestly a subtle mechanism well-suited to collective decision-making, it does not provide a satisfactory basis for the solution of the administrative problems which modern societies require. The fact that it has lasted for so long without major turmoil is both the result of the fact that there has been only a very slow realization, in many countries, that better and more systematic policy-making was a vital necessity, and of the fact that the bureaucracy, in European countries at least, has been competent and dedicated at the intermediate and lower levels: the machinery of the state has therefore operated without obvious daily difficulties. But the problems are being increasingly realized: these cannot be overcome, however, until cabinet government is reformed in such a way that the gap between government and bureaucracy is reduced and indeed disappears.

The Semi-Hierarchical, Semi-Pluralistic American System

It might be suggested that the American arrangements provide a solution to these difficulties, yet this is scarcely the case, as the United States government has not solved problems of policy-making and coordination through the presidency, but has in fact had to accept such a degree of autonomy among federal agencies that the concept of a united policy is often more apparent than real. Admittedly, the American government avoids in part the problems arising from the sharp distinction between those who are ministers and those who are not. At least in principle, the traditional penetration, deep into the federal bureaucracy, of men coming from outside, and willing to leave the job when a new president arrives, has the beneficial effect of introducing new blood and new ideas while reducing as much as possible the impact of the widespread view in Europe that the civil service forms a 'class' of its own. But this felicitous arrangement has been soured in the last few decades, as the federal bureaucracy gradually acquired more power in the society and the civil servants, anxious to increase their status as well as to build their careers, slowly undermined, in practice and in theory, some of the beneficial effects of what used to be known as the 'spoils system'. Indeed, as was pointed out in the previous Chapter, the increased requirement for technical know-how makes it most unlikely, even in a country as rich as the United States, that there will be enough men able to take over large numbers of positions in the bureaucracy. While perhaps practical if the changes of president were not also often accompanied by a change in the party in power or indeed the faction of the party backing the president, the more limited 'spoils system' which the United States now operates is both a heavy consumer of imaginative policy talent and a repeated hindrance to the long-term planning needs of the society. And, even the United States — for instance on energy problems — is gradually being made aware of the fact that it, too, requires long-term policy preparation and some consistency in these policies.

Meanwhile, the American government displays, not coordination between a number of departments anxious to follow a line, but marked divisions among bodies pulling in different directions and over which the president can throw only a semblance of unity by multiplying his agencies and increasing his own bureaucracy. The job of the presidential bureaucracy consists then in lengthy battles and in innumerable trade-offs as the various fortresses are strongly defended by the many interests which act as their clients. The United States government is, as was pointed out earlier, a 'government of strangers'. It is, indeed, a government of embattled strangers: drawbridges are rarely down — not a good recipe for coordination. Only the president can, occasionally, bring the departments to collaborate. No matter how strong the White House Office becomes, departments will always have more soldiers in the fortress — the federal civil servants — and more soldiers outside in the various lobbies. Political strength and authority are the only real means by which these feudal castles could be made to elaborate policy in a harmonious manner. But, as long as political authority in the government is concentrated in the president alone, and as long as much political authority is outside the executive, in the Congress in particular, the United States government will be characterized by autonomous and contradictory actions, and will rarely be concerned with long-term development. With fewer resources and an increasing reliance on public sector decisions, the American policy-making process must therefore come gradually to alter its exclusive dependence on the president and his staff if it is to remain efficient: but it is not apparent so far from where the change might come nor when it will come.

Multi-Level Governments in Communist Countries

It is, at least, not surprising that the United States governmental arrangements should have been so little followed: there are very few countries where political power is so decentralized; there have therefore been few countries where the various ministries of the national government have been able to count on so many friends outside to support their own case; and there have been few countries where the legislature has produced so many leaders whose sole course of action, if they wish to achieve power, is either to become president or to build, in Congress, a solid power base with which the president must contend. Thus, for better or worse, the United

States experiment remains truly unique in the contemporary world. But, at the risk of sounding impractical or of going beyond the bounds of acceptable lack of orthoxody, it must be said that perhaps the only way in which the American government could gradually repair some of its divisions would be to draw some lessons from the experiments which are being conducted in the Soviet Union and other Communist states.

Of course, it is patently clear that the Communist experiment in multi-level government has so far operated only in the tightly-knit context, not just of a single-party system making any change of government wholly impossible, but also of an 'establishment' which is fully protected by the *nomenklatura* method and ensures that only men and women who have proved their full reliability and their unwillingness — or inability — to challenge the prevailing values filter to the top. And there is much evidence, perhaps superficial, mainly circumstantial, but clearly very strong, that there is some relationship between the characteristics of the multi-level governments of the Communist countries and the closed socio-political characteristics of the party structure and of its recruitment patterns. Yet, there is also little doubt that, as an achievement, the multi-level governments of the Communist states provide at least a pointer to what might be attempted elsewhere. There is, at the top, a collective body, stemming from the party structure, which, while it does recognize the strength of the leader, also brings together a substantial number of men who are accustomed to work together both before being in power and after they are appointed. And the physical location of Politburo and Secretariat provides means by which informal exchanges occur daily between members: this leads to a manifest reinforcement of the inbuilt tendency of members to collaborate.

A group of politicians, not one man alone, is at the top of Communist governments: like members of a cabinet, the Communist Party elite both relies on the leader and is there in its own right. The fact that Politburo and Secretariat are so closely intertwined means that, unlike in Western parties and in Western governments, research and analysis do not take second place to the requirements of political expediency. It may be that, in practice, the very old hierarchy which has tended to rule Communist countries in the 1970s has given rather low priority to imaginative thinking about new policy developments; but it is at least possible, within the structure itself, for those who favour programmes to make a direct impact on the Politburo, while, in Western cabinet systems, the few non-portfolio ministers, if they were inclined to play such a part, would not have the backing of a large research body endowed with the prestige which, by its size and in view of its past role, the Secretariat of the Communist Party has in Eastern countries.

This is not the only advantage of Communist multi-level governments, however. By sharply distinguishing coordination and management duties of the executive from policy-making functions, Communist systems focus more clearly on the essential role of the 'administrative segments' of this executive. It has typically been fashionable to regard Councils of Ministers, in Communist states, as of little importance to 'real' policy-making, and it has been especially pointed out that the Presidiums have only a formal role. This is, perhaps, what happens, as there is little evidence, in one or the other direction, from which to draw firm conclusions. But the structure itself is interesting, since it both helps to distinguish between the coordination activities, which the Presidium does — or should — undertake, and which are characteristically in the hands of a sizeable number of vice- or deputy-chairmen, and the management activities which are the responsibility of individual ministers.

Yet, perhaps the most important advantage of the system which the Soviet and other Communist states have developed lies in the fact that there is no real distinction between politicians and civil servants. The 'administrative' government is composed, by and large, of civil servants who have moved up the ladder within the ministries; a considerable premium is therefore placed on technical ability and on administrative talent generally, whereas, in cabinet systems, these qualities are neither essential nor indeed specifically sought for in the selection of most ministers: and consequently there is probably a relatively limited desire on the part of the ministers to go beyond the level of technical and administrative decision-making and to be concerned substantively with policy-making and coordination.

Of course, this state of affairs does not altogether dispose of the distinction between 'politicians' and 'civil servants'; it brings civil servants higher up and into the governmental hierarchy, while the politicians proper reserve for themselves the positions in the Politburo and at the top of the Council of Ministers. Moreover, in the context of an authoritarian system such as the Communist system, it seems easier to operate a de facto osmosis by which those civil servants who move to the top are those who by nature are the most political, and constitute a hybrid of politicians and administrators. And finally, the whole system seems to be depend markedly on there being no alternation in power and on the existence of a political orthodoxy. If the civil servants had to be ideologically neutral, they could not as easily be picked to become ministers in view of their political or political-administrative skills, and the men at the very top would have well-known political views and therefore find the association with civil servants less easy and less smooth.

The Requirements of a Modern Government

This dilemma does exist: it was pointed out in the previous Chapter that the distinction between government and administration was one which very few political systems could avoid. Yet the value of the Communist experiment in this respect is that it shows the direction in which it might be possible to go in order to accommodate, at least to some extent, the requirements of a sophisticated management of society and those of complex coordination and policy-making in the government. If a liberal and pluralistic political system entails the opportunity given to the people to replace the men at the top through the alternation in the fortunes of political parties, efforts must be made to ensure that the policy-making, coordination and management consequences are not such that the advantages of a pluralistic and liberal system are viewed as too costly in terms of their administrative consequences for the society. Thus the arrangements must be such that both the political personnel is administratively as competent as possible and that it at least includes a group of men who are recognized as intermediaries between government and bureaucracy.

The first point entails a major rethinking of the basic structure of political parties. Here, too, the Soviet experience can be of interest to a Western environment. For it is not sensible on the part of Western countries to devise a system which divorces, as was pointed out earlier, the basic career patterns of most politicians from the type of skills which, when they are successful, these same politicians will have to display. Parties must base their recruitment process on selecting men having both a wide knowledge of administration and a capacity to handle managerial and policy-making matters. This does and will create tensions as a political party naturally wishes to draw its personnel in a representative manner from the groups and classes which vote for and participate in the organization. Admittedly, Western political parties are far from being fully representative, but, by stressing the need for these parties to give administrative talent a high priority in the recruitment mechanisms which lead men to the top, one creates yet a further incentive to reduce the representative character of political parties. The problem can be solved: it means broadly that the recruitment basis must be dissociated from the career structure; but the difficulty should not be overlooked if parties are to remain lively organizations while at the same time providing countries with the leaders and ministers which modern societies need.

What is clear, however, is that the ministers must cease to be drawn from a group of men and women whose administrative talent and competence is at best obtained by chance and is at worst almost non-existent. This means that there has to be a reduction in the priority given to campaigning, factional debates and easy and witty repartee, in favour of research, analysis and organization. The internal structure of parties must stress the importance of analytical skills, and it must give a premium to schools, work groups, pilot studies, and indeed high involvement in local government affairs, rather than to rallies, carnivals and conventions. And the structure of Parliaments and other legislatures must shift the major emphasis away from points which are scored in a facile manner towards analyses leading to a systematic assessment of problems facing the society: political activity no longer needs to be more circus-like than economic action or the most significant cultural endeavours. Only if a massive change occurs will the problems posed by the inadequacies of ministers in cabinet systems and other types of government begin to be overcome.

Meanwhile, an effort must be made to rethink the relationship between the ministers and the civil service elite. It is simply wasteful to view the two groups as antagonistic and as having only rather formal links. Clearly, the idea that civil servants need to be loyal to their political masters, whoever their political masters may be, whatever they think privately of the ministers' actions, is a form of hypocrisy, or of myth, which can only be dysfunctional in a general context in which highly complex technical matters require a true partnership and genuine reciprocal esteem by all those involved in the decision-making process. Even if it is believed to be truly difficult to find a solution, even if the current arrangements prevailing in cabinet systems do have the advantage of being cosy while any reorganization will create much soul-searching, it is simply wrong to continue on a path which breeds disgruntlement, fosters mistrust on both sides, and thus diverts everyone towards considering how best to circumvent the other man's actions rather than how to bring everyone together in a concerted effort.

For it seems possible to maintain unity between the government and the bureaucracy only if the civil servants share the ideology, indeed the programmatic outlook of the politicians. This can easily be done in the Soviet context because it is simply assumed — indeed positively stated — that there is a common ideological orthodoxy to which civil servants must adhere if they are to come to the top. If one wishes to translate, even in a diluted manner, such an arrangement to a pluralistic system, difficulties seem truly formidable. One solution, clearly the simplest one, is the American answer by which large numbers of men are purely and simply replaced if and when a new set of ministers comes to be selected. But such a solution is predicated on the broad general assumption that it is both possible and sensible to move in and out of the civil service and yet be competent to handle the broad problems of the society. This is perhaps true to an extent, as indeed it is valuable for both ministers and civil servants to have opportunities in opposition or in an academic environment to reflect about the best way of running the nation's affairs while having occasion to increase their technical competence. But, unfortunately, the modern American system is not just a wasteful, but an incorrect approach to governmental action. For even if the society has enough manpower to provide alternative teams way down the civil service line, a major problem would remain on the administrative side: civil servants must have the opportunity to move up to the top, to engage in real debates with policymakers and coordinators and thus to participate fully in governmental actions. Even a humanized version of the old spoils system is what its name states — a system based on 'spoils' — as if the bureaucracy was there to be plundered by the men from outside, not as if it was to be brought together, for a common action, by genuine leaders.

The solution must therefore be one which induces civil servants to be more than partly involved, in the strong sense of the word, in the activities of the politicians. There has to be an acceptance that top civil servants be partly politicized, though on the understanding that ministers have the choice of which civil servants to bring into their own circle. This means a difficult balance between the rights of civil servants to expect a good career and the rights of ministers to pick those whom they want. This means creating positions where civil servants less favoured by the party or group in power can retreat and yet be useful to the community and the public service: committees, commissions, enquiries, should give many opportunities for those who find themselves, temporarily perhaps, on the political sidelines.

Technically more competent ministers, helped by a substantial group of technically competent assistants and working in close contact with a higher civil service whose members are truly committed to the government's actions are thus the prerequisites of an effective management of the nation's affairs. But there must also be a group at the very top which, though composed in part of some of the ministers, must also include men and women who, together with the leader, are primarily engaged in policy-making and co-ordination; these must be backed by a substantial body of aides and specialists who will give the leader and the 'superministers' the advice which they need to carry out their tasks. This does not mean the end of the cabinet system, quite the contrary: the group at the top must remain collective; they have to be bound together by their policy aims and the whole group must be helped by the political strength of each of its members.

The major problem of modern government is to reconcile the needs of political representation with those of effective action in global policy-making and detailed management. In their various ways, collective governments and hierarchical structures, single-level and multi-level executives, all have attempted to grapple with part of the problem, but this has been done in an unsystematic and indeed empirical manner: governments have emerged in the particular context of a society. Little attention has been paid to the overall nature of the problems; little effort has been made to find an answer to the major contradictions — or tensions — between the various aims which have jointly to be pursued. The size of modern government and the magnitude of the problems facing the world have made such an approach redundant, indeed perhaps dangerous. It is high time that governments themselves considered their structure and looked for improvements, by resolving, not avoiding, the problems which they face. Taboos and myths have to be dispelled; there must be willingness to look in all directions to see what can be gained from experiments which, like the Soviet experiment, are too easily disregarded mainly because they are automatically thought to be worthless or repugnant. From a re-analysis of the problems of governmental structure can indeed come a solution to many of the difficulties which all governments experience in policy-making and administration and even a more general solution to some of the problems experienced in political life as it currently manifests itself in modern societies.

SELECT BIBLIOGRAPHY

This bibliography relates specifically to those works which have been concerned with the study of the structures of government from a general standpoint: for studies of individual governments, the reader is referred to bibliographies in standard works on the countries concerned. But individual studies are mentioned here when they provide at least an indirect contribution to the comparative analysis of governments; these are indeed often the only sources, given the paucity of general works.

L.S. Amery, *Thoughts on the Constitution*, Oxford University Press, 1964.

D.E. Ashford, *Policy and Politics in Britain*, Blackwell, 1981.

W. Bagehot, *The English Constitution*, Watts, 1964.

J. Blondel, *Introduction to Comparative Government*, Weidenfeld, 1969.

J. Blondel, *World Leaders*, Sage, 1980.

R.G.S. Brown and D.R. Steel, *The Administrative Process in Britain*, 2nd ed., Methuen, 1979.

Lord Bryce, *Modern Democracies*, Macmillan, 1921.

Z. Brzezinski and S.P. Huntington, *Political Power: USA/USSR*, Chatto and Windus, 1964.

P. Cerny and M.A. Schain, eds, *French Politics and Public Policy*, Methuen, 1980.

B. Chapman, *The Profession of Government*, Allen and Unwin, 1959.

L.G. Churchward, *Contemporary Soviet Government*, Routledge and Kegan Paul, 1968.

S. Cohen, *Les conseillers du président*, Presses Universitaires de France, 1980.

E.S. Corwin, *The President: Office and Powers*, New York University Press, 1957.

R.H.S. Crossman, Preface to Bagehot's *English Constitution*, Watts, 1964.

A. De Swaan, *Coalition Theories and Cabinet Formations*, Elsevier, 1973.

L.C. Dodd, *Coalitions in Parliamentary Government*, Princeton University Press, 1976.

L. Dupriez, *Les ministres dans les principaux pays d'Europe et d'Amérique*, 2 vols, Rothschild, 1892 and 1893.

G.R. Elton, *England under the Tudors*, Methuen, 1974.

R. Fenno, *The President's Cabinet*, Harvard University Press, 1959.

B. Headey, *British Cabinet Ministers*, Allen and Unwin, 1974.

H. Heclo, *A Government of Strangers*, Brookings Institution, 1977.

V. Herman and J. E. Alt, eds, *Cabinet Studies*, Macmillan, 1975.

R.G. Hoxie, *The White House: Organisation and Operations*, Center for the Study of the Presidency, 1971.

A.H. King, ed., *The British Prime Minister*, Macmillan, 1969.

A.H. King, ed., *The New American Political System*, American Enterprise Institute, 1978.

M. Lesage, *Les régimes politiques de l'URSS et de l'Europe de l'Est*, Presses Universitaires de France, 1971.

A.L. Lowell, *Governments and Parties in Continental Europe*, Harvard University Press, 1896.

J.P. Mackintosh, *The British Cabinet*, Stevens, 1962.

R. Neustadt, *Presidential Power*, Wiley, 1960.

O. Oyediran, ed., *Nigerian Politics under Military Rule, 1966-79*, Macmillan, 1979.

W. Riker, *A Theory of Political Coalitions*, Yale University Press, 1962.

R. Rose, *Managing Presidential Objectives*, Macmillan, 1977.

R. Rose and E.N. Suleiman, eds, *Presidents and Prime Ministers*, American Enterprise Institute, 1980.

F.D. Scott, *Sweden: The Nation's History*, University of Minnesota Press, 1977.

H.G. Skilling, *The Governments of Communist Eastern Europe*, Croswell, 1966.

G. Smith, *Politics in Western Europe*, Heinemann, 1972.

D.T. Stanley, D.E. Mann and J.W. Doig, *Men who Govern*, Brookings Institution, 1967.

R. Syme, *The Roman Revolution*, Oxford University Press, new ed., 1960.

N.C. Thomas and H.W. Baade, eds, *The Institutional Presidency*, Oceana Publishers, Inc., 1972.

M. Voslensky, *La Nomenklatura*, Belfond, 1980.

A. Wildavsky, ed., *The Presidency*, Little, Brown, 1969.

INDEX

JEAN BLONDEL

is Professor of Government at the University of Essex, and
founder and former Executive Director of the European
Consortium for Political Research/ECPR. His many publications
include *Voters, Parties and Leaders, A Reader in Comparative
Government* (1970), *Comparing Political Systems* (1972),
Comparative Legislatures (1973), *Contemporary France* (1974),
Thinking Politically (1976), *Political Parties* (1978), and *World
Leaders* (1980).